Please, Miss

BERNADETTE ROBINSON

The true story of a trainee teacher in 1960s Liverpool

D1337366

HODDER

First published in Great Britain in 2012 by Hodder & Stoughton
An Hachette UK company

1

Copyright © Bernadette Robinson 2012

A CIP catalogue record for this title is available from the British Library

ISBN 978 1 444 74138 4
Ebook 978 1 444 74139 1

Typeset by Hewer Text UK Ltd, Edinburgh
Printed and bound by Clays Ltd, St Ives plc

Hodder & Stoughton policy is to use papers that are natural, renewable
and recyclable products and made from wood grown in sustainable
forests. The logging and manufacturing processes are expected to
conform to the environmental regulations of the country of origin.

Hodder & Stoughton Ltd
338 Euston Road
London NW1 3BH

www.hodder.co.uk

For my darling husband Robby in appreciation of his encouragement . . . and for teaching me to use a computer!

For my family, especially my grandchildren, Oscar, Hugo and Sofia, who no doubt in years to come will give me hours of endless fun.

For Samuel, Lucy and James Brauckmann, for reminding me what fun it is to be with children.

I dedicate this book to all the people who as children had the ignominy of standing in the 'free dinners' queue.

Contents

Prologue

'Help! I need somebody. Help! Not just anybody . . .'

It's September 1965 and the Beatles are belting out their latest hit on the radio as I nervously get ready for my first day in teaching. I wriggle into my new black miniskirt, moving my hips in time to John Lennon's distinctive rasping voice. John's my favourite. I have a soft spot for him because he grew up round the corner from me in Woolton, Liverpool. 'Won't you please, please help me!' I join in fervently as I pull on my white knee-length boots.

Standing in front of the mirror, I backcomb my blonde hair into submission. I certainly need all the help I can get today as I'll be looking after a class of forty primary-school children and right now it feels like there's a swarm of butterflies fluttering up from the pit of my stomach. I'm not just nervous, though; I'm excited too. This job is everything I've ever wanted.

You'll have to do, I tell my reflection, taking a deep breath and grabbing my hairspray from the dressing table. The mist that bursts from the can is so cloying it makes me choke. Still, you can't keep a bouffant in place without a little assistance.

Running downstairs, I hear a rush of water from the kitchen tap as my mother fills the kettle.

'Do you want some toast?' she calls, without turning round from the sink as I come into the kitchen.

I can hardly think about eating, but I know Mum will make a fuss if I don't have something.

'Just one slice, please.'

I get a mug for coffee from the cupboard and Mum finally turns round and catches sight of me.

'My God, Bernadette!' she exclaims, her Irish brogue still clearly identifiable in her voice after more than twenty years in Liverpool. She looks disapprovingly at my skirt. 'I hope you're not going to sit down in that. I've seen curtain pelmets with more material in them.' I don't have time to argue with Mum this morning. I have a two-hour journey across Liverpool ahead of me to get to my first teaching job, a primary school on a council estate in Huyton. I want to be there early so that I can pin some nice, colourful posters on the walls and make the room seem warm and welcoming before the children arrive. A little surge of apprehension shoots through me. What if the children don't like me?

'Here,' says Mum, handing me some toast. 'Sit down and eat properly. If that skirt lets you sit down, that is,' she adds wryly.

I can only manage a couple of mouthfuls and a quick gulp of coffee before I'm off and soon I'm running past the redbrick terraces of Penny Lane to catch my bus. There's plenty of time to plan my day as the bus trundles slowly across Liverpool. The bag at my feet is stuffed with rolled-up posters for my seven year old pupils. I plan to put the bold alphabet A–Z on the back wall. 'A' for apple, 'B' for ball . . . 'T' for tiger is my favourite picture. The gleaming amber eyes of the big cat are both fierce and beautiful.

The bus is busy and I squeeze up closer to the window when someone sits down beside me. This is it, I think to myself. I've really made it. All through my childhood I daydreamed about becoming a teacher, and these secret dreams kept me going through some hard times. I used to get Mum's button tin out to play my favourite game. I'd open the lid and shake all the buttons out, watching the different sizes tumble onto the carpet. I recall a big red button from my sister Aideen's coat. Probably that coat was my eldest sister Helena's before it was Aideen's. Then it would be passed to me and finally to my younger sister, Kathleen. Black buttons, green buttons, suit buttons and blue buttons. Then the little silver button from our brother Andrew's sailor suit.

I'd pretend the buttons were children. I'd rank them in order of size: big buttons at the back and smaller ones at the front. They were my little class. 'Now, children,' I would say, assuming my kindest voice, 'if you're very good, I'll tell you a story.' I would sit for hours making up elaborate tales, just as I did at my primary school during rainy playtimes, when the teachers would ask me to sit on the stage and entertain the younger children. I loved books and stories, and I loved being 'teacher'. I always wanted my little charges to be happy. I couldn't wait for the day when I would grow up and make real children happy. And now, I think, gazing out of the bus window as the streets of Liverpool rush by, that day has finally come.

1

Winds of Change

The world was changing in the 1960s and I wanted my relationship with the children I taught to be very different from the relationship I'd had with my own teachers and parents. Children in the 1960s had more of a voice than they did when I was growing up, and I was happy to listen. I wanted to encourage them, nurture them, help them develop.

I was born near the end of the war, in 1944, into a Liverpool that had been the most heavily bombed British city outside of London. When I was travelling on the bus with my mum as a little girl, I recall peering out of the window at the bomb sites of the city, many of which hadn't yet been cleared. In fact, some never were demolished and the Bombed Church, which has no roof, exists to this day, standing testament to a period that changed the city's skyline for ever. Liverpudlians had to be very resilient in those war years and perhaps that's partly where the city's distinctive sense of humour comes from. It's a warm, vibrant place, full of wit and wisecracks and a sense of comedy that is firmly edged with black.

My parents were both from Ireland and moved to Britain after they married. My father's aunt married my mum's uncle, so my mum and dad met on the aunt and uncle's farm. Mum was a typical Irish matriarch and her word was law in our house. Any misdemeanours or cheek were dealt with immediately with the stair rod. Discipline was still an important concept in the post-war years and maybe punishment was emphasised a bit more than justice back then. We were never really encouraged to explain what had actually happened when we were in trouble. As children, we didn't expect to be heard. Whenever Mum approached the staircase in anger to get that bottom stair rod, we didn't hang around to give explanations! It was our cue to scarper as quickly as possible.

Once, I accidentally broke an ornament in the hall and was told to sit on the bottom stair. Here goes, I thought . . . quick swipe with the stair rod. What happened next still sends shivers down my spine, even as an adult. My mum picked up the telephone, dialled and then, after a pause, said, 'Is that Druids' Cross Orphanage?'

Another pause.

'May I speak to Reverend Mother, please? It's Eileen Tierney here.'

A longer pause.

'Hello, Reverend Mother. I have a very naughty little girl with me. Can you take her to the orphanage, please?'

I listened, wide-eyed, with a growing sense of horror.

'Oh good. What time can you come for her? . . . Yes, seven o'clock is fine.'

Then she put down the phone and went into the kitchen without even looking at me.

I ran upstairs, absolutely terrified, and sat on the bed for hours. Eventually, the others came up to go to bed.

'Aren't you putting your pyjamas on?' asked my sister Aideen.

I looked up at her, too frightened to explain.

'No,' I replied. 'I think I'm going somewhere.'

I stayed sitting on the edge of the bed and finally the landing lights went out and the house was still. Hours later, I decided that maybe Reverend Mother was having trouble finding our house, so I climbed into bed fully dressed, just in case she came for me in the night, and slept fitfully. Next morning there was absolutely no mention of it, and of course I didn't bring up the subject either! I've never forgotten the cold fear of those hours, waiting to be plucked from the security of home and the familiar, and thrown to the unknown mercy of the nuns in long, black habits at the orphanage. Perhaps that's why I always wanted to make children in my charge feel secure.

My four siblings and I ate very well as children, even though food rationing lasted well into the 1950s in Britain. We also had 3d in sweet coupons to spend on Saturdays, as sweet rationing remained in place until 1953. I think the emphasis on good, hearty food in our house was partly an Irish thing. I remember my mum taking us to Ireland on the boat to visit our relatives when I was about four. When my dad came to pick us up from the boat two weeks later, he noticed that all of his children, who were normally very slim, had suddenly ballooned out to fill our coats to bursting point.

'Goodness!' he said. 'You've all been eating well.'

'Right, you can take your coats off now,' my mum said as we drove away from the docks.

My dad watched in amazement as we wriggled out of them to reveal strings of sausages and packs of bacon tied round our waists. Adults were searched coming in from Ireland, but children were not. The whole experience was part of a childhood awareness that the good things of life were in short supply and that it was important to stock up when you could and also 'make do and mend'.

Like most women of the wartime generation, my mother did not like waste. We had a lovely collie dog called Trixie who we got from our milkman, Mr Coulthwaite, and Trixie would often help me out at dinnertime if I didn't want something that was on my plate. One evening I didn't want my mashed potato. Usually I managed to push the potato to the side of the plate and then, when no one was looking, surreptitiously take a handful and hold it under the table. Oh, that lovely lick, lick on my hand as the obliging Trixie polished it off! Unfortunately, though, on that night Trixie, who was prone to roaming, had not yet come in for the evening.

'If you don't finish that mashed potato, it's the back doorstep for you,' said my mum sternly.

Sadly, Trixie didn't arrive home in time to save me, so the back doorstep it was.

I sat there, gradually getting colder and colder, just looking up at the stars. The sky grew darker and I shivered, but it didn't occur to me to protest – or even to ask if I could come in now. Just as I was beginning to think I would be there all night, the door opened and Mum came out with the coal scuttle. She'd forgotten all about me.

'What are you doing there?' she asked in astonishment.

'You said to sit on the back step,' I replied.

'Well, I didn't mean all night! Off you go to bed!'

We lived in a big, Victorian, end-of-terrace house that had three large bedrooms on the first floor and two attic rooms on the top floor. The front attic room had a turret with a sealed door and we often heard noises coming from behind it.

'What's that?' I would whisper to Aideen, and then we would stand stock still and listen to strange scurrying and scratching noises from behind the door.

No doubt it was mice, but when we asked Mum, she said it was Father Christmas's workshop. It was such an exciting answer and I believed that until I was about eight. Of course, we adored Christmas as children and we used to cry when the tree was taken down. In fact, one year we all cried so much that my mum relented and it didn't get taken down until Easter, so perhaps there was *some* childish indulgence in the 1950s!

On the ground floor of the house we had what we called the front room, the middle room and the kitchen. The kitchen had a range, which Mum didn't use for cooking, but to heat the water. Every evening she would shout, 'Everyone out of the way!' and then dash from the kitchen to the middle room with a shovelful of hot embers, to start the fire for Dad coming in from his evening surgery as a GP.

My dad came from Monaghan in Ireland and was one of ten children. He had a very difficult childhood and it perhaps wasn't surprising that he carried a little bit of baggage from his own childhood into ours. His own father was a respectable headmaster by day but a demon at night, when he got home and reached for the bottle. He beat his wife, and his children were all terrified of him. When my dad was quite young, his brothers met him at the gate one day and told him to get something in his hands, sticks or stones, and to follow them. They lay in wait, and when their father staggered drunkenly up the path, they jumped him. He never hit their mother again.

My grandfather's cruelty made my father so anxious as a child that he developed a terrible stammer. You would think that his upbringing would have made him resolve never to frighten his own children, but he developed quite a temper of his own. Somehow his stammer made him seem all the more intimidating as he stuttered out, 'C-c-c-come here!' I was so frightened of adult authority that I used to run into the room, say, 'Goodnight, God bless,' in a rush, and escape upstairs as quickly as possible.

Sometimes, when you look at the past through the eyes of the present, the past can seem very harsh – almost cruel, but while my childhood was more austere than the one many children enjoy today, we really didn't expect anything different and didn't consider ourselves deprived in any way. Parents in the 1950s did their best, as they do in every generation, but people then thought very differently about the way children should be brought up. Until you were an adult, you certainly weren't encouraged to have much to say. In my parents' generation, for example, there had really been no such thing as 'teenagers'. There were children and there were adults. You left school and earned a living immediately and the world was run by hard work, discipline and no-nonsense values.

The result of a period in history of strict conformity – and the post-war years had certainly been that – tends to be rebellion. In my youth you could sense change coming the way you can feel rain on the wind. For me, there were some difficult years to get through first, years that taught me exactly what kind of person – and teacher – I did and didn't want to be. But I was so lucky to come from Liverpool. As the home of the Beatles, Liverpool felt like it was at the very heart of the revolution. Finally, young people would have a defined place in the world. Lively, vibrant clubs would spring up and throb to the beat of an exciting new popular music, music that to our parents was just anarchic noise. Fashion would no longer be dictated by clothing coupons, and hemlines would reflect a new sense of daring. Life was going to be different; we knew it. And I, for one, couldn't wait to be part of it.

2

Growing Up Overnight

'Bernadette!' hissed my big sister Aideen.

'What?'

I had my head stuck in a book as usual and barely even looked up at Aideen, who had popped her head round the living-room door.

'Come and see!'

I put my book down and followed her into the hall and upstairs. Dad had obviously been up to the loft. On the upstairs landing were the big trunks in which Helena and Aideen used to pack their things when they went away to convent boarding school in Dublin. Aideen was two years younger than Helena and I was two years younger than Aideen. Then there was a four year gap to my little sister Kathleen and a one year gap between Kathleen and the baby of the family, Andrew.

The trunks were still covered in a film of dust from their summer in the attic and at first I didn't understand why Aideen had dragged me up to see them. She looked at me expectantly.

'What?' I said.

'There are three!'

We stood in silence for a minute. I was only ten years old, and just about to start my final year at primary school, but we both knew what this meant. I didn't want to think about it.

'Come on,' I said, tugging on Aideen's sleeve. 'Let's go and play with the puppies.'

Trixie's constant roaming meant she was often pregnant and recently she'd had another litter. We always loved it when the puppies were first born, eyes still locked shut. These puppies were a few weeks old now, but every bit as adorable. Aideen and I tiptoed into the front room and looked at the cute little black-and-white bundles, all huddled together in the basket. They really made our hearts melt and we knelt down to run our fingers gently over their soft fur.

'They're gorgeous,' whispered Aideen.

The puppies began to move, clambering over one another to get to Trixie's teats.

'Girls,' my mother's voice called from the kitchen.

I looked at Aideen. I bet Mum wanted us to peel the potatoes.

'Girls!' my mum shouted, more insistently this time.

'Quick,' I said, pulling Aideen by the arm. 'Scarper!'

We ran, closing the door quietly behind us, and didn't stop until we reached the wall round the back of the house where we always met our gang. Aideen and I collapsed over the wall in a fit of giggles, panting. Soon a group of children gathered round us. There were about twenty children in the street who all played together, ranging from four to twelve years old. It was a close community and the women in the street would tell the children to call them 'auntie'. One day I went in and told my mum that a neighbour of ours had made a kind offer.

'Auntie Rose says would you like some of the cakes she's just made?'

'She's not your auntie!' retorted my mother. 'You have dozens of aunties in Ireland and you don't need these made-up ones. They're just knitted aunties!'

Knitted aunties! My mother always had very colourful expressions. She was an elegant woman who dressed well and I think she enjoyed her status as the local doctor's wife and kept a certain distance from some of the other women.

Luckily we had no such social divisions and played with the children in the street every evening, come hail, rain or snow. We had a lot of freedom because there was hardly any traffic in the road at that time, and from that point of view at least, it was a wonderful time to be a child. In fact, my dad, being a GP, had the only car in the street and it was such a status symbol that I can still remember the number plate – GKD 545!

The only other 'traffic' was the morning visit from Mr Coulthwaite, the milkman, with his horse and cart. The noise of rattling bottles as the cart trundled down the street was more reliable than an alarm clock. One poor girl in our street, called Muriel, had to run after the horse with a bucket and shovel, gathering up manure for her mother's roses. I felt very sorry for her, but the boys, with typical male sensitivity and sympathy, nicknamed her 'Shitty Muriel'!

'What shall we do?' asked one of the gang. 'Shall we play on the go-karts?' Most children in the street had a makeshift go-kart of some description. In our house, we all shared one that had been made by my mother. They were usually made out of doors and Mum had heated a poker until it was red hot and then burned a hole in the door to make it fit the axle, which came from an old pram.

'No, let's play Froggie, Froggie,' I said, because it was my favourite game and we hadn't played it for ages.

Aideen was elected Froggie and stood on one pavement, while the rest of us lined up on the far side.

'Froggie, Froggie, may we cross your golden water?' we all chanted together.

'Not unless . . . you're five years old,' shouted Aideen, and two of the little ones took a triumphant step forward. The object was to be the first person to cross the golden water, and whoever got there would take over as Froggie.

'Froggie, Froggie, may we cross your golden water?' we repeated.

'Not unless . . . you're wearing a red jumper,' responded Aideen.

I took a great big leap forward, so big that I shot past the little ones who had stepped forward in the last round.

'Hey,' protested one young boy to Aideen, 'you only chose that because your sister is wearing a red jumper!'

'No she didn't!' I jumped in indignantly.

'Yes she did! That's cheating!'

And so we squabbled and giggled our way through a long summer afternoon of street games, making our own entertainment and staying as far away as possible from the separate world of adults. We were happy in our own world, fulfilled. We only needed each other to have fun.

When we returned home that evening at teatime, however, it was obvious all was not well in the adult world and Mum was in a foul mood.

'Where did you get to?' she demanded, as she banged the pots about for dinner, but we kept quiet and luckily she didn't ask any more because just then there was a shout from the front room and Helena came running in.

'Where are the puppies?' she asked.

'They've all gone to good homes,' said my mum. 'I took them this afternoon. You knew that we couldn't keep them all for ever and they're big enough now to go to homes of their own.'

'Awwww,' we chorused sadly.

Tears sprang to my eyes, but we all comforted each other with the idea that at least they had nice families who would look after them. Mum had made sure of that. Some other children would now have the fun of raising a little puppy.

It had been a nice warm day, but it was nearing the end of summer and by evening the air had turned sharp and chilly. After we had cleared up the dinner dishes, my mother sent me out to the coal house to fill the scuttle. My father would be in soon and we always tried to make everything as nice as possible for his arrival. He could be quite grumpy after evening surgery. He only had one evening off a week, on a Thursday, and we used to take the telephone off the hook and put a notice on the door asking callers to come to the back so that he wouldn't be disturbed.

Tonight was Wednesday and he would soon be home, so I went out with the scuttle to do as I was told. I don't know what prompted me to look in the old steel bucket that was out in the back yard. It had a piece of wood placed securely over the top and a large brick on top of that, so I had to make an effort to get into it. What made me? I suppose it was just a child's natural curiosity, something my career in teaching would later give me a lot of insight into.

I bent down and pulled off the brick. Then I removed the piece of wood that acted as a lid and suddenly dropped it in horror. To this day I am not sure how I managed to remain silent. Underneath was a nightmare scene. The six puppies that had been tumbling over Trixie earlier in the day had been drowned in the water. Their little bodies were bloated, and they looked up at me with fixed stares in their eyes.

I didn't understand how my mum could have done it. I wanted to scream. I wanted to run into the house and shout, 'Why? Why?' but I didn't. It wasn't a child's place to question, and anyway, this was just another example of my mother's pragmatism. You have to place her response in the context of that time. When your generation has cried over lost fathers, lost brothers, lost friends, brought down in foreign lands, perhaps you don't have many tears left for a few dead puppies. But being a child, I didn't see it like that at the time.

For a moment I stood rooted to the spot, just staring into the water. Then I slammed the piece of wood back over the bucket so that I couldn't see the contents any longer. My heart was hammering painfully and I felt sick, but I carefully replaced the brick as if it had never been touched. I went to the coal and filled up the scuttle, then walked back in as if nothing had happened, keeping all my feelings locked tightly inside.

'What kept you?' said my mother, but I couldn't look at her in case I broke down.

I didn't tell the others, and wouldn't until we were all adults. At bedtime, as I climbed the stairs, I felt glad that I could retreat to the safety of my own bed and be left alone for a bit. At the top of the stairs, I halted suddenly, confronted by the three trunks. I had forgotten all about them. I stared at them, then ran to brush my teeth. I got ready for bed quickly, burrowing deeply under the blankets, and when the light was put out, I turned my head into the pillow and cried for the poor dead puppies.

There was another image that kept springing into my mind in the darkness, though: the three school trunks sitting on the landing. On the way past, I had noticed that they had been wiped down and had fresh labels stuck on them. 'Helena', 'Aideen' and 'Bernadette'. So it was definitely true. Nobody had said a word about what was to happen to me, but this told me everything I needed to know. I wouldn't be going back for my last year at primary school as I had thought. I would be going to the convent in Dublin.

3

Hairy Moments

It was Saturday morning and Aideen and I carefully braided our long, brown hair into plaits. All four Tierney girls had the Irish-colleen combination of brown hair and blue eyes. The trunks were still on the landing, but we just ran by them without talking about what might soon happen. There was at least a week of holiday left and we were in a good mood because we had pocket money that we were going to spend in the sweetshop after breakfast.

'Look – I can nearly sit on my plaits,' said Aideen. She was proud of the fact that her hair was longer than mine and she couldn't resist drawing attention to it at times.

'Well, I *nearly* can,' I said.

Mum shouted to us as we left the house, clutching pennies in our hands, 'Aideen! Bernadette!'

We looked at one another on the doorstep. What now?

'Yes, Mum?' Aideen called back.

'No chewing gum!'

'OK!'

We banged the door behind us before she delayed us any further and ran down the street to the sweetshop.

'Packet of chewing gum, please,' said Aideen instantly, placing her pennies on the glass counter with a clatter.

'Packet of chewing gum, please,' I repeated, putting mine beside hers.

A tray of sweets was pulled out from the counter and we chose some chews too, which were handed over in a small paper bag. We started on the sweets the minute we got out of the shop.

'When you come to school . . .' Aideen began. My stomach lurched at her words and I looked up at her fearfully. I didn't like it being spelled out that I was going to the convent. If it wasn't said, maybe it wouldn't happen. '. . . you have to give some of your pocket money to the black babies,' Aideen continued.

'Why?'

'Sister Clare at school told us about a baby who was born in Africa,' confided Aideen, who was enjoying sharing her knowledge with her naïve little sister. 'A guardian angel called Wopsie looked into the baby's eyes and saw its little black soul and said, "If that baby dies before it is christened, it will go to Limbo and it can never get into Heaven."'

'Never?'

Aideen shook her head. 'It will just float around in the sky for ever.'

At primary school, we had been told not just about Heaven and Hell, but about Purgatory, a sort of no-man's land where souls went to be cleansed before they were good enough to get into Heaven. It sounded to me like a great big spiritual waiting room in the sky. I didn't fancy it much, but this Limbo place sounded even worse. At least in Purgatory you knew you were getting to Heaven eventually.

The sheer cruelty of the concept of an innocent baby being banished for ever because its parents had committed the unpardonable sin of failing to get some holy water poured over its forehead baffled me. It still does.

Aideen's story whirled round in my head as I tore open my packet of chewing gum and then I came up with a question – as I always did.

'What do you give the money for the black babies for? Can you buy them out of Limbo?'

'Sister Clare says we can save the babies by giving money to the priests who go out to Africa to save them from Limbo. When you pay five shillings, you get a black baby all of your own and they call it after you.'

I looked at Aideen in astonishment.

'Does the black baby come to stay with you when it's yours?'

'Don't be silly!' said Aideen scornfully.

We were so busy talking and chewing as we walked home that we didn't notice until it was too late that there was someone standing on our doorstep.

'Bernadette, it's Mum!' said Aideen in a stricken voice. 'We need to get rid of the gum!'

'I'm going to swallow mine,' I said in a panic.

'You can't do that!' said Aideen. 'Mum says if you swallow it, it sticks all your insides together.'

Stuck-together insides seemed preferable to Mum's wrath, so I hastily took a big gulp.

'Gone!' I said.

Aideen surreptitiously took hers out of her mouth and stuck it the only place she could think of in a hurry – on the back of her right plait. Mum didn't notice as we walked past her and we breathed a sigh of relief.

That afternoon we spent with the gang, including our little brother, Andrew. Unlike us girls, Andrew was never sent away to boarding school, even when he was older. Mum said it was just that my father worried about his girls being in the city, but I always wondered about that. Dad had longed for a boy and I think he was a bit disappointed when he had four girls one after another. Andrew was the jackpot at the end of a long wait. The day he was born, my dad's friend Tom came round to celebrate and played the same tune on the piano over and over again.

'When you come to the end of a perfect day . . .' he sang.

Eventually, poor, exhausted Mum staggered downstairs and slammed the lid of the piano down.

'It is *not* a perfect day!' she snapped.

It was to my dad, though.

Even if Andrew was the icing on the family cake, he wasn't treated more indulgently than the rest of us – as was proved that night. After dinner my mum doled out jobs for us all.

'Andrew and Kathleen, you clear the table,' she instructed. 'Helena, you wash the dishes, and Aideen and Bernadette can dry.'

We all moved immediately, apart from Andrew, who was sitting with his back to Mum. The next thing, Mum was giving him a clip on the back of the head.

'Andrew, do what you're told!' she said.

Andrew jumped but didn't say a word.

After clearing the table, he disappeared upstairs. He shared an attic room with Kathleen at this time, and when she went up, she found he had locked the door. Kathleen stomped back downstairs.

'Andrew won't let me in the room,' she complained.

Well, there was a bit of coming and going after that, with Kathleen running up and down the stairs reporting Andrew's consistent refusal to open the door. Eventually, my mother lost her patience.

'You tell Andrew that if he doesn't open that door, your father is coming up!'

That would normally have been enough to frighten Andrew into compliance, but Kathleen came down yet again and my father hauled himself out of his chair in exasperation. We were all terrified. Andrew was really pushing his luck.

My dad was quite overweight and we heard his heavy footsteps thundering on the staircase, then the bang on the bedroom door. We tiptoed onto the stairs and watched from a point of safety.

'Open the door, Andrew!' shouted my dad.

When there was no answer, I remember Dad's face changed. There was a momentary shadow of panic. He kicked the door open and it fell across the bottom of Andrew's bed. Andrew never moved. He was fast asleep and hadn't heard a thing. In fact, what none of us had realised was that Andrew didn't hear a thing a lot of the time but was too frightened to say. It was only after this incident that he got the operations he needed to help him hear.

You might have thought a doctor would have noticed that his own son was partially deaf, but by the time he got in at night, I don't think Dad wanted to hear a single word about aches and pains and illness. He had never wanted to be a doctor in the first place and had only studied medicine because his bullying father had made him.

That was probably why he also didn't notice that I had a painful childhood tumour on my wrist. My mother used to tell me not to be a baby when I yelped if she grabbed it in the bath, but my older cousin, who did paediatrics, realised what it was. It was the kind of tumour you get on the brain, like a bunch of grapes with red worms in, and it was removed and put in a jar in the children's hospital in Liverpool. I've still got a scar, but I have never had any bother since.

If we thought it was going to be a quiet evening after all the excitement with Andrew, we were quite mistaken. On Saturday nights my mum would bind our hair with rags so that we would have ringlets for going to Mass the next day. When Mum called me and Aideen to come for our turn, we skipped off without thinking. Aideen went first and Mum took the bands off the ends of her pigtails to brush out her hair. A minute later we heard an exclamation of disgust.

'Aideen Tierney, what on earth is this in your hair?'

She had discovered the big blob of chewing gum Aideen had stuck on her right plait. The gum had stretched over the ends of her hair, working its way upwards and matting it into a horrible, sticky mess.

All hell broke loose and Aideen was sent to bed in disgrace.

'What have I told you about chewing gum!' Mum ranted.

I kept very quiet indeed and hoped my stuck-together insides wouldn't give me away too.

'Never mind,' I said to Aideen, giving her a big hug at bedtime.

Next day, Mum took Aideen down to Miss Finnie's, the hairdresser on Penny Lane. I had my nose up against the front-room window waiting for her to come back and I gasped when she appeared. Her beautiful long hair, of which she was so proud, was now about two inches below her ears. I loved Aideen and I felt sorry for her losing all her treasured tresses. I gave her one of my sweets that I had saved for during the week. As I discovered when I became a teacher, a degree of rivalry between children is natural, but I am a little ashamed to say that whenever Aideen annoyed me, as inevitably sisters sometimes do, I couldn't resist a dig.

'Look at this, Aideen,' I would say casually, 'I can nearly sit on my plaits!'

All week the trunks had remained on the upper landing, but the day came when my mum started to pack them. I watched silently as my clothes were taken from drawers and cupboards and placed in neat piles inside my trunk. Still nobody said a word, but I knew I was about to embark on the biggest adventure of my young life.

4

Convent Blues

'Bernadette Tierney, get that look off your face! You are as bold as brass!'

Sister Clare looked me up and down, her stern face framed by her wimple. There wasn't a single wisp of her hair visible, nothing to soften her appearance, and the severity seemed to emphasise her hooked nose. I looked back at her in astonishment. What had I done? I had no idea what 'bold' meant.

It had been the same ever since I arrived at the convent, an imposing three-storey building in extensive grounds in the suburbs of Dublin. I was terrified on my first night and cried myself to sleep. From the start I didn't fit in. I was a very enquiring child, but unfortunately, this was somewhere inquisitiveness was discouraged. In the nuns' world, it was not a child's place to question, but I couldn't help myself. Questions just blurted out of me. I didn't mean to be cheeky when Sister Clare talked about Jesus walking on water. I simply wanted to know why he didn't sink.

'How could Jesus do that?' I had asked curiously.

'He just did – and don't you be so bold,' Sister Clare had retorted.

I was glad when a knock came at the door and the nun's attention was diverted from me at last.

One of the senior girls came into the classroom.

'Excuse me, Sister,' she said, handing over a card. 'Here's the spiritual bouquet for Sister Rose.'

Sister Rose was an elderly nun who had passed away a few days before and prayers had been said repeatedly for her. Sister Clare now wanted us all to sign the card.

'Write down how many spiritual ejaculations you will do for Sister Rose,' she instructed, 'and remember, girls, that it's to help her soul get into Heaven.'

'Please, Sister . . .' I said.

Sister Clare shot me a withering look.

'. . . what is an ejaculation, Sister?'

I thought Sister Clare was going to explode. Her face went purple and she almost ran to her desk to take out a thick black strap.

'Bernadette Tierney, come out here!' she shrieked.

I think she thought I was being deliberately rude, but I was just bewildered. On my first, lonely night at the convent when I had cried myself to sleep, I had comforted myself with the thought that at least there would be no stair rod here. Little did I know it would be replaced by this fearsome-looking belt.

'Hold out your hands!' she commanded.

She gave me five of the strap and I walked back to my desk, hands stinging, but none the wiser about what constituted a spiritual ejaculation.

As I sat down, I felt a nudge in my back and I turned round.

'It's just a simple prayer that you say over and over,' whispered the girl behind me, Breda. 'Like "God is love.

God is love. God is love." Or "Jesus, Mary and Joseph." You say it about a hundred times and then you write on the card that you have done a hundred spiritual ejaculations. And if we do enough, she gets into Heaven.'

Well! What a very odd system, I thought.

Many years later, at a dinner party, my friend Bette and I were recalling all this and a Jewish friend, Sonia, almost choked to death on her smoked salmon when Bette mentioned that we did ejaculations for dead nuns. Just like I had all those years before, Bette forgot – though in her case no doubt on purpose – to mention the word 'spiritual'.

'How old do you think she is?' my new friend Breda whispered as we lay in bed and watched Sister Clare disappear down to her cubicle at the bottom of our dorm. The dormitories – there were seven in total – were all on the top floor of the school and housed twelve girls each.

'Ninety?' I said.

'No!' snorted Breda.

'You're right,' I said. 'Ninety-four!'

We turned our faces into our pillows to stop Sister hearing our giggles.

'No more talking!' she said, snapping out the lights.

In fact, Sister Clare must have been a relatively young woman, perhaps in her thirties. The walls of the cubicle where she slept were made of a thin wood and when she had a candle, it lit up her silhouette behind the partition. We were fascinated by this and used to watch the shadows on the wall avidly when she took off her veil. We knew that under their veils, the nuns' hair was very short, almost completely shaved, and we were curious about what that would look like.

What was even more mysterious was what went on in Sister Clare's head. The nuns' view of the world was truly baffling at times. It was Halloween that night and as soon as Sister Clare left the room, we started telling ghost stories. There was one girl who was a fantastic storyteller and she could scare the life out of us all. She probably went on to become a writer. When it was her turn, we all listened to her, mesmerised, as she told a story complete with sound effects. Creaking doors, hooting owls . . . she threw in the lot. I was so frightened that I jumped out of my bed and into Breda's and the two of us sat huddled together, listening and trembling.

Suddenly, Sister Clare bustled in and the beam of her torch swept over the room and came to rest on Breda and me. Anyone else would have seen two innocent ten-year-olds listening to a story together, but she saw something else.

'Look at you two and not a pillow between you!' she scolded. 'You, out!'

As a child, I didn't really understand her anger. It was only years later that I felt a rush of sadness. Why would you think like that about two naïve children? But anything that could possibly have a sexual connotation was heavily censored in the convent and they even stuck pages of the biology textbooks together so that we couldn't read them. There was also that old advice given to generations of Catholic schoolgirls about not wearing patent shoes. Men could see your underwear, the nuns insisted. Well, only if they had their X-ray specs with them!

We were tired the next day after staying up telling stories, but it was an early rise as usual to attend daily Mass at 7 a.m. with the nuns. As we traipsed into the convent chapel with its hushed interior, the outlines of the religious statues looked a little frightening in the flickering candlelight. Breda and I dipped our fingers into the melted wax of the candles at the back, popping the greasy residue into our mouths and chewing it all through the service. It was the closest we were going to get to chewing gum.

Sunday was my least favourite day of the week. There were eighty boarders at the school, but with day girls, the numbers rose to a couple of hundred. I so envied the day girls, who could go home in the evening. Sundays seemed very bleak without them coming in to give us gossip and news from the outside world. A long day stretched ahead with only two hours of the dreaded embroidery – or 'embuggery', as we called it – to look forward to. I had enough tray cloths to open a teashop, but they were always polka-dotted with blood because I kept sticking the needle in the wrong place: straight into my fingers.

It was also letter-writing day. ' "Dear Mammy and Daddy," ' Sister Clare wrote carefully on the blackboard in her elaborate looped script. We copied it dutifully onto our writing paper. I had never called Mum 'Mammy' in my life. I vividly recall my first Sunday at the convent, when I'd looked around the room at the rest of the girls scratching away with their nibbed pens on the paper. Once I'd started, though, I'd got into the swing of it: writing a letter was just like telling a story and I'd poured out everything that had happened in my week.

'Now, girls,' said Sister Clare, 'when you finish your letter, I want you to conclude it with these words . . .' She picked up the chalk again and wrote as she talked. ' "I . . . remain . . . your . . . loving . . . child," ' she finished with a flourish. 'Then put your own name at the end.'

I wrote the words, signed my name and put my pen down.

'Please, Sister, I've finished,' I said. 'May I have an envelope now?'

'Bring it here, Bernadette.'

I walked to the front of the class and handed her the letter. I soon discovered that all letters were censored when Sister Clare began to read mine. She glanced up at me as she read, then back at the letter. A frisson went round the room. Sister Clare's disapproval was almost tangible. When she finished, she reached for another sheet of paper.

'Sure, your mammy and daddy don't want to hear that kind of thing, Bernadette, do they?' She handed me the fresh paper. 'Now away and write another one.'

I heard the rip of paper as I turned away and took my new sheet back to my desk. I reached my seat just in time to see the remnants of my letter fluttering into the waste-paper basket at her feet. I sighed and picked up my pen. 'Dear Mammy and Daddy . . .' I wrote again.

* * *

My early years in the convent were difficult and I found it hard to adjust. I always longed for more warmth and more love, but as I got older, I stopped searching for it. I saw little of my sisters because we were in different classes and dormitories. In fact, boarding school felt like a prison and Breda and I took every opportunity to escape in any way we could. For example, we both hated hockey – oh, those dreary hours on soggy fields with mud-caked shoes and bruised ankles! – but made ourselves play for the simple reason that the hockey team were the only ones who were legitimately allowed out of the convent. We used to get the bus back to school from matches and there was an ice-cream bar called Cafolla's next to the bus-stop. If we had time, a group of us would go in there and order a knickerbocker glory and four spoons.

As teenagers, other interests took over and offered a diversion from the strict regime of the nuns. Obviously there weren't any real boys to catch our eye in a convent boarding school, but there was Elvis! I wrote to him when he was stationed in Germany, and when a letter arrived for me with a German postmark, I was thrilled. Breda and I ran into the grounds to open it.

'What does it say?' she asked excitedly. 'What does it say?'

My eyes quickly scanned the letter, but disappointment awaited. It wasn't from my beloved Elvis at all; it was just an acknowledgement from Colonel Parker, his manager.

Pop music had arrived and I was well and truly smitten. I loved the exciting beats, the energy, the way adults tutted and viewed it as a dangerous and subversive influence. When I was a senior pupil, I was the only girl in the school to have a secret radio. Until, that is, one disastrous night when I was lying in bed with my earplug in – in those days you only had one.

'Can I have a go?' whispered Breda from the bed opposite. 'Just for a minute,' she pleaded quietly, leaning across the gap between our beds.

'Of course,' I said, though to be honest I could hardly bear to miss a precious minute of my favourite pop show. I listened to pop music as much as I could and when the days at the convent were tough, I'd think to myself, Only five more hours to go until Radio Luxembourg!

I took out my earplug and reached under my pillow for my battered old radio. 'I'll give it back if Elvis comes on,' promised Breda.

My radio had come close to being discovered when I'd put my earplug in and listened to the radio in the study room while I was doing my homework. The programme I was listening to had been interrupted to announce that Pope John XXIII had died. You can imagine the impact such news would have in a convent and I poked the girl sitting in front of me.

'The Pope's dead,' I whispered.

She passed it on and eventually it reached the front row. Sister Bartholomew, or 'Old Barty', as we called her, who was supervising, noticed that there was something going on.

'What are you girls whispering about?' she demanded.

'It's the Pope,' said the girl in front of her. 'He's dead.'

'How dare you say a thing like that!' retorted Sister Bartholomew, but before she could say any more, the door opened and Sister Aquinas – whom we called 'the Egg' because of her freckled oval face – bustled in. After a whispered conversation, Sister Bartholomew looked curiously at the girl in the front row.

'How did you know the Pope was dead?' she asked.

I held my breath and gripped my radio. Oh, please don't let her say anything!

'I-I . . .' stuttered the girl, '. . . I just had a feeling!'

She was probably revered as a seer by the nuns from that day on!

My eyes were closing in the dorm when I heard Breda whisper again, 'Bernadette! Bernadette!'

I opened my eyes and she was holding out the earplug. 'Elvis!' she said.

I was bolt upright in an instant and reaching for the ear plug. 'Return to Sender'! Breda grinned at me as I 'danced' on the bed. ' "I gave a letter to the postman. He put it in his sack," ' I mouthed at her in the half-light and she collapsed back onto her pillow, grinning.

The trouble was, I collapsed back onto my pillow too. After Elvis, I drifted off back to sleep and disaster struck. The earplug got ripped out as I turned in bed, the volume dial went up, and music blasted out into the dorm. I woke with a terrible fright, heart hammering, and made a grab for the radio, turning it off as quickly as possible, but it was too late. A minute later Sister Clare came out from her cubicle and bustled up the dorm, switching the lights on as she went.

'Who was responsible for that?'

There was silence.

'Well . . .?' said Sister Clare. 'I'm waiting, girls.'

Still nobody said a word. They wouldn't tell on me and Sister Clare bristled at the defiance. I could tell things were going to get nasty.

'Unless somebody owns up,' said Sister Clare quietly, 'then I am going to have to punish the entire dormitory.'

A groan went round the room.

'That's not fair,' one brave soul muttered.

'There will be detention tomorrow at—'

'It was me, Sister.'

I couldn't let the whole dorm be punished because of me. All eyes swivelled towards me and I lifted the radio out from under my pillow. Sister Clare silently held out a hand and waited. It broke my heart to hand it over. It was my friend, my lifeline. Breda looked on, horrified, and flashed me a look of sympathy.

Sister Clare glared at me. 'Bernadette Tierney,' she said grimly, as she walked away with my precious radio, 'I might have known.'

In the last two years of school the nuns began their recruitment drive, talking to seniors about vocations and how, as a nun, you could help people to learn about God. They didn't try too hard with me because I think they realised 'Miss Bold as Brass' was a lost cause! I knew exactly what I was going to do, as I had always known:

I was going to be a teacher. Four or five girls would join the order each year and I wasn't really surprised when Aideen was one of them. She always had a much stronger faith than I did.

It was strange to have her staying on at the convent, now dressed in a habit, for my final years at school. I was never malicious and would never have hurt Aideen, but I did have a strong sense of mischief. The corridors and stairs in the school were all highly polished and it was the job of the novices and postulants – first- and second-year nuns – to clean the school. They were not allowed to speak at all in their first year and they seemed to spend most of the day on their knees, whether praying or scrubbing.

One day Aideen was polishing the staircase as I came down. I knew she wasn't allowed to speak to me, so I just smiled and dropped a piece of paper in front of her. As she picked it up, she didn't need to say anything: it was all in the narrow-eyed stare! We both laughed about it later – it really was a very funny moment – but I suppose it also illustrated why my lovely sister was a nun and I wasn't!

On my last day of school there were no farewell parties, but a few girls were crying as the fleet of parents' cars arrived to take everyone home. Not me! I was ecstatic. My trunk was collected to go home on the ferry and I only had a small case with me because I was catching the bus to stay with one of my Irish aunties for a while. I linked arms with Breda and we walked down the school drive, singing at the tops of our voices a little ditty we had made up about our teachers, including Old Barty and the Egg:

> *No more Irish, no more French,*
> *No more sitting on a hard school bench.*
> *Kick up tables, kick up chairs,*
> *Kick Old Barty down the stairs.*
> *If the Egg interferes,*
> *Knock her down and box her ears!*

At the bottom of the drive, I turned to my dear friend Breda, who'd helped me through so many dark days. 'I'll always keep in touch with you, Breda, but I'm never coming back here,' I said.

And I didn't.

5

The Casbah Waltz

'Where are you off to, dressed like that?' asked my mother suspiciously.

It was the summer I left school; I was eighteen and living back at home. I had taken special care with my appearance that night. I was dressed in a navy and green tartan mini-kilt, my hair was freshly washed and dried, and I had applied a pale pink gloss, the colour of cherry blossom, to my lips.

'I'm just going to Billy Martin's,' I said, hoping she wouldn't spot the faint, inconvenient blush that coloured my cheeks. I had spent enough time with nuns not to be a very good liar.

Billy Martin's was a school in Liverpool where young people learned to dance. Ballroom mainly, so Mum thought I was off to practise my waltz and I wasn't going to disabuse her of the notion.

'Don't be late,' she said, and I could hardly believe my luck that I wasn't going to be interrogated further.

I think her mind was probably on other things. My sister Kathleen, like us, had been sent to the convent boarding school in Dublin, but that very day a letter from Reverend Mother had thudded onto our mat. 'Dear Dr and Mrs Tierney,' it began, 'we would appreciate it if

Kathleen did not return to the school in September.'
There was no indication of her crime. Nothing was
spelled out. That was not the nuns' way.

Kathleen's misdemeanours were to offer her an escape
route from Dublin. However angry my parents were, the
result of her expulsion was that she was going to stay at
home and attend the local grammar school. Kathleen was
thrilled, but she was wisely keeping a low profile that night.

'Wish I could come,' she had said enviously, swinging
her legs as she sat on the edge of my bed and watched me
get ready.

'You'll be lucky if you get out of this house within a
month,' I joked, building up a thick black layer of
mascara on my lashes.

Kathleen sighed and lay back against the pillows. Then
she giggled. 'Still,' she said, 'at least I don't have to go
back to Dublin!'

I turned from the dressing table curiously, the mascara
wand poised mid-air. 'What exactly did you do?'

'Oh, nothing.'

'Come on, Kathleen. I won't say!'

Kathleen pushed herself up with her elbows and
looked at me, her mischievous, grey-blue eyes dancing.
Of all of us, Kathleen was the one who tended to dare to
do what she wanted. She could be quite clever about it.
For example, she once deliberately pressed a crease down
the side of my dad's trousers so that she wouldn't be
asked to do the ironing again.

She motioned with her hand towards the door and I
closed it before she spoke.

'Mary Reilly and I found Old Barty's prayer book in the chapel,' she explained. 'We took it back to the dorm and wrote stuff about her in it.'

'What stuff?'

'Just stuff.'

'Kathleen!'

'Oh, all right . . . About her and Father Coyle.'

My hand flew to my mouth and I suppressed a snort of laughter.

'Don't say!' said Kathleen.

'Well, don't say where I'm really going tonight, then!'

Kathleen knew I wasn't going anywhere near Billy Martin's. I was going to number 8 Hayman's Green and I was trembling with excitement at the very thought. As I left the house, I heard a knock and looked up to see Kathleen grinning from the upstairs window and waving. I waved back and winked at her.

My friends and I got the bus to West Derby and were just about to ask for directions when we saw a throng of teenagers heading in the same direction. We joined the crowd and ended up in front of a big Victorian house, half concealed by trees, which that night seemed to us to be the most exciting place in the world. We headed down the driveway and joined the queue that was snaking out of the door.

This was the Casbah Club, founded by Mona Best, mother of Pete Best, who was the original drummer in the Beatles. (Two years after the Beatles formed, Pete was sacked by the Beatles' manager, Brian Epstein, and replaced with Ringo Starr.) In the late 1950s Mo had opened up the cellar of her home, ordered in crates of Coke and a coffee machine, and young people now crammed in to listen to the new groups that were springing up all over the city at that time. It was a huge house, with numerous bedrooms, and the story was that Mo was the first woman in Liverpool to get a mortgage. Apparently, she had sold all her jewellery and put the money on a Lester Piggott horse that had romped home at 33–1. The horse was called Never Say Die, which seemed very appropriate for Mo.

She was a formidable force: big, buxom and dark-haired with a personality to match. She was not the kind of woman you argued with; in fact, someone once said that if Mo told you on a Tuesday that it was Sunday, you would have no choice but to agree with her. That night she was stationed on the door collecting the tickets – pink for the girls and blue for the boys – and generally making sure there was no nonsense. The first band to play at the Casbah had been the Quarrymen, a group that had John Lennon, Paul McCartney and George Harrison as members. By now, though, they had left and formed the Beatles and tonight we were going to hear them play and decide for ourselves if the buzz about them was justified.

The club itself was a warren of narrow corridors and low-ceilinged cellar rooms, so the effect was small and intimate – or, more accurately, cramped! We paid our money and descended into the cellar, a wave of heat rising to meet us. There was no ventilation and after a while it was hard to breathe down there, but we didn't care. The sweat . . . the noise . . . the screams . . . it was all part of it. We crammed in together just as John Lennon leaped onto the small stage.

'We are the Beatles and we are going to play some rock and roll!' he shouted. The crowd went wild, screaming so loudly we could hardly hear the opening notes to the music.

The walls of the Casbah were painted with white gloss, apparently because John Lennon, who had helped Mo decorate, mistook it for emulsion. The sticky walls took quite some time to dry properly in the damp environment. John was studying art and a few weeks before opening night, he had also painted the ceilings of the cellar rooms that were to be used as the coffee bar and dance area. He painted pot-bellied figures at first, but Mo didn't like them.

'I'm not having that,' she said. 'Paint over them.'

He did as he was told and instead did an Aztec painting, which is still there. There was also a spider room, in which a painted red spider stuck in a white web was the backdrop to the stage. Paul McCartney painted a colourful rainbow on one of the ceilings, and the coffee bar's ceiling was covered with silver stars, stuck on by all the members of the band. Sotheby's recently valued those stars at £2,000 each – if they could be prised off the ceiling.

Perhaps if I had not gone to boarding school, or if I had gone to a mixed school, the effect of the Casbah would not have been quite so profound on me as it was. Everything about that night – the noise, the crush, the sweat on the walls – signalled freedom to me. My life had been so closely regulated, a world of incense and prayer, of rules and strictures, and here I was in a cellar listening to the most raucous, unrestrained music I'd ever heard in my life – music my parents would hate, which made it all the more appealing. I felt alive in a way I had never known before, new feelings bubbling up inside me until I felt I would explode with excitement.

And there was a lad. A cute-looking lad in drainpipe jeans who leaned against the brick walls and winked at me whenever I caught his eye. I didn't need him to talk to me. It was enough to know that in the whole crowded room, someone had noticed me. My hair was damp, and sweat trickled down my back, but I felt that this dark, dingy cellar was the centre of a new universe.

I didn't want to leave the Casbah, but we had to catch the last bus home. I hardly listened to the chatter of my friends around me because I was daydreaming the whole way back about what my life was going to be like now that school was over. This was only the beginning. Now I was back in Liverpool, I would go to teacher-training college, visit clubs, be free. I would educate children and change lives.

'Are you listening, Bernadette?' asked one of my friends.

'No,' I said, and they all laughed.

I wasn't too late home and Mum was still doing some ironing when I got back.

'Did you have a good time?' she asked.

'Oh, yes! It was fantastic!'

Mum looked at me in surprise. 'You sound a bit hoarse. Have you got a sore throat?'

Oops! All that shouting!

'A little bit. Might be coming down with something,' I said vaguely.

'No wonder, going about dressed like that,' she said, eyeing the mini-kilt. 'I had no idea you were a keen dancer,' she added, thumping the iron down on the board.

'Mmm.'

'I used to love going dancing,' she said, developing that nostalgic glint in her eye that all mothers get when they start reminiscing. 'The music . . . and the dresses! So feminine and elegant. Unlike you lot!'

I wrinkled my nose and stuck my tongue out at her and she half smiled, despite herself. She was still so mad with Kathleen that I could tell she was feeling quite well disposed towards me.

'So can you waltz now?'

'Oh, yes,' I said, 'I can waltz.'

It was true. That night I could waltz on air. It was just lucky she never asked me to show her!

6

The Four Buddies

I felt like Billy No Mates. It was September 1962, my first day at teacher-training college, and all around me there were chattering college girls, catching up after the summer holidays and squealing with laughter. We were all dressed similarly, most of us wearing our college scarves, which were navy with light blue stripes. I was so proud of that scarf! It was my badge of freedom. I was finally grown up, and when I wore it, I felt as if I was on my way to where I wanted to be. While I may have looked just like the others, though, I didn't feel part of the crowd. Having gone to school in Dublin, I didn't know a soul here and inside, I was desperate for acceptance. The few friends I did have left in Liverpool weren't training to be teachers. I shoved my hands deep into my duffle-coat pockets and tried to look nonchalant.

It was just assumed that having gone to a convent school, I would now train in a Catholic college and teach in Catholic schools when I qualified but I wouldn't have minded where I taught. My eye caught a group of girls standing round the main noticeboard and I went over to see if I could find out where I was meant to be. I had worn glasses since I was ten and was very short-sighted, but I didn't want to put them on. I squinted up at the board.

'Excuse me,' I said, smiling shyly at a pleasant-looking girl with short curly black hair who was talking to her friends. 'Do you mind if I just move in there past you to see the board?'

The girl returned my smile as she moved aside for me and I scanned the lists of names. Ah, there I was . . .

But as I scribbled down a quick note of the building and room number, I became conscious of the dark-haired girl looking curiously at me and trying to shift her position to get a better look at my face.

'Bernadette?'

I swivelled round in surprise. As I looked at her, something clicked in my head. She had eyes that were as blue as cornflowers . . .

'Tweet!' I exclaimed.

Tweet's real name was Ann Burd and I hadn't seen her since primary school.

'Bernadette Tierney!' she laughed. 'Where did you disappear to? We all wondered what had happened to you. Nobody told us that you weren't coming back for the final year of primary school!'

'Nobody told me either,' I said ruefully, remembering with a sudden rush of clarity the impact of those three dusty trunks on the landing.

Tweet's eyes widened when I told her what had happened.

'Oh, poor you!' Then she grinned. 'But never mind,' she said, linking her arm through mine and leading me off to our first class. 'You're back now!'

It was as easy as that.

*   *   *

'Maggie!' I hissed. 'Sister Alphonsus is coming!'

Maggie Gee shot out of her chair as if a gun had been fired, tripping over the bag at her feet. She had a book in her hands that looked as if it had suddenly turned into a hot potato as she looked around wildly for somewhere to put it. In her panic, she thrust it under the cushion of her seat and hastily sat back down on top of it at a rather lopsided angle.

There was a group of us sitting drinking coffee in a soft-seated area of the college and we all grinned at Maggie as she looked expectantly at us.

'Oh, sorry, Maggie,' I said innocently. 'It's not Sister Alphonsus after all. It's just Tweet in a black coat!'

'Bernadette Tierney, I'm going to throttle you!' said Maggie, pulling the book out from under the cushion and taking a swipe at me with it.

'What's going on?' asked Tweet, throwing herself into an empty chair.

'Maggie's reading *Sex and the Single Girl*,' said my friend Annie Stauss, a vivacious blonde with sparkling blue eyes who was always full of fun.

'Still?' said Tweet, raising her eyes. She turned to Maggie. 'What chapter are you on?'

'Two,' said Maggie.

'Two!' said Tweet in disbelief. '*Two?* Maggie, you've been reading that for a month at least!' She looked at her with mock suspicion. 'So that's why you want to teach nursery-age children. You can't read!'

'Ha, ha,' said Maggie good-naturedly.

'Look at that,' I said. 'The cover has an endorsement from Joan Crawford.'

'Well, she should know what she's talking about, anyway,' murmured Annie. 'She's been married four times! Or is it five?'

'What does the book say, Maggie?' I asked. Having gone to a girls' convent school, and now finding myself at an all-female college, I needed all the help I could get to unravel the mysteries of men.

'No! We don't want to know!' exclaimed Tweet, who was a bit more sensible than the rest of us.

' "Chapter Two," ' read Maggie, ignoring her. ' "The Availables." '

'What are they?' I asked.

'You have to list all the men you know and put them into categories. Listen . . .' She began reading from the text. ' "The Eligibles . . ." She looked up at us, expecting some names, but we all stared back blankly. We didn't know any Eligibles. That was the problem. ' "The Eligibles But Who Needs Them," ' continued Maggie.

Well, we might know a few of them.

' "The Don Juans . . . The Married Men . . . The Homosexuals . . . The Divorcing Man . . . The Younger Man . . ." '

Annie raised a perfectly arched eyebrow. 'Pass . . .' she murmured.

'Is there a category for just *any* man?' said Tweet plaintively.

'The trouble with us,' sighed Maggie Gee, 'is that we're at an all-female college.' She closed the book and started gathering up her things. 'Need to go. I'm supposed to see Sister Alphonsus about my assignment.'

'Here,' I said, a mischievous idea suddenly occurring to me, 'you don't want Sister Alphonsus to see your book, Maggie. Give it to me and I'll stick it in your locker for you.'

'Ta,' said Maggie, and the array of bracelets on her wrist jingle-jangled loudly as she threw it to me. Then she wiggled her way down the corridor in her tight leopard-print miniskirt and white heels.

'Hey, Maggie,' shouted Annie, and Maggie turned. Annie motioned onwards with her arm. 'Straight on for Lime Street!' she called.

Lime Street was the red-light district and we used to tease Maggie about her blonde beehive and colourful outfits, the gold lamé gloves and sparkling bling. It was all good-humoured; one of Maggie's greatest attributes was her sense of fun and she never took offence. She put her hands on her hips and made a face at Annie, before walking off with an even more exaggerated wiggle.

I took a sheet of paper from my bag when she'd gone. 'Right,' I said, 'I've got an idea. Who can write like a nun? I want to put a note in Maggie's locker.'

We spent the next half-hour composing a variety of notes, supposedly from Reverend Mother, but decided in the end that simplicity was best.

' "Margaret," ' the note read, ' "I have found a very offensive book in your locker. Please come and discuss this with me at five o'clock outside the library. Reverend Mother." '

Poor Maggie nearly had a heart attack when she looked in her locker that afternoon and found the note but no book.

'What am I going to do?' she wailed.

We all pretended to be shocked.

'Oh, I am so sorry, Maggie,' I said, trying to keep a straight face. 'I didn't know Reverend Mother did inspections of the lockers or I would never have put the book in there.'

By late afternoon Maggie was twitching nervously. She had wiped all trace of lipstick from her mouth and was pulling the leopard-print mini down over her backside, trying in vain to make it more respectable.

'Lost cause, Mags,' said Tweet.

'Bernadette,' said Maggie desperately, looking at my low-heeled strap shoes, 'you take the same size shoe as me. Can we swap for ten minutes while I go and see Reverend Mother?'

I obligingly took off my shoes and gave them to Maggie, slipping my feet into her white stilettos.

'God, Maggie! How do you walk around in these all the time?' I tottered precariously for a few steps but ended up shuffling like a child in her mother's too-big shoes.

Maggie took a deep breath. 'Better go or I'll be late.' She looked around. 'Where's Annie?'

'Dunno.'

Tweet and I exchanged a glance and I almost laughed. We knew exactly where Annie was.

'Wish me luck,' said Maggie, and she was off down the corridor, still tugging at the back of her skirt.

'Quick!' said Tweet when she disappeared. 'We need to run round the other side to get to the library before her.'

Tweet shot off, with me in less than quick pursuit.

'Tweet! Wait!' I hissed, hobbling in her wake in Maggie's impossible shoes. Eventually, I pulled them off and ran barefoot to catch up.

When Maggie reached the library, she found a nun in full veil waiting for her. What she didn't know was that the rest of us were hiding behind the bookcases, with our hands over our mouths, smothering giggles.

Maggie didn't even wait for 'Reverend Mother' to demand an explanation. She walked straight up to her and immediately began talking nervously.

'I'm very sorry, Sister,' she said contritely. 'It's not my book. I'm just looking after it for a friend.'

Behind the bookcase, we were doubled up, but Reverend Mother was saying nothing. I could see Maggie looking down at the floor, then glancing quickly up again. Something wasn't right here. Reverend Mother was wearing Dr Scholl's sandals and had bright red nail polish on her toes!

'Annie you bitch!' shouted Maggie.

It was indeed Annie, dressed in an outfit we had borrowed from one of the student nuns on the pretext of playing a nun in an opera production. We all tumbled out from behind the bookcases, beside ourselves with laughter, and Maggie couldn't help good-naturedly joining in.

'Here,' I said, handing her both her shoes and her copy of *Sex and the Single Girl*.

Maggie's confidence and bravado quickly returned. We played pranks on each other all the time, and she would doubtless get her own back!

'What's the next chapter, Maggie?' asked Tweet.

'"How to Be Sexy,"' said Maggie.

We all whistled.

'I think,' said Maggie, slipping her feet into her stilettos and shaping her lips into a grotesque pout, 'I can afford to skip that bit!'

It was good to have a wide circle of friends at college, and I loved training to be a teacher, but there were four of us who gradually became closer and we called ourselves 'the Four Buddies'. There was the crazy blonde, Annie Stauss, Geraldine (whom we called 'Jellybean'), Barbara Mc and me. Annie, Jellybean and I were all quite similar – always full of mad schemes and mischief – while Barbara was the quieter one of the group and perhaps a little more sensible, like Tweet. They usually acted as a restraining influence on the rest of us when we got out of hand!

Jellybean was very musical and went on to become quite well known as a singer, but she hadn't discovered her abilities until she went to college. Her father, who had played the saxophone and was a 'Wall of Death' rider, had scarpered years before and Jellybean lived in a flat with her mother, who was very bohemian, and her sister Pat, and brother John. They had a piano in the flat, but there had been no money for fancy stuff like music lessons. When Jellybean was at college, however, she discovered a wonderful talent for the piano. She switched to a slightly different course from the rest of us, specialising in music. She had to practise hard because she was starting from scratch, but she loved it and was so naturally gifted that she came out with a degree in music.

The four of us haunted Liverpool's Bold Street, where there were lots of coffee bars, like the El Caballa and La Bussola. Our social lives revolved round these cafés during the day and the smoke-filled clubs like the Casbah and the Jacaranda at night. When the Beatles formed, they played in both those clubs, but it was the famous Cavern that they became most associated with. Like the Casbah, the Cavern was in a cellar. It was used as an air-raid shelter during the war and was said to have been inspired by the famous Parisian jazz club le Caveau.

We did get to see the Beatles in the Cavern, though it didn't turn out quite as we expected. One lunchtime in 1962, not long after we started training to be teachers, we all wound our way downstairs into the tiny club with its bare, rough brick walls and curved tunnel-like ceiling. We sat in a quiet corner because we didn't want to be noticed. You were supposed to buy the Cavern's food if you ate there, but we were too poor and had smuggled in our own sandwiches.

'Oh, I can't wait for this,' said Annie, trying to surreptitiously unwrap a packet of sandwiches that was nestling in her bag.

'What, a limp cheese sandwich?' teased Jellybean.

'No! The Beatles!'

The club was dimly lit and Jellybean peered into Annie's bag. 'Oh God, Annie, you put tomato in it! It will be all soggy and disgusting.'

Annie shrugged and took a big bite, then looked at Jellybean and laughed. 'You're right,' she said.

'Disgusting. But it's going to be worth it. Do you think they'll sing "Love Me Do"?'

'Love Me Do' had been the Beatles' first hit, released a few months earlier, and while it had only peaked at number seventeen, we had all loved it. As it turned out, however, not only did the Beatles not sing 'Love Me Do', they didn't sing anything at all; they only played their instruments.

'What's going on?' we asked one of the staff. 'Why aren't they singing?'

'Sorry, girls,' he replied. 'You need a special licence to sing at lunchtime. You'll have to come back at night.'

We couldn't afford to, though, and somehow we seemed to miss our chance because the Beatles' last appearance at the Cavern came just a year later. I had seen them at the Casbah, but the others hadn't and were bitterly disappointed.

'Never mind,' I consoled them, trying to look on the bright side, 'at least we *saw* them.'

We were always broke at college, but I didn't care. After years of incarceration at the convent, I felt rich in other ways. For a girl who had resorted to surreptitiously listening to Radio Luxembourg under the blankets in her Dublin dorm, Liverpool felt like the centre of the universe. Even the Rumblin' Tum Café was heaven. I loved the way the jukebox blared out the latest hits. I loved the buzz and the chatter and the camaraderie. Most of all, I loved the freedom.

Sometimes we would take our college essays to write there, and the contrast with the hushed regime of Old

Barty's homework classes couldn't have been more marked. It gave me a little surge of happiness every time I realised how different my life now was. I hummed along to the music, the hiss of coffee machines as background percussion, and scribbled happily as the rain splattered against the windowpanes and ran in rivers from the gutters. For ten pence we got a slice of toast and a mug of coffee and the only problem was making it last for a thousand-word essay. We nursed our coffees for as long as possible, but we would usually got chucked out eventually.

'Come on round to Rodney Street,' Jellybean said one day when we were looking for somewhere to go. 'I found a really nice café called the Centurion there the other day.'

'Rodney Street!' exclaimed Annie. 'Isn't that very expensive?'

Rodney Street was Liverpool's equivalent to London's Harley Street. It was a very well-to-do area with fine, listed Georgian architecture and was home to consulting rooms of many different specialists. The Centurion was attached to an antique shop, and we sat there all afternoon, writing furiously, without anyone coming near us. We did, though, see a very scantily clad girl disappear upstairs.

'She'd give Maggie a run for her money,' murmured Jellybean to me across the table, and I laughed.

Eventually, the waitress came over with a coffeepot.

'Would you like some more?' she asked.

'Actually, we can't really afford another,' I replied apologetically.

'You're OK,' she said. 'No one's looking,' and she kindly filled up our cups.

'Isn't this place friendly?' whispered Barbara Mc.

Annie looked up from her essay. 'Have you noticed how many posh businessmen have been coming in and out?' she said, as another pinstripe-suited man disappeared upstairs.

'That girl who went up was a bit strangely dressed,' said Jellybean thoughtfully, chewing on the end of her pen.

'Must be another bit to the café upstairs,' said Annie. 'Bet it's expensive!'

I don't know what it was but the rest of us just looked at one another.

'What?' said Annie, and then she suddenly clicked.

Gentlemen. Upstairs. Scantily clad girl.

'Let's get out of here!' I said, gathering up my things.

We were poor students trying to eke out our grants, but there were some things at which even we drew the line!

It was just a smile. A stranger's smile across a room. At nineteen, I had no idea how significant that stranger would become.

It was a Saturday night and all the Four Buddies were together because Annie was having a party at her house. Wherever I turned, the stranger seemed always to be in my eyeline.

'Who's the dark-haired guy leaning against the wall?' I whispered to Annie, intrigued but slightly disconcerted by the unflinching dark-brown eyes.

She glanced up. 'That's Jaime,' she said. 'He's Spanish.'

By this time Annie had extended her Eligibles list and was going out with a boy called Fred. Jaime was Fred's friend. He was shorter than my usual type – only a couple of inches taller than me, in fact – but quite charismatic, his olive complexion giving him an exotic warmth next to the lily-skinned Liverpool lads.

Next thing I knew, Jaime was at my shoulder and Annie was introducing us. Music thumped steadily in the background and I had difficulty shouting above it, but I discovered that he was one of seven children whose family had moved from Spain when he was ten. His English was fluent, but his mother had never learned English, so the family all spoke Spanish at home. Jaime's accent was a curious hybrid of Spanish and Scouse inflections.

He was a year older than me and worked for a shipping company. His job, he told me, was to translate the ship's manifest and then go on board with the documents. I didn't get the impression his job was very important to him, though. Jaime seemed intriguingly contradictory to me: he was laid-back in his attitude to life, and had a fantastic sense of humour, yet there was such an intense quality about the way he spoke and interacted with me.

'Can I take your phone number?' he asked at the end of the evening.

I hesitated. My dad insisted that we didn't give out our phone number to any friends because the line needed to be free when he was on call and he didn't want it to ring when he wasn't on duty. Dad would go mad if I started getting calls from strange men. But Jaime's dark eyes were watching me intently and for some reason I couldn't say no.

'Have you got a pen?' I asked.

Jaime fished in his pockets and brought out a cigarette packet from one and a pen from another, and proceeded to write my number down on the packet.

'I'll call you,' he said, and smiled.

On Monday Annie sought me out first thing.

'Remember Jaime?' she said.

I nodded.

'Well, you certainly made your mark,' she laughed. 'Poor guy went to Mass four times yesterday hoping to bump into me!'

'What on earth did he do that for?'

'Apparently, he forgot that he had written your phone number on his cigarette packet and threw it away. He wanted me to give him your number again.'

Four Masses! I was flattered. By this time I didn't even go to Mass once on a Sunday. Although my parents insisted that we all went to church, they weren't especially religious. My mother sent us all to Mass on a Sunday morning while she stayed at home and made lunch. When we came back, she would ask questions to make sure we'd been, like 'What colour were the priest's vestments?' Now that we were older, we would go to the pub and then nip into the church on the way back to pick up a newsletter and check out what the priest was wearing. 'Right, purple this week,' we'd all agree.

By Tuesday Jaime had phoned. It was a long time after that I discovered that on the night we met, he went home and told his sister Marie that he had met the girl he was going to marry. I did sense that he was keen, though, and a few weeks after our first meeting there was a knock at the door. I opened it to find a florist's van parked outside.

'Miss Bernadette Tierney?' said the delivery man.

I nodded, too surprised to speak.

He handed over the first bouquet I'd ever received in my life. It was a rustling mass of cellophane and extravagant ribbon bows, and nestling inside was an array of bright yellow and burnt-orange flowers that glowed like a blast of sultry Spanish sunshine. I closed the door behind me and buried my nose in the flowers, sniffing deeply. My mother came into the hall, her eyebrows shooting up in surprise at the sight of the flowers, but she disappeared again without saying a word.

I would need to tell Maggie Gee my news. My list of men now had a single name on it. But was he, as *Sex and the Single Girl* would demand to know, just an 'Available' or a genuine 'Eligible'? Only time would tell.

7

Keeping Order

The day came during our training when we were let out of the lecture theatre and into schools with real children. I was so excited at the prospect. This was what I'd dreamed of ever since I lined up those buttons from my mum's tin on the carpet. I had lavished care on my 'children' back then because I knew that was what kids wanted. At least, it was what I wanted and I was just acting out my secret fantasies. Our house had been full of kids rushing in and out, so there hadn't been much time to focus on each of us individually. If I could have secretly changed my life, it would have been to include more cuddles and have more notice taken of me. Not in a spoiled-brat, attention-seeking kind of way; I was just a little girl who longed for love. Now I was grown up, I felt I had a lot of love to give children who might feel just as I once had. I understood them. For me, the intense emotions of childhood hadn't simply faded away. I remembered them as if they were yesterday.

How I was actually going to translate all these good intentions and emotional responses into something effective in a classroom was another matter. Next door to our training college was the demonstration school. When I was a child, one of our primary-school classmates used to go to 'the Dem', as it was called, and I thought it was a very strange name for a school. It was only as a student that I understood.

Every morning these children in their brown uniforms were frogmarched over to college, where our tutors would demonstrate how to teach different subjects, like maths, English and science. We just watched, but when the next group arrived, one of the students would be selected to give a lesson. In some regards, it was a good way to learn to teach, but it was certainly laboratory conditions. It didn't prepare us for the harsh reality of schools. The children in the Dem were so docile and well behaved it was unbelievable. We thought, This teaching lark is going to be a doddle!

Crash!

At the back of the class, a chair toppled over in the general chaos and a shower of pink, mauve and yellow tulip petals rained down onto the desks. A voice rose shrilly above the din.

'Miss, he's got all my petals!'

Bang!

'Oi! They're mine! Give 'em back or I'll batter yer!'

A doddle? I'd been for root-canal treatment that was more agreeable than this.

I was on my very first teaching practice and had been placed in a senior primary class. It was a school that was situated next door to a gas works and the stench permeated everywhere. Playground duty was a nightmare, but the children didn't seem to notice the noxious smell. I suppose they were used to it. Gas wasn't the only thing ready to explode round here . . .

For the first week the class teacher had stayed with me while I taught, but now I was on my own. I had started with such high ideals. I was teaching a biology lesson and had gone to the expense of buying enough tulips for every child to have their own, so that we could learn the different parts of the flower. I thought they would enjoy the novelty. The idea was that the children would gently remove the petals and stick them into their books. The foolishly optimistic word here was 'gently'. The petals were ripped from the stems before I could even finish explaining the task!

'Gerry Matthews, give me tulip back or I'll deck yer!' roared Bernie, a big, heavy-set lad who already had the cut of a junior Mafia leader.

'I don't have yer stupid tulip, soft lad! It were Johnny!'

'Fight! Fight!' chanted a delighted duo of mischief-makers in the corner.

'Boys, sit down this minute,' I said, hoping that if I kept calm, order would be restored. It was as if I hadn't spoken. Nobody took the slightest bit of notice.

Never mind the War of the Roses, this was the War of the Tulips. A few of the boys started hitting each other over the head with the flowers and soon the sound of shouts and uproarious laughter rang round the room. It was mayhem, with even those children who were normally reserved getting overexcited and joining in.

The nauseating smell of gas leaked through the open windows, contributing to my growing headache. 'Polly, shut the windows, please,' I said desperately to a quiet girl in the corner. 'The rest of you, sit down!'

Nobody paid the slightest notice. Children have an animal instinct about authority and who's 'just' a student. I had completely lost control and was taken by surprise at how quickly it had happened. One minute I was in charge of a class of relatively well-behaved children, the next I had a near riot on my hands.

'SIT DOWN!'

Even I jumped. The door had been thrown open and Miss Thompson, the class teacher, had walked in. Instantly, you could hear a pin drop.

'I could hear you down the corridor . . . Now sit down and be quiet,' she said sternly. She pointed a finger at the back of the class, making a beeline for the ringleaders. 'Gerry Matthews, Bernie Taylor . . . out! I might have known I couldn't leave you for two minutes.'

Bernie ambled slowly to the front of the class like a disgruntled bear, followed by Gerry, who immediately began protesting his innocence.

'Aarh ray, miss,' he said with aggrieved innocence. 'It wasn't me—'

'Don't you "aarh ray" me, Gerry Matthews,' snapped Miss Thompson.

'Aarh ray' was a very versatile Liverpool phrase, used frequently by children in myriad contexts. If they heard someone had died, they would say slowly, 'Aarh ray,' in a soft, sad voice, but if they were told to go to the other side of the playground after a fight, the same phrase would be used with loud indignation. It was a phrase I would hear a lot during the course of my career!

'Miss—'

'Bernie, not another word,' said Miss Thompson, and there wasn't.

Could I ever exert control like that? I don't know what that class learned about biology, but I learned something important that day and decided a younger age group might suit me better. In actual fact, my disastrous lesson with the tulips was just lack of experience – the kind of thing that happens to most teaching students at some point or another – but it dented my confidence for a while. Then I realised something. Learning isn't a straight line. It's a bumpy one with ups and downs along the way – and learning to teach is no different.

Having said that, knowing your strengths is important and even after one teaching practice the obvious was staring me in the face. It was small children towards whom I instinctively gravitated and I noticed that in turn they gravitated towards me. Young children were fun. They made me laugh. They made me want to protect and nurture and help them. When I went back to college, I had a word with my tutors. From now on, I said, I wanted to specialise in infant teaching.

My romance with Jaime blossomed in the following months. Annie and I sometimes worked in a bingo hall for a pound a night and Jaime would often wait outside for me and we'd go to the Wimpy for a burger and milk-shake, or to a late film. We didn't have the best of introductions at each other's houses, though, which would later be the subject of much hilarity. The first time I went to Jaime's house, his sister Maria and his mother were in the middle of a full-blown Mediterranean argument. I could hear the raised voices the moment we came in, and as we opened the kitchen door, a jar of strawberry jam went flying past my ear and splattered against the wall. The thick red jam glooped down the wall as we all stared at one another in horror.

'Who is this?' demanded Jaime's mum.

It was my introduction to Spanish volatility!

Jaime was always a gentleman about seeing me home and he would catch the last bus from near my house. One night we spent rather too long saying goodnight – Romeo and Juliet had nothing on us – and we looked up to see the last bus coming down the road. Jaime jumped out and waved his arms, but the bus sailed by.

We just looked at one another.

'What on earth are you going to do now?' I said.

Jaime shrugged. 'Walk?'

'You can't do that! It's much too far.'

I looked at my watch. Mum and Dad would be in bed.

'Come with me,' I said, 'and be really quiet. You can sleep in the kitchen.'

We tiptoed in and I pushed two chairs together and left Jaime to sleep with a blanket over him. Unfortunately, my dad was called out in the middle of the night and came downstairs to find a complete stranger asleep in his kitchen.

'Who the hell are you?' he demanded, snapping on the light.

Poor Jaime nearly died of fright.

'I'll go,' he said, after stuttering out an explanation.

Amazingly, my dad, who always refused to let us have visitors in the house, told him grumpily to stay where he was. By the time he got back, Jaime was away for the first bus and I made myself scarce for the next couple of days!

Even though I was dating Jaime, my friendships remained important to me and I saw plenty of my college friends. Annie was the only one of our group who 'lived in' at the halls of residence. The halls were down at the River Mersey and the road up to the bus-stop was dark and a bit creepy at night. Consequently, the rest of us often bunked in for the night with Annie, making sure that no one knew we were there, as it was strictly forbidden to have people stay overnight. Actually, I think they were probably referring to boyfriends, but we didn't take any chances. When we got off the bus from town after college, we would go to the chip shop and get a 'six of chips'. Then we'd buy a loaf of bread so that we could have chip butties for supper.

When we got to the halls, if anyone was at the main gate, Annie would have to think of a diversionary tactic. Fortunately, she had a very lively imagination and would suddenly say, 'I think someone is hanging around in the bushes over there.' The caretaker would go off to check and that usually gave us a chance to make a run for it, and when we arrived at Annie's room, we would collapse on the bed, shrieking with laughter. We could probably all have just walked in the main door, but we had a well-developed sense of drama.

One day a girl called Vee invited Annie and me round for dinner at her house on a Friday night. We didn't really know her that well, but it was nice of her to invite us and we politely accepted. It turned out to be the strangest of experiences. Vee lived in an area called Old Swan, so Annie came to my house and we got a bus from Penny Lane. We eventually found the house and were greeted by Vee and her mum. Bizarrely, though, all through the meal, if there was the slightest noise outside, the two of them would freeze.

'Is that dada?' her mum would say, and we would sit in silence, waiting.

Annie and I just looked at one another across the table, eyes widening.

'No, it's not,' her mum would finally decide, and everyone would breathe out and resume eating with relief.

By the fourth time Annie and I were beginning to feel a bit unnerved.

Afterwards Annie said politely, 'Can we do the washing-up?'

'Oh, that would be lovely,' said Vee's mum.

We carried the dishes into the kitchen and were dismayed to be confronted by at least a week's worth of washing-up, including congealed porridge pans, frying pans and tons of greasy plates. We spent almost an hour washing and drying them before hearing the click of the side gate. Vee came dashing in to us at the sink.

'It's dada!' she whispered. 'Can you leave now?'

We grabbed our coats and she virtually threw us out of the front door. Annie and I laughed all the way to the bus-stop. Vee's dada must have been just like mine: a force of nature.

Even forces of nature can be quelled, though. Little did I know that by the next day, I would have a terrible shock about my dad. The whole evening at Vee's had been so strange that Annie and I had decided to go on to the Jacaranda, a club in Slater Street. The plan had been that I would stay that night at Annie's house rather than travel home, so we knew we could be as late as we liked.

It had been such a good night because I loved the Jacaranda. It was another tiny, brick-floored cellar night-club that was dark, smoky and noisy – just the way I liked it! The Jacaranda was actually the first club that the Beatles performed at when they got together, and it was owned by their first manager, Allan Williams. My mother had banned my sister Helena from going there because she heard people smoked pot. If they did, I didn't know anything about that. Like most teenagers, I just loved the live music and the dark, bohemian glamour of it.

Like the Casbah, the walls of the Jacaranda had artwork done by the Beatles, bold ornamental patterns and strange haunted faces inspired by African and Polynesian art. Most of it had been painted by Stuart Sutcliffe, the original bass player of the Beatles, who had left the group before they became really famous to concentrate on his art. Stuart had subsequently died of a brain aneurysm in the middle of an art class in Germany, at the age of just twenty-two. It was a sad story, but his artwork in the Jacaranda really set the atmosphere of the club. Allan Williams once described it as 'the black hole of Calcutta set to music' and that just about summed it up.

After a fantastic night Annie and I got back late and were looking forward to a lie-in, but early next morning there was a pounding at the door.

'What on earth is that?' I asked sleepily, opening one eye and squinting into the light.

Annie stumbled out of bed and went over to the window. There was a guy on a motorbike with a visor looking up at her. Annie lifted the windowpane.

'Go away!' she shouted grumpily.

'I've got a telegram,' he replied. 'For Bernadette Tierney.'

I jumped out of bed and ran to get the telegram, completely baffled as to what it might be about. I ripped it open and discovered it was from my mother.

'Come home. Daddy ill,' it said.

I should have known, really. You don't send a telegram just because someone's a bit sick. I took two buses and a train to get home.

'How's Daddy?' I said as I walked through the door.

My mother looked at me in total shock for a moment. 'He's dead.'

It was so sudden, so stark, that I couldn't really take it in. We didn't shout or scream or even cry. Not immediately. It was almost as if we had gone beyond emotion, into a strange place of disbelief where we had pressed a button and the world had simply stopped. Daddy had been such a dominating presence for all of us. He was the person the house's activities revolved round. How could he simply be gone? Mum and I stood stock still, as if we were waiting for someone to press the button again, for the world to resume and everything to be back to normal, but it never, ever would be.

Aideen came over from the convent in Dublin for his funeral, but she was not allowed to stay at home. I felt so sad for her. A funeral is such an ordeal, but while the rest of us were able to stick together as a family after the traumatic events of the day, Aideen had to go to a local convent, where she knew nobody, to stay the night. I didn't like to think of her alone in there. Things would change later, when her convent rules became much more relaxed, but that day it brought home to me that Aideen no longer belonged to us. The nuns had gained a sister and I had lost one.

My dad was only fifty when he passed away, but he smoked and drank and was overweight. In the weeks to come Mum found his diary. She handed it to me silently. The pages were full of notes and blood-pressure read-ings, little squiggles and exclamation marks at the side of the page if there was a particularly worrying measure-ment. He had tried going on a diet, but he hadn't been very successful and now it was too late. All that was left were pages of scribbled notes. Looking at them, I felt sad. I think that he knew that he might not have long to live and I wondered about the secret fears that he had carried, and the extra pressure that must have heaped upon him.

Money was tight after he died and the following summer I went to work in a factory during the holidays. My grant had run out weeks before and I certainly needed the money, but the whole experience also ended up providing me with an insight into my dad. The job was making perfume boxes for Hypnotique and Electrique Christmas gift sets and my first two weeks were spent on 'the punch', where I had to punch holes in sheets of acetate. There was a whole gang of students employed, so it was a bit more fun, but in general the place was pretty awful and at first the women who worked there refused to speak to any of us.

'If it weren't for you lot being here making the boxes,' one of them said, 'we'd get lots of overtime later in the year.'

We had our uses in the end, though. The first lunchtime one of us asked the boss which room we could eat our sandwiches in. He looked quite bemused and didn't bother to answer. So when the lunchtime hooter went, we just followed the other workers. Where would they lead us? A staff canteen? A cloakroom? Not exactly. Our lunchtime restaurant was the toilets. They all sat themselves on the floor and proceeded to eat their butties.

There was no way we were eating our lunch in the toilets, so we went outside and sat in the rain by the railway line. A nice young student called John started going on about workers' rights and what a disgrace it was that these people had no proper staff facilities. Within a day or two he had started rallying the workers. One of them asked us if we would support them if they threatened strike action for better working conditions. To a person, we said yes.

Fortunately, it didn't come to that and the management reluctantly agreed to allocate a room for us at lunchtime. From that moment on all of us students were accepted as part of the workforce. The best two weeks for me were spent in the packing room with Manfred Mann blaring out on the radio. 'Come on without, come on within, you ain't seen nothing like the mighty . . . Everton,' as the girls there sang lustily.

My job in the factory was only temporary, but it taught me a lesson. It was a means to an end – I really needed that money – but despite making some friends there, I knew I didn't want to do it for ever. I realised fully how lucky you were in life if you had a job that inspired you, that made you want to get up in the morning. I thought of my father and, for the first time, understood him.

Dad hadn't wanted to be a doctor. He had wanted to study languages and only took medicine because his own father had forced him to. He had died doing a job that rubbed like an ill-fitting shoe, and while he could walk, it was painful. Growing up, we had trodden on eggshells around him because he always seemed to be on a short fuse. Now I realised that he had spent his whole life living someone else's dreams and maybe it wasn't surprising that he carried so much anger around inside him. In my heart, I made my peace with him.

I knew how lucky I was: I knew what I wanted to do with my life, had always known. I wanted to teach children, and if I worked hard, I would be allowed to do just that. Nobody would stop me in the way my dad had been stopped. Coming out of that factory, my determination had never been stronger and I worked hard. When I finally got that all-important piece of paper saying I was qualified, I felt completely fulfilled. That's why, as I listened to 'Help' on the radio that very first morning, I couldn't wait to get started, despite my nerves. I knew I didn't just have a job; I had a vocation. I was going to change lives.

8

Leakin' Shoes and Rumblin' Tums

When I stepped off the bus in Huyton that first morning, I found myself in what could only be described as a concrete jungle, a dismal sprawl of high-rise flats and ugly graffiti, with small groups of young men mooching around on street corners with nothing to do. I felt sorry for the people forced into blocks of flats, stacked on top of one another like biscuit tins, who could do little to make their living environment more pleasant. There were very few houses that had gardens, and those that did tended to have discarded baths or broken tellies rusting disconsolately in the rain. The people here were trapped in every way. There were only a few dingy shops, and the prices they charged suggested Dick Turpin's descendants were alive and well and trading in Huyton. It was daylight robbery.

While it wasn't a pretty place, there was a lot of spirit about Huyton. The people were warm and humorous, and there was a sense of community because everyone was facing the same problems. They were in it together. I was looking forward to teaching here and I was pleased that I would have a familiar face in the school: my vibrant friend Maggie Gee had got a job here too.

The young lads hanging around Huyton with nothing to do had a bit of a twinkle in their eyes as they watched the girls go by.

'Eh, love,' one of them shouted cheerily as I walked towards the school, 'do you need a hand with that bag? It looks heavy!'

'No, thanks – I can manage!' I grinned.

It was still early when I got to the playground that first morning, and as I crossed the yard that was to become so familiar in the coming months, I saw a lonely little dark-haired figure kicking stones with shoes that had seen much better days. It wasn't his shoes that made the biggest impression on me, though. It was his strange hat. I didn't have my glasses on and I squinted at the outline in the distance. I just couldn't figure it out. What on earth was that perched on top of his head? As I drew closer, I realised to my horror it was a sanitary towel, stretched across and then tied under his chin.

I walked over and gave him a big, reassuring smile.

'Hello,' I said. 'What's your name?'

He looked at me with big, soft brown eyes. 'Joey, miss,' he replied solemnly. 'You the new teacher, miss?'

I nodded. 'First day, Joey, so I'm a bit lost. Do you think you can help me?'

He nodded back, eyes shining in his pale little face like two round, dark pennies. Children love to think they can help adults and Joey was so proud to have a job.

'Come on, then,' I said. 'Come and show me where everything is.'

As we walked towards the school, I said as casually as I could, 'What's that on your head, Joey?'

'Earmuffs, miss. I've got the earache and me mum says I've gorra wear 'em.'

'Hmm,' I said thoughtfully. 'I can see they're very useful, those earmuffs, but do you know what?'

'What, miss?'

'I think I felt the rain coming on as we came into school, and while your earmuffs would be very good for dry days, I think they're maybe not so good for rainy days. What do you think?'

Joey nodded.

'Well, let's see what else we can find for you,' I said. 'Can you show me where the lost-property box is?'

Joey led me down the corridors until we came to the cloakroom, where there was a brightly coloured box in the corner, stuffed full of hats and scarves, discarded gloves and forgotten jumpers. After a quick rummage around, we found a bright blue balaclava.

'Do you like this one, Joey?'

'Yeah. That's Everton, innit?'

A wad of cotton wool in each ear and he was 'made up', which I soon discovered in Scouse-speak meant pleased! Joey had gained a bright blue balaclava and I had gained a friend for life, a right-hand man who would run to carry my bags when he saw me in the morning and who stuck loyally by my side whenever he could.

'Now, would you like to come and help me pin up my posters before the bell goes?' I asked, and was rewarded by a beaming smile.

I was glad I had brought some posters to decorate the room because I have to say it was all a bit unprepossessing. The school was no more than a series of old wooden huts in an L-shape, containing eight classrooms. The only brick building was the one where the teachers' staffroom and the head teacher's office were situated. It sounds almost Dickensian now, but my classroom had a stove in it, lit by the caretaker every morning.

'What do you think, Joey?' I asked, as we stepped back to admire our handiwork on the wall.

'Looks great, miss,' he said enthusiastically.

'Which is your favourite picture?'

'The tiger!' he said immediately.

I smiled. 'Mine too.'

When the bell rang and the class trooped in, the children eyed me curiously. It's one of the things I like about young children: the honesty of their interaction. Often, they tell a thing the way it is, without artifice. 'I like your shoes.' 'I don't like your scarf.' 'Why is your hair sticking up?' They sat down quietly while they checked me out and there was that strange moment when forty pairs of eyes swivelled onto me and just waited. I was like a conductor in front of an orchestra. I realised they were waiting for me to raise my baton – and then the music would begin!

There is nothing quite like a particular smell for taking you right back to a place and a time. It had been raining quite heavily by the time the bell went and the huts smelled damp, of steaming clothes and stale urine, because as I discovered, some of the children wet the bed but weren't washed afterwards. Some of the houses had baths, but the local joke was that in this area, the bath was where you kept the coal. On rainy days like today, when the classroom windows got steamed up, the smell got worse, but after a while you became almost immune.

There was a big fireguard round the stove, so I told the children to take their wet things off and hang them over the guard. Soon the room sizzled with the stench of steaming socks, which had turned grey with the grime and rainwater that had leaked into their shoes. Some of the children didn't even have socks and just had their bare feet stuffed into their shoes.

'What's that?' I asked one little boy, as his bare foot emerged from his shoe with a soggy grey lump of matter on top.

'It's cardboard, miss,' he said. 'From me mum's corn-flake packet,' he added, seeing my mystified look. 'You know . . . to stuff the holes in me shoe, like.'

Well, I hadn't known, but I did now. Many of the children had holes in their shoes and they had to try their own repairs. They were gorgeous children, they really were, but they were also poor little ragamuffins with holes in their trousers and snail trails of snot on their sleeves. I wanted to gather them up and take them home with me to make sure they were all right.

'I can't do these sums for me belly rumblin',' I heard one little boy called Charlie murmur to his friend Ben halfway through the morning.

'What did you say . . . Charlie, isn't it?' I asked, and he looked up, startled that I'd heard, then blushed scarlet.

'Nothin', miss,' he said.

'He's just hungry, miss,' said Ben.

'What did you have for breakfast, Charlie?'

The question seemed to mystify Charlie as much as if I'd asked him, 'How high is the Eiffel Tower?' Or, 'What angle does the Leaning Tower of Pisa lean at?' Breakfast? What breakfast?

'Pencils down, everybody,' I called, and there was a clatter of wooden pencils rolling into the grooves on the desks. The class looked at me expectantly.

'Hands up if you had breakfast this morning,' I said.

Only a few put their hands into the air. What I discovered was that many of the children got themselves out in the morning because their parents were unemployed. When they didn't have a job, I suppose it was easy for some of the mums and dads to lose motivation and they often didn't bother getting up until later in the morning.

'I've got a good idea,' I said. 'I think maybe I should keep a packet of biscuits in my desk for when any of us gets a bit hungry.'

Charlie and Ben looked at each other as if their ship had just come in.

It was still raining at playtime and the children peered out into the sodden yard and drew pictures on the window-panes. By lunchtime, though, it had faired and I walked up to the local precinct to buy a slice of ham to put between the two pieces of bread I'd brought to school for my lunch. As I stood in the queue, there was a woman in front of me with about five children in tow, all school age.

'Have you got a bag of bones with plenty of meat on?' she whispered to the butcher when it was her turn to be served. 'It's for the dog,' she added.

The butcher turned round to have a look, and I saw one of the children peer up at her mother excitedly.

'Eh, Mam,' she said eagerly, 'are we gettin' a dog?'

A distant memory returned to me of schooldays at the convent. When it came back to me as I ate my lunch, it helped in a way to understand what the children I taught felt like. It was obvious my class had a different experience of childhood to those from more affluent homes. I hadn't ever been malnourished or dirty and bedraggled in the way that they were, but I had occasionally been enviously hungry at the convent. When I first went there, my only experience of boarding school was from the books I constantly had my nose stuck in. In books, boarding school was one big jolly round of midnight feasts and tuck shops, and food boxes from home stuffed with slabs of homemade cake and chocolate bars. What a wheeze! The reality was somewhat different.

There had been some girls from very wealthy families at the convent I attended, girls whose fathers ran successful businesses and had plenty of money to spare. Then there were the country girls from the farms. If you became best friends with a country girl, you had it made. Their parents would often arrive in big Dormobiles with food stashed in the back. Great big juicy hams that would make you drool as you watched the lucky recipient cut chunks of meat from the bone. They ate in front of the rest of us, while we watched silently and enviously, and filled up on porridge and Irish soda bread.

We sat at the same tables to eat, but the country girls disappeared to their lockers at breakfast. They brought out homemade butter, then spread it thickly on their bread, a big, primrose-yellow wedge of creamy deliciousness. It was quickly brought home to me that there were the haves and the have-nots in the world and they sat side by side. I didn't think much of such a system. I didn't think it should be allowed. There was one girl at my table who had two eggs a day, while the rest of us had none. I used to watch her tuck in, and with the Christian charity that the nuns has instilled in me, I chewed my bread enviously and thought it would serve her right if she dropped dead from high cholesterol!

On my second morning I stopped at a shop on Penny Lane before I got on the bus and bought two packets of digestives. Milk wasn't supposed to be given out until ten thirty, but to their delight, I sat the children straight down and gave them a drink and a couple of biscuits because so many of them hadn't had any breakfast. They beamed as if I had provided a three-course feast. Some of them hungrily gobbled up several biscuits within minutes, like poor, half-starved little pups.

One of them was Robbo. He was a cute little boy with an unruly shock of blond hair that always looked like it could do with a good brush. In fact, he looked like a little Faganite out of *Oliver Twist*: bright, charming and funny but streaked with grime and dressed in tattered clothes.

As Robbo came out to put something in the bin at my desk, I noticed as he walked back to his seat that he was wearing threadbare khaki shorts. They had a hole in the bum and he wasn't wearing any underpants. Poor Robbo. I didn't want to draw attention to him, so I asked him to come and help me with some books in the big stockroom at the bottom of the classroom.

I must confess I was a little hesitant about opening the door to that stockroom. The head teacher, Miss Barnes, had come into my classroom earlier that morning to see how I was getting on and I had been in there looking for pencils. Miss Barnes was a tiny, rather prim little figure, but tough as steel. She was always dressed immaculately in straight skirts and blouses and high heels.

'Always send the children into the stockroom if you want something,' she had advised.

'Why?' I'd enquired, puzzled.

'Rats, dear. The children are used to them, but you may not be.'

I had never seen a rat in my life, but I remembered one of my mother's phrases, 'Never corner a rat or it will go for your throat!'

When I took Robbo in, I tried not to look into the corner of the stockroom in case I saw any gleaming eyes staring back at me. This morning I'd brought in a box, labelled 'Accident Box', which contained a supply of fairly decent old trousers, underpants and socks gathered from friends and family in the summer before I started teaching.

'Your trousers have got a hole in them, Robbo,' I whispered. 'Would you like to choose a pair from my box?'

Robbo nodded, looking at the box with such excitement that you would have thought it contained the best of designer gear instead of other people's cast-offs. He picked out a nice pair of Marks & Spencer trousers and some underpants, and put them on. During the day I noticed him stroking the material on his trousers with a contented smile on his face, so I couldn't understand it the next morning when he turned up in even worse clothes than the day before.

'Robbo, where are the trousers I gave you yesterday?' I asked.

'The tallyman come, miss.'

I had no idea who the 'tallyman' was, so I said nothing. At playtime an older teacher explained it was a debt collector.

'My dear,' she said, 'don't let them take anything decent home, because if you do, you'll never see it again.'

Nevertheless, I was determined to help this poor soul, so later that day I took Robbo into the stockroom again and asked him to choose more clothes.

'Do you know what would be a good idea, Robbo?' I said. 'Maybe in the morning you could come in here and put these clothes on, and then at home time you can change back into your home clothes.'

'OK, miss,' he nodded, with a very wistful expression. He knew *exactly* what I meant. As a teacher, you quickly understand how empowering knowledge can be, but I must say I felt sad when I saw Robbo's knowing look. He was so young to have experienced all the difficulties he already had, to have such an adult level of understanding and acceptance. Robbo, with his big heart and dirt-engrained fingernails, made me realise what a sheltered background I came from, how much I had taken for granted.

One thing was for sure, I told Jaime when I met up with him that weekend and poured out the experiences of my first few days, it was my job to teach these children, but they would also teach me.

9

Free as a Bird

Halfway down Penny Lane, the bird table I was carrying for my class was beginning to feel like a bad idea. It seemed to get heavier the further I carried it, and the rough wood of the stand was already forming calluses on my hands. It was the start of my first full week of teaching and I had a grand plan.

Come on! I urged myself. It will be worth it, won't it? I imagined the children's enraptured faces when a host of colourful birds hovered round the table, wings fluttering while they pecked at the seed. This would help the children see that even if their housing estate wasn't the most beautiful, Mother Nature could brighten any corner.

I struggled on and off my two buses – much to the amusement of the conductors – and then hauled it through the estate at the other end.

'Miss! Miss!'

There was the sound of running feet behind me and then Joey appeared, panting, at my side, wearing bright red wellingtons.

'Wow, Joey!' I said. 'I like your wellies.'

'Me mum 'ad a win at the bingo, miss,' he said, beaming with pleasure that I'd noticed.

'Well, aren't they smart?' I said admiringly.

Joey bounced along beside me, the wellingtons scuffling along the pavement as if he was trying to keep them on.

'They look a wee bit big, though,' I said. 'Do they fit?'

'Mum said they'll last longer.'

He looked at the cumbersome bird table. 'Will I carry it for you, miss?'

'It's maybe a bit heavy.'

'I'm dead strong, me! Honest, miss!'

I smiled. 'I'll bet you are, Joey. Tell you what, how about I carry the front and you carry the back?'

The bird table was more an awkward shape than seriously heavy, so between the two of us we managed to get it to the school, where I was immediately surrounded. It had been the same last week: a little cluster of bedraggled children would run to meet me and gather eagerly round as I walked through the playground.

'Eh, miss,' they'd say, 'are you all right?'

Me all right? Having that morning left my warm, end-of-terrace house, with all its windows intact and tasty sandwiches in my bag for lunchtime? Yes, I was all right. So many of them were not. However bad things were, though, there was a certain pride in not acknowledging that their lives were less than they might have been. They just stood in the free-dinners queue and got on with it.

It was Monday morning, a time in the week that, when I had more experience, would make me groan because of the dreaded dinner register. The ordinary register came first and if a child hadn't turned up by nine forty-five, we had to mark them absent. I soon learned to use pencil because so many would appear around ten o'clock saying Mum had 'overslept'.

That first Monday morning, the deputy head explained to me that an 'F' next to a child's name in the register meant they received free dinners, so I shouldn't ask them for dinner money. Fair enough, I thought, and resolved not to draw attention to that fact. Those without an 'F' were called out to me one at a time.

'Have you got any dinner money?' I would whisper.

They usually handed it over wrapped up in a piece of old newspaper.

My discretion was wasted, though. When lunchtime arrived, the deputy head rang a bell. 'All free dinners over here!' he roared.

I was horrified. It was as if they were lepers! They might as well have had a big sign on their backs and a stamp on their foreheads. Why? I thought. Do they get a different meal? As it turned out, they got exactly the same meal, so I could never understand the segregation. It seemed an unnecessary humiliation to me and I never got used to it. Not that everyone understood what was going on. One day during this process, I felt a little pull at my sleeve and a tiny mite, who I realised from her name badge had just started school, looked up at me.

'Am I a flea dinner?' she asked.

'I don't know, sweetheart,' I said, taking her hand, 'but let's find out.'

I came into teaching with such high ideals, but though I had only been working for a few days, it was hard to know how to help these children. It all felt a bit overwhelming. What could I do in the face of the dreaded tallyman and the free-dinner queue? I couldn't buy them all new clothes, or find them nice clean houses to live in, or feed them good healthy food, or be there at home to make sure they got a good night's sleep.

I would soon realise that I had the most precious gift in my possession that any of them could ever be given, and that was a good education. The best thing I could do for these children, if I really wanted to change their lives, was to give them the tools to change it themselves. I believed passionately in that, and still do. I was determined that unless a child had special needs, they would leave my class able to read and write properly. Whatever it took, I would do. I wanted my pupils to love books, and if a child didn't – and lots of little boys, in particular, were not interested at all – then I would create a special one for them. Joey's reading book. Mary's reading book.

'What do you like best, Joey?' I would ask.

'Trains, miss.'

'Right! Let's make a reading book about trains.' Anything to get them reading.

I also loved storytime, just trying to make children engaged and interested in the stories that we read in class and improving their vocabulary along the way. I always got a kick out of reading aloud to children and watching their reactions. They can be so unguarded and instinctive in the way they respond, and their pleasure is always obvious.

Something happened during my first full week at Huyton that really brought home to me how important it was that these children learned to read and write. I realised it was their only route out of poverty. It was actually an adult who taught me the lesson, and that was very important, because it reminded me that these cute little children in my care were going to grow up one day and then people wouldn't think they were cute any more if they couldn't read and write. They would just label them illiterate. Jenny, the cleaner for my classroom, showed me just how distressing these children's futures could be if they didn't get a good education.

I came across Jenny after my first art class with the children. I enjoyed teaching art and Monday afternoon was set aside for painting. That week we painted birds because of our new bird table. Afterwards I laid all the colourful masterpieces to dry over the units at the windows.

The next morning I came in to find that the cleaner had stuck the chairs on top of the paintings when she had cleaned the floor. There were marks all over them so the paintings were ruined and the children were disappointed.

'Never mind,' I said. 'We'll do them again and I'll leave a note for the cleaner this time.'

I left a note stuck on my classroom door which read, 'PLEASE do not put chairs on the children's paintings.' Next day, I was stunned to see the chairs were again stuck to the artwork. Right, I thought, I'll wait and try to talk to her personally.

Unfortunately, it was a long wait because she started at the other end of the school, but at long last she arrived at my room. She was young, and looked to be in her late twenties, though there were dark smudges round her eyes that suggested she was kept up at night with young children, or perhaps worked too many hours to make ends meet. I suppose I expected that someone who had so deliberately ignored my note would be difficult to deal with, and I am ashamed to say I was less friendly than I might normally have been.

'Excuse me,' I said, a bit frostily, 'I left a note for you on my classroom door on Monday evening. Did you read it?'

A pink flush spread across Jenny's neck.

'Well, no,' she said. She sounded tentative rather than defiant and I was slightly taken aback.

'Why not?' I asked, much more softly.

'I'm sorry, miss, but I can't read.'

Her answer certainly took the wind out of my sails and I felt so guilty at the thought that I might have caused her any embarrassment.

'Did you not learn to read at school?' I asked tentatively.

'I skived off most of the time,' she replied.

What a waste, and how important to make children engaged and interested in school.

'It must make life very difficult for you,' I said gently.

Jenny's eyes filled up. 'My little lad is starting to bring home reading books and I have to keep pretending I am too busy to hear him read. I haven't even told my fella that I can't read.'

'You know, it's never too late to learn,' I said.

'I don't know how . . .'

'Maybe I could teach you?'

A rush of such hope flooded through Jenny's face that it brought a lump to my throat.

'Oh, yes, please . . .'

'OK,' I said. 'Let's start today. Forget about the cleaning . . . I won't say anything.'

Fortunately, Jenny's son was on the same reading scheme as our school, so over the next few weeks she managed to stay a book ahead, mainly memorising it at first, but she took to it very quickly and could soon put a simple sentence together. She was really eager to learn because she had a reason to – and that reason hadn't been there when she was at school.

The important thing as far as I was concerned was not so much that being unable to read had limited what job Jenny could do – though it had. Far more importantly, it had limited her relationship with her husband and her young son. What greater pleasure is there than having a small child snuggle into you with their reading book? It was a joy Jenny had nearly missed out on and I didn't want that to happen to any of the children in my classes. I didn't want their lives to be limited in any way. When they clustered round me in the morning asking if I was all right, I wished I could mend the holes in their shoes, and the rips in their clothes, but instead I concentrated on doing the most important thing I could – and that was to teach them to read.

All that first week we talked about which birds might come to the table.

'Miss,' said Robbo, 'will we get any eagles?'

'I'm afraid not, Robbo. You don't get eagles in the city, but maybe I could see if I could find a picture of an eagle for the wall. I think we'll just see some little birds, but that will be nice too, won't it? Sparrows . . . and chaffinches, maybe . . . and wagtails. Does anyone know what colour wagtails are?'

There was silence. Then Mandy, a little blonde girl with round glasses and long pigtails, spoke up. 'Blue?' she offered hopefully.

'No, Mandy, but well done for taking a guess. Wagtails are black and white, and they are very cute little birds because their tails dip up and down when they move.'

'Miss,' said Joey, 'what about vultures? Will we see vultures?'

I think they were a little confused about wildlife.

I folded large pieces of card into a book and wrote on the front, 'Visitors to Our Bird Table.' Each child was to have a turn looking out at break and then either draw or write about the visitors that they saw. On Friday, just before home time, I got the children to tidy up the class-room, then sat them down.

'Right now, let's have a look at our bird book,' I said brightly, opening it up. I was surprised to see that it looked a bit empty. There didn't seem to be much recorded there.

' "Day one," ' I read aloud. ' "Today a rat come to our bird table." '

Hmm.

'"Page Two,"' I continued quickly. '"A nuther rat cumed to the table."'

By Friday's entry not a single bird had been spotted visiting our table. End of bird table!

I lugged it all the way back through the estate and manhandled it onto the two buses again, this time back to Penny Lane. Thank God for Friday!

'Hey, love,' said the bus conductor cheerily, 'do you always carry a bird table around with yer?'

I smiled weakly, then peered out through the bus window, head resting wearily against the glass. I had survived my first full week, but this changing-lives lark . . . maybe it wasn't going to be quite so easy after all!

10

On the Bounce

Isn't it wonderful when someone says they care enough about you to want to be with you for the rest of their life? When Jaime proposed, the little girl inside me who had always longed to be loved reappeared, reached up her arms and said, 'Yes, please!' We had known each other a couple of years by now, and I had grown to love him dearly. He was so funny and kind. Lots of friends were beginning to get engaged and settle down too. Barbara Mc was going out with a butcher and we were all agog when she told us how he had taken her home and pressed a little parcel into her hand. As we listened to the story, we thought she was going to say it was an engagement ring. Not quite: two pork chops – which I guess signals true love from a butcher. But Barbara did marry him, and both Jellybean and Maggie Gee were now spoken for too. Maggie, being Maggie, had not settled for the mundane: she'd bagged herself an Elvis impersonator teacher, called Bill Ogden.

Around that time I became friendly with Nora, the secretary of the local secondary school in Huyton. She was older than me, but she travelled from the same side of the city and I got to know her because we often ended up on the same bus. After we'd been travelling together for some months, she asked if I would like to come to her house the next Saturday for lunch. I was a little surprised, because we were travelling companions more than bosom buddies, but I liked Nora and I'm a sociable person, so I agreed to go.

'There's someone I want you to meet,' she added rather mysteriously, as she got off the bus.

You never know, do you? You never know when the seemingly incidental little things in life will suddenly blow up into something significant. When I walked down Nora's street that Saturday clutching a bunch of spring daffodils for her, I was curious about who she wanted me to meet, but I had no idea that the mystery guest would end up posing a big dilemma in my life.

It was an ordinary Wednesday – grey skies and occasional drizzle – with nothing much to distinguish it. Until Jeannie arrived in class.

'My dad's coming to get you, miss.'

Jeannie was gazing up at me solemnly, her grey-green eyes peering out anxiously from underneath a fringe that was slightly too long.

I must have misheard.

'What was that, Jeannie?'

'My dad, miss. He's coming to get you.'

'Why?' I asked, my mouth suddenly going dry with fear. Jeannie was lovely, an elfin little girl with pale skin and fine features and a mass of auburn curls that she kept tied back in a ponytail. Her dad was less lovely. He was built like the side of a house and, judging by the smell of alcohol that always seemed to accompany him, he made regular and generous contributions to the brewers' benevolent fund. If Jeannie's dad was coming to get you, you didn't really want to be around when he arrived.

'I don't know why, miss,' said Jeannie. 'He just said he was. I tried tellin' him . . .' Her voice trailed away.

I spent the rest of the morning jumping every time the classroom door opened. I popped in next door to see Maggie Gee, now Mrs Ogden, for a bit of reassurance. Teaching hadn't toned Maggie down one iota. She was still in tight skirts and stilettos, full of confidence, but when I told her my predicament, she went very pale.

'Jeannie Martin's dad?' she said. 'Oh my God, Bernadette!'

So, I thought, I'm on my own!

No knock came at the door, though, and by lunchtime I decided that maybe I had misunderstood what Jeannie had said, and by two o'clock I was almost feeling calm.

Then suddenly, with a crash, the classroom door was flung open. A burly, red-faced man slewed in.

'Eh, you . . . over 'ere,' he slurred.

'Me?' was all I could manage to say, my voice an octave higher than usual.

'Why did you 'it her?'

'It wasn't her, Dad!' Jeannie shouted. 'I told you it was the dinner lady.'

Oh, thank God, I thought. The dinner ladies could look after themselves better than I could. They all seemed to shout as if every child was deaf, and some of them were a bit rough and ready. In fact, one or two looked like they could go ten rounds with Muhammad Ali, so Jeannie's dad would be meat and drink to them.

With that, Jeannie's dad reeled towards the door. 'I'll have 'er!' he shouted.

Outside the door, Miss Barnes drew herself up to her full height of five feet nothing. (Plus six-inch heels.) The school secretary had alerted her to the fact that we had an intruder, a parent up 'on the bounce', as we called it, and she was waiting to intercept him. It was like a Chihuahua squaring up to a Rottweiler. Jeannie's dad could have ripped her to pieces, but I had to hand it to her – Miss Barnes was tough in her own way. She really knew how to handle difficult parents.

'I'm asking you nicely to leave the premises,' she trilled.

'And I'm telling you to fuck off,' he yelled. 'No one hits my kids – except me.'

In the distance, we could hear the wail of police sirens. The secretary had panicked and dialled 999 and before long a young constable arrived.

'Come along now, sir,' he said.

Now that the heat was off me, I couldn't help noticing the constable was very handsome and he couldn't resist eyeing up all of us younger members of staff, lined up at our classroom doors to watch the commotion.

'He's been abusive and has used bad language,' said Miss Barnes, in her best ladylike voice. She might be as tough as old boots underneath, but she could be very prim when she wanted. In fact, it was part of her technique.

'What did he say, love?'

'Oh, I couldn't repeat it,' Miss Barnes demurred.

'OK, love, I'll write a few words down in me book and you tell me if that's what he said.'

I think he was beginning to enjoy himself and he was certainly playing up to his female audience. With a grin over his shoulder at us younger ones, and making eyes at Maggie Gee in particular, Constable Swagger wrote down a word and showed it to Miss Barnes.

'Did he say this, love?'

'Oh, no!' replied Miss Barnes, eyes widening.

'Well, what about this?'

'Oh, oh my goodness, no!'

By the time he'd showed her the third word, I thought we were going to have to bring in the smelling salts and lavender water. They were clearly not words Miss Barnes was in the habit of using, though I suppose it's never too late to expand your vocabulary.

It reminds me of a story a friend of mine told me about teaching in a convent junior school. One of the nuns from the senior school was walking across to the chapel when she saw a rabble of children dragging a child towards her.

'He sweared, Sister. He sweared!' they said excitedly, desperate to be the virtuous bearers of scandalous news.

'Right,' she said, putting her hand on the little boy's shoulder. 'The rest of you, run along. I'll deal with this.' She crouched down to the young boy's level. 'Now,' she said solemnly, 'did you swear?'

He nodded his head.

'What did you say?'

A shake of the head.

'What if I spell out what the other children said you said. Will you say "yes" or "no"?'

A nod of the head.

'S-H-I-T,' she spelled out.

'Yes, fuck,' he sniffed.

Jeannie was not the only child by far in that school whose life was blighted by alcohol (and I certainly met a few teachers over the years whose lives were too). There were many problems that kids faced in this area, but of course all of them were made worse if booze was involved. Some children were astute and knew what was going on if one of their parents was a heavy drinker, but for others, alcohol caused fear and confusion. What is a young child supposed to think if they find their mother slumped behind a door? Often, they assume she's ill and get frightened that she's going to die and leave them all alone.

Many of the children came to school smelly each day because they weren't being cared for properly at home. You could smell as high as a ripe cheese and it didn't make you stand out particularly in this school. Yet during my first term at Huyton there had been one little girl, Margaret, whose problems had been so extreme that she'd caught my attention. She could have been such a pretty little girl with her long, black tresses and big blue eyes, but her hair was always dirty and unkempt, straggling untidily down her back because it was unbrushed. She clearly wet the bed, and on many occasions I had to take her across to the toilet block to wash her hands and face. The soap in the containers there was disgusting – cheap and far too abrasive for the children's delicate skin – so I kept a special bar of soap and a flannel in my bag for times like this.

On PE day, when the children had stripped off, I noticed that Margaret's underwear was quite filthy. I quietly took her into the stockroom and showed her my 'Accident Box' of clothes.

'Now, I'll leave you here to choose some nice clean knickers and then you can give me those ones you have on and I'll wash and dry them for you before home time,' I told Margaret.

I was a bit worried about offending parents and having them come up to the classroom on the bounce, but I couldn't just leave Margaret in such dirty clothes. A few minutes later she reappeared from the stockroom wearing pretty pink knickers, a matching vest and a big smile. I was so grateful to friends for all their children's cast-offs. To the children in this school, they were as good as new.

As the term went by, Margaret was increasingly late arriving at school.

'My mum overslept,' she would say.

She had two older brothers who were taught by Maggie. I mentioned Margaret's timekeeping to her in the staffroom and she said the boys were always late too. Something was obviously going on, but none of us was sure what. Miss Barnes decided to ask the school nurse to visit, using the fact that Margaret had nits in her hair as an excuse to call at the house. The next day the nurse reported back.

'I think Dad has gone off and Mum may be drinking,' she said.

We got in touch with social services, who said they would monitor the situation. 'Keep an eye out for any bruises,' we were told, 'and try to get the children to talk to you about what's happening at home.'

We did try, but Margaret didn't say much, and if her older brothers were asked questions, they immediately clammed up. Children can be very loyal, and even when their home life is difficult, they don't want to jeopardise it. It's all they have.

Over the coming weeks I paid close attention to Margaret, and though I didn't notice any bruises, she certainly wasn't any cleaner. The breakthrough came on the last day of term, just before Christmas. The children had their Christmas party and Miss Barnes had arranged that after the children had gone home, we would have a staff party. I had brought a bottle of wine to school and my mum had made some mince pies, some for the children and some for the staff. That morning, when I arrived in school, I put the bag of goodies down by my desk. With their natural curiosity, nearly every child in the room came to look in that bag. However, when Margaret looked in, her reaction was different from the others.

'That's booze,' she said uneasily.

'Well, it's wine,' I said. 'It's for the teachers' party, after your party.'

Margaret wasn't happy. Her eyes clouded over. 'If you drink that, you will fall over,' she said, and there was real panic in her voice.

'Tell you what – I'll only drink one glass and then I won't fall over,' I replied, trying to soothe her.

'You can't do that,' Margaret insisted. 'If you drink it, then you will keep drinking it.'

'Well, maybe the best thing is if I don't drink any,' I said, watching her intently. 'Would that be better?'

She seemed pacified by that and went on to really enjoy the children's party. When I mentioned to Miss Barnes what had happened, I think she came to the same conclusion I had and she got straight on the phone and rang social services. I felt awful then. What if I had misinterpreted what Margaret had said? What if her mother didn't have a problem with alcohol and I was just being interfering?

When I'd returned to school in January after the Christmas holidays, there was no sign of Margaret or her brothers. I went straight up to Miss Barnes's office to ask her what had happened.

'They were taken into temporary foster care over Christmas,' she replied.

My heart sank. I felt so responsible. Was it my fault that they had been taken away from their mum, right before Christmas, and was it the best thing for them? How could you judge whether a mum who wasn't coping was better than no mum at all? The children didn't reappear in the coming months, and it seemed such a shame that they had had to leave the school as well as their mother, but the school nurse gave me regular updates. She told me that social services were trying to keep the three children together and were looking for a permanent foster mother. I got a heavy heart every time I thought about this broken little family and I just hoped that the children were together and not pining for their mum.

I didn't actually think I would ever see Margaret again, or find out what happened to her. As it turns out, I was quite wrong about that.

Nora's was a neat terraced house near Penny Lane with vibrant red windowboxes that singled it out from its neighbours. The gaily coloured spring flowers in the boxes danced lightly in the breeze and I heard a dog bark inside as I pushed the bell.

Through the glass of the door I saw the small, round shape of Nora bustle down the hall and she smiled welcomingly as she opened the door.

'Oh, how lovely!' she exclaimed as she saw the daffodils. 'Thank you so much. Come on into the kitchen. Lunch is nearly ready.'

I could see through the open door that there was someone sitting at the table reading a paper.

'This is my son, Anthony,' said Nora. 'Anthony, this is Bernadette.'

'Pleased to meet you, Bernadette,' said Anthony, and two warm, blue eyes rested their gaze on me. He was dark-haired and attractive, and had a smile like Nora's: warm and somehow reassuring. Hmm, I thought. He's nice!

I remember that we laughed a lot during lunch, but I made sure to mention Jaime's name because I didn't want to be disloyal. I guess that in itself was a sign that I knew there was some instant chemistry. When I spoke about Jaime, there was a momentary awkwardness, a sudden change in temperature.

'He's my fiancé,' I explained.

Then Anthony smiled.

'Lucky Jaime,' he said, and after that the conversation resumed its natural flow.

Anthony worked for Boeing and had a flat at St Anne's-on-Sea, but he was also a keen sailor and kept a small boat on the lake near Fornby.

'Oh, that must be lovely in the good weather,' I said.

'It is,' said Anthony. 'Why don't you come next Saturday and I'll take you out on the lake?'

'Good idea,' said Nora. 'You'll enjoy it, Bernadette.'

The invitation seemed very natural, was made in front of his mum, Nora, and didn't feel in the least like a date, so I smiled and accepted. After all, what harm could there be in going for a boat trip on the lake with a friend?

11

Reading It Right

It was mid-morning and I sat at my desk, chewing on my pen top thoughtfully and watching the class work. I didn't often sit at my desk. I liked to be out among the children and would usually work my way round, sitting beside them on the small chairs and helping anyone who was stuck. Today, though, I needed a few minutes to watch and to think. I had a problem and his name was Daniel.

Daniel was a bright boy, I knew that, but while he was very good with numbers, he really struggled with words. He had a straight blond fringe and big blue eyes that seemed luminous when he was doing sums, as if all his enthusiasm and aptitude for number work switched on a light in his brain. He simply glowed.

Today I had left him with three other children and a big box of sorting toys. There were small cars, boats, houses and figures, all very attractive and brightly coloured, which is no doubt why so many regularly went missing! The task I gave them was to group all the red objects in twos, all the blue ones in threes and all the yellow ones in fives. I knew it was a simple task for Daniel and I watched as he raced through his work.

When I came back to their table ten minutes later, I asked them one at a time to tell me what they had done.

The other three simply told me how they had sorted the objects into twos, threes and fives.

'Now, Daniel, tell me what you found out,' I said.

'Well, here I have twelve groups of two and that makes twenty-four. Here I have ten groups of three and that makes thirty. And over there I have eight groups of five and that makes forty,' said Daniel solemnly. Then he stared very intently at the groups of objects, completing the calculation in his head, and I could see his eyes were now so bright they were sparkling.

'That makes ninety-four altogether,' he concluded confidently.

'You are *such* a clever boy,' I said, and gave him a big hug. 'Now, while the others continue with this, I'd like you to come out to my desk with your reading book.'

It was as if I had switched Daniel's light off. Reluctantly, he picked up his reading book and came out to my desk, but his beautiful blue eyes had dulled. He opened the book and falteringly read a few words. I could see he was labouring in a world where nothing was clear for him. Back in the 1960s we didn't use the word 'dyslexia', yet I knew there was something wrong even if I didn't have a label for it. I watched Daniel closely as he read, observing his emotional reactions as much as listening to the words. He was uncomfortable, a bit sad, perhaps even a little angry. He was simply making up the story as he went along. He was turning the pages over, but the words he was saying bore no relation to what was actually written on the page.

I could see Daniel's frustration building and I really wanted to help him. Because so little was known back then about reading difficulties, it really was a case of trial and error. There was no reference book I could look up, no expert I could approach, and so I had to act on instinct. In the coming weeks I did a lot of clay work with Daniel, and as it turns out, that's often the approach used now with dyslexic children. He liked plasticine and I would get him to roll it out and make words with it. I think it works because it's a very physical way of learning. The words become an object, something that can be handled, and because he was intelligent, Daniel learned to form the words very quickly.

Many dyslexic children can only 'see' words if they have a picture in their minds that they associate it with. If you show a card with the word 'television' on it, and include a picture of a television, the word goes into their minds as a picture. That's why dyslexic children often have much more difficulty with conjunctions like 'and' or 'but', which have no visual reminder, yet can learn long nouns, like 'telephone', quite easily.

I made Daniel a special reading book, and with a lot of patience, over the next few months his reading slowly improved. Language would never be his strong point, but I could see that with a bit of effort, he would get by. He had a single, teenage mum, but his grandmother was very involved in his upbringing and she used to come up to the school regularly to discuss his progress with me and find out how she could help.

'You are trying so hard to get him interested,' she said gratefully. 'Thank you.'

'I know he can do it,' I said. 'He's a very bright boy.'

Sometimes it takes many years before you know as a teacher whether you have influenced your pupils' lives. There are few instant answers in education. All you can do is hope that you have started a process, lit a light, made a difference. It would actually be another ten years before I got to know that all that early work with Daniel had been worth it, that he had made it. I bumped into his grandma in the supermarket and she had wonderful news. Daniel had been accepted by Oxford University – to study maths, of course! Despite his initial reading difficulties, Daniel was going to make a success of his life. I knew that if we had not addressed his reading problems early on, he could have switched off and dropped out, and his life could have gone in another direction entirely.

And so, as it turned out, could mine.

Anthony's boat skimmed across the surface of the lake, and I trailed my hand in the water as warm sunshine mingled with cooling spring breezes on my face. It had become something of a pattern: for the last month or so I had gone out on Saturdays to the lake with Anthony. One week Nora had come too, so I told myself that it was all very casual. None of it meant anything.

Today we were alone and Anthony seemed lost in thought. I had the feeling that he was building up to something. It provoked an unfamiliar emotion in me, a mixture of nerves and dread but excitement too. I wanted two things simultaneously: for him to speak and for him not to.

I leaned back and closed my eyes, letting the warmth dance on my eyelids, as the boat rose and dipped.

'Bernadette?'

I shielded my eyes with one hand and squinted into the light at Anthony.

'I got some news at work this week.'

I straightened up. 'What?'

'I got a promotion.'

'Congratulations! That's wonderful news, Anthony.'

He didn't smile and I looked at him, puzzled. 'Why didn't you say before?'

'It's in Seattle.'

'Seattle! In the United States?'

He nodded. I hardly knew Anthony, and I wasn't sure what I was feeling, but if I was honest with myself, I knew that I wasn't completely pleased at the idea of him leaving.

'So how do you feel about living in America?' I asked slowly.

He shrugged. 'How would you?' he asked lightly.

I hesitated, uncertain how to interpret the question. Did he mean if I was going myself or if I was going with him . . .?

'Bernadette, come with me!' Anthony blurted out before I could reply. 'Marry me!'

In that moment I realised I had created a little glass bubble of deception around myself and Anthony. I had pretended that we were just friends, that there was nothing more, and I honestly believed it. How capable we are of deceiving ourselves! But when he asked me to marry him, that delicate glass bubble shattered into a thousand pieces and I saw that however much I wanted to deny it, there was something more. I felt instantly guilty when I thought of Jaime.

'Anthony,' I started, 'I'm getting married in August to Jaime . . . That's just four months away. Everything is planned . . . I can't . . .'

'You can if you want to,' he said simply.

I knew that was true, but I was young and scared and I couldn't respond to the speed of this. I knew that I liked Anthony but I didn't yet know how much. How could I? We hadn't had a chance to explore the possibilities of what there might be between us. It could be nothing . . . or everything . . . and I had to decide if I wanted to gamble on which of those it was.

'But how would I get a job out there?' I asked.

'You wouldn't need one,' he said. 'I'll look after you, Bernadette.' Something told me he would. Anthony was a grafter. I would never want for anything, but I wasn't very materialistic and the way to my heart was never going to be money.

The sun dipped behind a cloud and we were in shade now. I shivered slightly. How had I allowed myself to sleepwalk into this position? I was on a boat, on a lake, with no way to simply walk away, with a man I barely knew who wanted me to marry him.

'I can't do it to Jaime,' I said. 'All the arrangements . . .'

'Better now than later,' said Anthony bluntly. 'Bernadette, you have to do what's right for you. Whatever that is. Just promise me you will think about it.'

'I'll think about it,' I promised, and I felt a rush of fear about what those deliberations might mean.

Anthony turned the boat then and we headed back in near silence, both of us lost in our own thoughts.

Everything was changing. The Four Buddies were beginning to make their own separate ways in the world. Barbara Mc married her butcher that year and moved away from the area. Jellybean, too, had plans to move with her new husband-to-be and had got herself a job teaching music in a prep school. By August there would only be me and Annie left – if I didn't go to Seattle. Annie taught in a primary school on the Woodchurch estate, a housing scheme that was not unlike Huyton. There was a vacancy coming up in Woodchurch in September and in the months leading up to the summer Annie regularly encouraged me to put in for it.

'It will be like old times,' she said.

At home, my mother wanted to downsize. It was a few years now since my father had died and she felt our end-of-terrace was too big. Aideen was still in the convent in Ireland. Kathleen was still at school in Liverpool and Helena, who had studied radiography, was already married. Andrew, too, had decided to move on. He had graduated from Oxford and was going backpacking round the world. The night before he set off, he spent ages making notices for hitchhiking. 'France.' 'Italy.' He got more ambitious as the evening wore on. 'India,' he wrote. 'Australia.' I laughed at the time – wrongly, as it turned out: he would make it to every one of those destinations.

I dropped him off at the M6 and I can see him still, a hippy figure in his jeans and purple tie-dye T-shirt, his hair flowing to shoulder length and his bare feet stuffed into flip-flops. God knows what my dad would have made of him! In his bag he had one change of clothing and a spare pair of flip-flops. I had a lump in my throat as I watched him . . . my little brother. Part of me was frightened for him, but a quick wave over his shoulder and Andrew was gone, setting off on the adventure of his life.

I knew I could do the same. If I wanted to be as adventurous, as carefree, as Andrew, I could head off to America, but I had too many things to tie me to Liverpool, and as time wore on, it became increasingly clear to me that I should continue on the path I was on. I might be young and a little bit confused, but that was natural. Each week was a week closer to the wedding and I knew that I couldn't let down Jaime. Anthony was fantasy, but Jaime was reality, and when I was with him, I fell under his spell all over again. I loved him and I didn't want to hurt him. I also loved teaching. I just couldn't imagine a life without it.

It was hard telling Anthony of my decision. I felt sad for him starting out for America all alone, but he was a lovely man and I knew he would soon find someone to share his life. Meanwhile I threw myself into making my plans with Jaime work. Anthony's proposal had forced me to think through exactly what I wanted and I was totally committed to our future. It was all the more important now that things worked out and that I proved to myself that I'd made the right decision. We rented a flat in Arrowe Park in Birkenhead to move into after the wedding, and as it was near the Woodchurch estate, I applied for, and got, the job beside Annie. I had only been at Huyton for a year, but the travelling had already taken its toll. Now my daily two-hour commute would be replaced by a ten-minute walk.

Though it would be more convenient, there was of course sadness to be leaving my first school. I was still working hard with Jenny, my cleaner, teaching her to read. We were at the stage now where she was asking me to help her with the local paper.

'My fella reads it every evening,' she explained.

Before she went home in the evening, we would work at memorising the headlines, even if she could not read all the words in the story. A few weeks before I left, she told me that the evening before, she had been able to read out the headline over her husband's shoulder: 'Pensioner mugged on way to shops.'

'Isn't that dreadful?' she had said. Her fella had agreed with her.

Jenny was so proud of her achievements, and in turn, I was proud of her. She looked deflated when I told her I was leaving, as if all the stuffing had been knocked out of her.

'I don't want you to stop learning, Jenny,' I urged her. 'You've done so well that you must keep going. Go to night classes.'

'But what will I tell my fella?' she asked.

'Tell him you're doing cookery . . . or Spanish,' I said. 'Tell him anything you like. Just don't stop learning to read. You've got too much potential for that.'

At that, Jenny's confidence seemed to return and she smiled gratefully at me. I am not sure anyone had ever told her before that she had potential, but she did.

On my last day at Huyton I could scarcely bear to say goodbye. Joey and Robbo, my two right-hand men, hung about in the yard until I left. At the gate, I bent down and gave them each a quick hug before they headed home.

'Work hard,' I said, 'because when you're big men, I want to hear how well you've done.' The last things I remember are the slap of Joey's wellingtons on the pavement as he ran off, and a glimpse of Robbo's grimy hands as he solemnly shook mine.

12

Father Jock

My wedding to Jaime took place that August, 1966, in the local Catholic church – my mother wouldn't have stood for anything else even if I had wanted it – and since my dad was dead, one of my mother's brothers, my uncle Tom, gave me away. Spain being a Catholic country, at least I didn't have the problems with Jaime that some of my friends did with their boyfriends. One of my college mates had gone to tell her parish priest that she wanted to get married to a non-Catholic and was given some rather stark advice. 'Away and find a nice Catholic boy and then come back,' he said, shooing her off the premises, as though falling in love was like ordering a Chinese meal from a takeaway. I'll have a number forty-seven, please.

A dressmaker that my mum knew made my wedding dress from white brocade. Although the 1960s were a time of changing fashion and daring hemlines, wedding dresses back then tended to be a bit more demure than some of today's creations. Mine was quite a simple design: long-sleeved with a modest scoop neck and a fitted waist. Annie was my bridesmaid, along with my sister Kathleen and Jaime's sister, Maria. I'm not a very formal person, so if it had been left to me, I'd probably have gone for a simpler affair for my wedding, but my mum insisted on the full works with morning suits. 'We mustn't spoil the ship for a ha'p'orth of tar,' she said.

I didn't know it until later, but Jaime and Maria crashed on the way to the wedding. Thankfully, the only real damage was to the car, but Maria's wedding preparations were all in vain. She had been to the hairdresser's that morning and had opted for a very elaborate 'up do'. By the time her hair had wrestled with the windscreen, it looked like she had a demented pancake on top of her head, with bits falling everywhere. Poor Maria! I was slightly surprised when I saw her because she was usually quite fastidious. Goodness me, I thought to myself, Maria hasn't gone to much trouble with her hair today!

A few weeks after the wedding Jaime and I went to a party. I was very happy, a newly married young woman basking in the confidence that brings, and I enjoyed chatting to people knowing that my husband was somewhere around. Afterwards, though, Jaime seemed unhappy.

'Who were you talking to in the kitchen?' he asked.

I was taken aback. I couldn't even remember. There were so many people at the party.

'Well, you were laughing. What were you laughing at?' he said.

I reassured him, but part of me felt a little sad – and anxious – that he needed that reassurance when we had only recently married.

'You'll be the new teacher, then? Miss Barnes's replacement?'

The voice was loud and booming, with a strong Scottish accent. Father Jock MacDonald was from Edinburgh, a ruddy-faced man with white hair and a cheery smile.

'Bernadette Cubells, Father,' I said, holding out my hand. It felt strange saying my married name, like I was a new person and this was a fresh start.

Father Jock screwed up his face in surprise, in a way that was to become very familiar to me in the coming months.

'Bernadette Cowbells?' he said doubtfully.

'Bernadette Cubells,' I said, a little louder this time. We were in the staffroom of my new school in Woodchurch and I didn't like to shout. People were already beginning to look over.

'Bernadette Bluebells!' exclaimed Father Jock. 'God save us, Bernadette, what kind of a name is that? Are you from the Moulin Rouge?'

Over Father Jock's shoulder, I could see Annie doubling up.

'No, Cubells, Father!' I said even louder, and Father Jock's hand lifted to his ear to turn up his hearing aid.

'CUBELLS!' I roared, and Father Jock jumped.

By now Annie was completely helpless.

'It's Spanish,' I added.

It was my first day and in addition to the new head teacher, Mrs Simons, the parish priest was one of the important people to meet. Father Jock may not have been an official teacher, but the local church had huge influence in Catholic schools at that time and the priests were forever in and out of the classes, questioning the children on religion. My time at the convent had left me less than enthusiastic about formal religion. It wasn't God I objected to; I just wasn't that keen on some of his representatives on Earth! But Father Jock, with his dodgy hearing and gruff kindness, was one of the few I grew to have real affection for.

'Best of luck now, Bernadette, and I'll be along in the next few weeks to see you,' said Father Jock, handing me my religious syllabus for the year and taking his leave.

'Come along, Meez Bluebell,' murmured Annie in a phoney French accent after he'd gone. 'I weel show you to your classroom. Zees way, pleeze!'

My new school in Woodchurch was not unlike my old one in Huyton. It was perhaps more mixed, with some good neighbourhoods in the school's catchment area, but in general it faced many of the same problems. The council estate was the result of one of the first post-war 'slum clearances' in Merseyside, which had changed the skyline of the area for ever. On paper, this was progress. Houses that were unsanitary, that had no inside toilet or running hot water, were bulldozed. Around a hundred thousand people were moved from their homes and placed in new developments on the outer circle of the city.

Unfortunately, of course, this wasn't just about new buildings; this was about families and communities. These were people's homes that were being razed and they had memories and associations and family connections that could not be so easily knocked down and replaced. The anger and resistance that flared up were reflected in Liverpool folk music, and the song 'Back Buchanan Street' summed this up with the mixture of nostalgia and defiance so typical of Liverpool.

> *A fella from the council*
> *Who's just left planning school*
> *Told us that we have to move*
> *Right out of Liverpool.*

Destruction is so much quicker and easier than construction. You can knock things down easily enough, but what do you replace them with? There weren't enough houses to cope with this massive social change. Temporary prefabricated houses had to be built to provide shelter, and of course the dreaded high-rise flats began to spring up. In Woodchurch, young families were moved out of terraced houses where they had grown up, and where they had extended families in neighbouring streets, to high-rise buildings where they didn't know a single person. Once, when a little girl was injured in the gym at school, I went to speak to her mum in one of those flats.

'Isn't your view nice?' I said, trying to be positive. You could see for quite a distance round about and could just make out some grass on the horizon, though admittedly you might have needed your binoculars to do so.

'No,' she replied dejectedly, 'it's not really.'

I felt awful. I hadn't wanted to seem patronising and it was just my attempt to be upbeat.

For many young mothers in particular, there was a real sense of isolation in these houses. 'I always had me nan to run round to when I was worried about the baby,' one young mum told me. 'She always knew what to do.'

High rises were also a far from ideal way to live when you had prams and young children to contend with. One morning, at about ten o'clock, a mother appeared in my classroom with three children. One was in my class and there were two other younger ones in a pram.

'I'm so sorry we're late, miss, but the lift has been vandalised again and I had to bounce the pram down twelve floors.'

What an effort!

'Please don't worry next time,' I replied. 'Just stay in until the lift is repaired.'

She looked horrified. 'Eh, miss,' she said, 'that's much worse!'

'Robert, please get down from there!'

I must have said it a hundred times in the first few weeks at my new school. Robert simply couldn't stop climbing. He climbed nimbly to the top of fences in the playground, onto shelves in the classroom, swinging like a monkey from one surface to another with amazing dexterity. Robert was an energetic little boy with sandy-coloured hair and freckles and a cheerful, open face, but he frightened the life out of me.

I introduced myself to many of the parents when they

came to pick the children up in that first week and I was keen to speak to Robert's parents.

'Hello,' I said, smiling brightly when I saw Robert's dad had come to pick him up. 'Can I just have a quick word?'

Robert's dad sighed when I told him my concerns. 'We've tried,' he said, 'we really have. We just can't stop him climbing anything he comes across!'

As we spoke, Robert ran towards us, straight through his dad's legs, then climbed up onto his shoulders and swung from his neck. I had to laugh. If his dad couldn't stop him, what chance did I have? I realised that Robert's energy and his need to clamber to the top of any fixed structure were just part of him, his special skill. That's what I love about children: they all have their own special, unique talent. It doesn't have to be academic. As a teacher, it was up to me to help them discover what that special skill was, to nurture it into something that would enhance their lives. I wanted to inspire them, to let them know there was something out there in the world just for them.

My new class of six year olds was stuffed full of characters, just as my old one had been. Apart from Robert, there was Joseph, a wild young boy with lively eyes and a tongue that never stopped talking. There was something almost feral about him; he reminded me of a little wild cat. I couldn't help having a real soft spot for Joseph, though. I usually did for the naughty boys! I noticed that many of the more difficult children had dads who weren't at home. A lot of them worked in Spain, apparently.

When I commented on that to Mrs Simons, she just smiled at my naïvety. 'Yes, dear,' she said. 'That will be Spain, Walton Jail.'

In those first weeks I took a look at the syllabus Father Jock had given me. For a lot of families, life was a question of survival and I can't say teaching religion was top of my list of priorities. I was respectful of religion – I had grown up a Catholic and had a sister who was a nun after all! – but unless we were going to have a miracle on the scale of the feeding of the 5,000 in Woodchurch, I wasn't sure how to make the religious syllabus relevant to these children.

I saw my theme for the year was 'God, Our Loving Father', which made my heart sink. I couldn't teach that! Some of these children came into school with their tender young skin stained with ugly purple and yellow bruises meted out when their fathers rolled home from the pub in a less than loving mood. Even on a purely practical level, I really wasn't sure that telling them God was just like their dad would win many soldiers for the Lord's army.

Since I'm not a great one for rules and regulations, I decided to teach a variation on a theme. God is out there somewhere and He hopes that everything is good for you. I knew that Father Jock would soon be paying me a visit and one afternoon, a month or so after I started, a sharp knock at the door heralded his arrival.

The class all rose to their feet, unbidden. 'Good afternoon, Father Jock,' they chorused in singsong fashion.

'Good afternoon, children,' said Father Jock jovially. He looked at me with a faint twinkle in his eye. 'Good afternoon, Mrs Cowbells,' he said quietly.

I smiled, but I was dreading this. My religious teaching had hardly been textbook Catholicism. I knew Father Jock would be looking for the children to know the answers straight out of the official catechism, just as the nuns had in the convent. In fact, I remembered catechism tests very well.

'What is God?' one of the nuns once asked a dumfounded classmate of mine.

Silence.

'God is love!' shouted the nun, slapping the girl as she did so.

Well, that proves it, doesn't it? God is love. Whack.

Thankfully, Father Jock seemed far more amenable.

'Now, children,' he said, 'let's see what you have been learning with Mrs Cubells these last few weeks. Raise your hand if you know the answer.'

The children looked back innocently at him, eager to please, as Father Jock took a well-thumbed catechism out of his pocket.

'Right,' he said, 'who made you?'

Silence. Not a single hand in the air.

'Come on now, don't be shy,' encouraged Father Jock. 'You laddie – you with the pale blue jumper – what do you think?'

'Er . . . me mum?' came the reply.

'He said, "God," Father,' I translated hurriedly.

'Very good,' said Father Jock, fiddling with his hearing aid. 'Right now . . . what is God?' he continued. 'The wee lassie at the back . . .'

'I dunno.'

'What was that?' he said, putting a hand to his ear.

'She said, "God is love," ' I offered hastily.

'Grand,' replied Father Jock.

If he ever got a hearing aid that worked, I was in trouble.

More difficult questions with longer answers posed more of a problem – 'Why did God make you?' for example. The answer was, 'God made me to know Him, to love Him and to serve Him here on Earth, and be happy with Him for ever in the next.' Quite a bit for a five-year-old to take in!

'Actually, Father, we haven't covered that yet because it's quite deep and needs a lot of thinking about, doesn't it? We wouldn't want the children learning it parrot fashion, would we?'

'No, no,' he agreed. A little doubtfully, I thought.

But God, My Loving Father was certainly looking after me that afternoon. As we conducted our very deep philosophical discussion on God and the purpose of creation, the bell for afternoon playtime rang. I breathed a sigh of relief and began to fuss over Father Jock.

'Come on, Father,' I said, 'why don't you come along to the staffroom with me and I'll make you a good strong cup of tea, just the way you like it. I'm sure I can find you a chocolate digestive to go with it.'

'Ah, Bernadette,' he said cheerfully, 'you're a grand lassie, you really are.'

Near the end of my first term in Woodchurch, Maggie Gee, who had stayed at Huyton, called me. Would I like to go back for the nativity play? I never turn down an opportunity to go to a nativity play and I thought it would be nice to go back and see how everyone was getting on. It was a long journey from Birkenhead back to the estate, but I turned up in plenty of time. As I walked in, the smell of the place hit me once again. Chalk . . . plasticine . . . dampness . . . and urine. Some things never change!

A cluster of children recognised me and gathered round to say hello as I walked into the hall, and then I heard a voice behind me.

'Hiya, miss. Are you coming back to teach us?'

There was something familiar about that voice. I turned round and could hardly believe my eyes. Margaret! Margaret, the little girl with the filthy underwear and the mum who we suspected drank too much. Margaret whom I thought I would never see again.

She looked completely transformed. She was wearing a lovely navy dress with a little white collar, and her bedraggled black hair was now gleaming and plaited into two fat pigtails and tied with bright red ribbons.

'No, Margaret,' I said, 'I'm afraid I'm not coming back. I live too far away now. I am *so* pleased to see you!'

And I was. It looked like all the worry about what had happened to her had been for nothing because she was clearly thriving.

'I love your ribbons,' I said.

'My new mum bought them for me,' she said.

'Do you like your new mum?'

'Yes,' said Margaret. 'She tells me and my brothers stories about when she was a little girl, just like you used to do, and she makes lovely cakes like your mum did.'

I smiled. So she and her brothers were all together still. As we chatted, I noticed that the rest of the children were beginning to get ready for the performance now.

'Are you in the choir, Margaret?' I asked. 'Because they're just sitting down.'

She turned and walked away a few feet, then came back. She looked all around before cupping her hands to my ear.

'I don't wet the bed any more,' she whispered.

I gave her a quick hug. 'That's wonderful,' I whispered back.

As the lights went down, I felt overwhelmed with relief. While I felt great sadness for Margaret's mum that she had such a lovely little girl yet wasn't able to care for her, now Margaret was clean, happy and well looked after. At least I knew that I hadn't been responsible for breaking her heart by having her removed from her own home. I had thought of her so often since last Christmas, but I didn't need to worry any more.

Children's Christmas concerts always engender such a lovely feeling of goodwill, and during the performance I couldn't help thinking of the generosity of that foster mum who had opened up her home to three children so that they could be kept together. After the nativity I heard from Miss Barnes that they had been placed with permanent foster parents who had been looking after children with problems for nearly twenty years. The foster mum said that once she took children in, whatever difficulties might arise, she was committed to them until they were sixteen. She never gave up on them. People like that deserve medals.

13

At the Chalk Face

Some days in teaching you secretly feel like you deserve a medal too. Working with young children is funny, rewarding, inspiring . . . and downright exhausting! It wasn't long now until the end of my first term at Woodchurch and I must admit I was ready for a holiday. Even so, Christmas was my favourite time of year with the children and I loved decorating the classroom with them. In both Huyton and Woodchurch, it was a time when everyone really pushed the boat out. They might have had no money for the leccy bill, but there were lights and decorations everywhere. Santas stood at the sides of houses, reindeers flew across rooftops, and while it was certainly gaudy, it was also cheery and life-affirming.

Many of the parents there paid into clubs all year, but they still went into debt at Christmas and I often used to feel very sorry for both parents and children.

'Remember,' I used to tell the children, 'just ask for one small thing and perhaps you will get a surprise.'

Hoping to run some energy out of them, I took my class to the hall for PE and Sam was the first one ready. Sam was a quiet boy but very intense, the kind of child you knew felt things very deeply. He was a watcher rather than a talker, and children like that can easily get overlooked in a classroom. I always tried to remember to give him some undivided attention when I could.

'What do you want for Christmas, Sam?' I asked him, while we waited for the others.

'I've seen a windmill in the toyshop,' he said, eyes shining. 'It lights up and goes round and round.'

'Oh, that would be a lovely thing to have,' I agreed. 'I do hope Santa brings it for you.'

'Miss! Miss, look at me! I'm inside out!'

The voice was behind me and when I turned, Robert was hanging upside down like a monkey from the climbing frame.

'Wow, Robert,' I said. 'I wish I could do that.'

His flushed, upside-down face grinned back at me. 'It's easy, miss! I could teach you!'

You needed eyes in the back of your head with Robert. A few minutes later I heard his voice behind me again.

'Miss, I can nearly touch the ceiling!' he shouted.

I spun round, not wanting to see what I knew I was about to. Robert was standing fearlessly at the very top of the climbing frame, bolt upright. My stomach lurched. If I shouted or made him panic, he could easily fall.

'Right, Robert, come down *very* slowly,' I said, trying to keep the panic from my voice.

Within three quick moves he had swung himself down deftly and was right beside me, chatting away.

I decided to keep away from the apparatus that day – my heart couldn't take it – and divided the children into teams for games. They were always sorry when PE was finished, but as I lined them up, I offered another incentive.

'It's nearly playtime,' I said, 'but I've got a story to read to you afterwards. Would you like to hear all about a little gingerbread man?'

Joseph's eyes flashed with interest. 'Is the little gingerbread man a vampire?' he asked hopefully.

Joseph, I had recently discovered, stayed up late with his teenage mum watching horror movies.

'No, Joseph,' I said, 'the little gingerbread man is not a vampire.'

'Is he a—'

'No, he's not a zombie either,' I interrupted quickly, anticipating his next question from experience.

After playtime I sat the children down for storytime, then realised Robert was missing.

'Where's Robert?' I asked, looking around the room. It was beginning to feel like a difficult day.

'In the storeroom,' the children chorused.

'What's he doing in there?'

'Looking for crayons.'

I went into the storeroom at the end of the class and looked around.

No Robert.

'He's not in the storeroom,' I said, puzzled.

'He is, miss! Miss, he's in there – I saw him!' shouted Joseph, who had been very voluble all morning. He ran the sleeve of his grey jumper along his nose, leaving a glistening path along the wool. I don't think the children had ever heard of hankies.

'Miss! I saw him!' he repeated. I don't know what Joseph had had at playtime, but the way he was fizzing round the room, I suspected it might have been cola and Smarties.

'Yes, thank you, Joseph,' I said wearily.

Puzzled, I went back into the storeroom and peered around. A sudden movement made my eyes lift upwards.

On the top shelf, near the ceiling, Robert was rummaging busily through boxes. Oh God, not climbing again! If he fell from there . . .

'Come down, please, Robert. You shouldn't be up that high.' My voice sounded calmer than I felt.

In seconds Robert had swung his way down from the mountaintop of shelves.

'Found some, miss,' he said, beaming and holding out some packets of fat coloured crayons.

It was hard to be cross with Robert. He wasn't being deliberately naughty. Climbing was just his thing and he simply had no sense of danger. But, of course, every teacher has to have a sense of discipline to enable a class to function in an organised way and create the right environment for children to learn in. For me, discipline was never a big issue because the children I taught were so young, though I'm not sure today's six- and seven-year-olds are quite so easily quelled.

At last I had everyone sitting round me and I began to read 'The Little Gingerbread Man'. It was one of my favourites. Children always enjoy being read to, and they love repetition, so the story's chorus of 'Run, run as fast as you can, you can't catch me – I'm the gingerbread man!' was always a winner. Joseph listened intently until

I got to the part where the baker's wife opens the oven door and out jumps the gingerbread man.

'Miss, was he working when he went in the oven?' Joseph asked.

I looked up from the page.

'Sorry? What do you mean by "working", Joseph?'

'Was his arms and legs working when she put him in the oven?'

'Do you mean, was he alive when he went in the oven?'

He nodded.

'No, he wasn't alive, Joseph. We wouldn't put someone who was alive in an oven, would we?' I did wish Joseph's mum would stop the horror movies!

The children sat enthralled when I continued the story, until I got to the end.

'And then . . .' I said, pausing for effect, '. . . the fox gobbled up the little gingerbread man!'

There was a gasp.

'Aarh ray, miss,' protested Joseph. 'That's dead tight!'

Joseph had difficulty concentrating and was difficult to pin down – the kind of child you might nowadays suspect had attention deficit disorder – but he was warm and engaging and easy to love. Mark was an altogether darker proposition. Every so often you would come across a child who seemed more disturbed than naughty, and it could be very sad to know that they were likely to end up in serious trouble one day.

Mark was quite a good-looking boy, big for his age but

inclined to bully those who were smaller than him. One lunchtime the children began to put their things away. I could see Mark was up to no good. His arm kept snaking out on the sly and punching other children.

'Stop that, Mark!' I called sternly, when I caught him. 'If you do that again, you will end up on the naughty chair.' The 'naughty chair' was around long before 'Supernanny' Jo Frost publicised it on television, and in most cases, the threat of it was enough to restore order. If it wasn't enough, keeping the culprit in at playtime worked quite well, particularly if their friends stood smiling in through the window.

Children are funny little creatures, though. Even the naughty chair garnered its own mystique. A few minutes later a lovely, well-behaved little girl called Jenny, who wouldn't say boo to a goose, sidled up to me.

'Miss,' she said quietly, 'do you think one day I could have a go on the naughty chair?'

Mark would not be told that day. He really was a very odd little boy, quite bright, but aggressive. When I saw him punching yet again, I took him aside.

'When you come back this afternoon,' I told him, 'I want to see a different boy. Christmas is a happy time, and this afternoon, when we get our work finished, we're going to hang some decorations. But anyone who's naughty won't be allowed to help.'

I was glad when the bell went. Temporary peace!

That afternoon, when the children returned after lunch, we made a winter frieze with different scenes . . . one in the countryside, one in the town and one at the seaside. We had a block of flats with Christmas trees in the window for our winter scene.

'What shall we include at the seaside?' I asked the children.

'Sand!' shouted one.

'Shells!'

Then I heard Mark shout something: 'The moon!'

'That's a nice idea. Why the moon, Mark?' I asked him.

'Because it regulates the tides.'

He was certainly smart, but when I saw him punch his neighbour yet again, I finally lost patience.

'Right, Mark,' I said. 'I've told you again and again today to stop punching people. I'm afraid you're going to have to miss this afternoon's break.'

When the bell went for playtime, the other children trooped out while Mark stayed behind. As I sat down beside him, he looked at me coldly, in a most un-childlike way.

'When I'm an adult,' he said, 'I'll come back and murder you.'

It took my breath away, but I did wonder sadly what it was in Mark's background that made him behave in that way. I didn't get a chance to find out because his family moved away shortly after.

In general, children mirror what's around them. I do remember one little boy who kept swearing. I spoke to his dad when he came to pick him up after school and had barely got the words out when he swung round to his son. 'Hey, you!' he shouted. 'How many bloody times do I have to tell you not to swear in school?'

After Mark's little outburst, I was desperate for the end of the day, but there was one more challenge ahead. There was a knock at the door and through the glass I saw the school nurse. I had completely forgotten she was due to come. I groaned inside but smiled as welcomingly as I could and turned to the class.

'This is the nurse from the clinic who has come to see what shiny hair we all have,' I told the class brightly.

They all looked at each other like I'd told them spacemen had just arrived from Mars. Eh? Shiny hair? They knew fine well she was the nit nurse.

'Nurse can have a look at my hair first,' I continued enthusiastically, thinking I was setting a good example. As she trawled through my hair with a fine-tooth comb, I kept a constant, encouraging smile plastered to my face.

That smile soon cracked.

'Sorry,' the nurse whispered in my ear, 'but you've got nits.'

I still remember the awful smell of the Derbac-M that I had to keep on my hair all night.

A male colleague who taught next door to me got so paranoid about catching nits from his class that he resorted to drawing a chalk circle round his desk. The children were not allowed to step over the line and they used to throw their exercise books over to him. When he marked them, he would shout out a name and they would dash out to catch the book. Turns out the children thought it was great fun, but I'm not sure they realised why the 'game' was played. I wasn't one for keeping my distance. I couldn't let it stop me giving a child a cuddle if they needed it.

When the nit nurse identified a child with a problem, they were given a letter to take to the clinic for treatment. Nowadays, a general letter goes out to parents saying, 'There is an incidence of nits in your child's class. Please check your child's hair and take appropriate action.' I'm sure most parents would prefer to be told up front. Many young parents don't know how to spot a nit, but me . . . I'm an expert with a fine-tooth comb.

I was looking forward to getting home and perhaps I was a little sharper than usual getting the children ready at the end of the afternoon! They were all lined up, waiting for the bell.

'Where's your coat, Joseph?'

I knew Joseph got a Local Authority clothing allowance. All the children on free dinners did and they had to go to the same outfitter's in town, where they would end up with identical grey duffle coats with red lining.

'It's gone, miss,' he said.

'What do you mean, it's gone?'

'Miss, the tallyman came, miss.'

Poor Joseph. He could be difficult, but he was up against it.

I had a teaching assistant in that afternoon and she caught my eye. 'This one's been a right S-O-D today,' I told her, nodding at Mark.

The bell rang. We opened the door to reveal all the parents waiting outside. Joseph, who was constantly curious and never missed a trick, looked up at me.

'Miss, what's an S-O-D?'

Oh G-O-D.

'Now,' I said to Joseph, thinking quickly and, of course, completely ignoring his question, 'let's have a quick look in the cloakroom because I think this morning you lost an S-O-C-K. Or was it an S-H-O-E? I ushered him over quickly to the coat pegs. His grandma was picking him up that day and when she came over, I announced, 'We've been looking for his S-H-O-E.'

All I could do was pray that he had forgotten the original 'S' word. Fortunately, I heard no more about it and Joseph skipped off quite happily. I went back into the classroom with relief. Some of the stragglers, including Jenny, were still there as Mrs Simons, the head, came up and handed me an envelope. Ah, compensation! Good timing. Jenny looked up at the envelope with interest.

'Please, miss,' she said. 'What is in that envelope you were given?'

'That's just my pay cheque, Jenny,' I told her. 'The money I get for working.'

'Oh,' she said curiously, 'where do you work?'

I couldn't possibly imagine.

14

Holy Smoke!

A little ring of smoke gathered round Father Jock's head as he contentedly settled back in an armchair in my sitting room with a cigarette. Because Jaime and I lived in the parish, he occasionally popped round to see us, though he never complained that he didn't see much of me in his congregation!

'I thought I'd come and have a wee word about the christening next week.'

I was to be godmother to a friend's baby and Father Jock was taking the service.

'Jaime not in?'

'He'll be back shortly. Cup of strong tea, Father?'

'Oh lovely. Thanks, Bernadette. I always say it – you're a good lassie!'

I laughed and bustled into the kitchen.

'God save us, who's that?' I heard Father Jock call. I popped my head round the doorway to see him holding a framed photograph that had been sitting on the shelf beside his chair.

I grinned. 'That's my brother, Andrew.'

'He's a hippy!'

'He certainly is, Father. A flip-flop-wearing hippy. He's in Tahiti just now.'

'Haiti?'

'Tahiti,' I said loudly, enunciating clearly.

'That's what I said – Haiti.'

'TAHITI!'

'Oh, Tahiti.'

I often wrote to Andrew with news from home and was always relieved to hear back from him. He slept for so many nights on a beach in Tahiti that he woke up one morning surrounded by tourists staring at him and taking photographs. '*Ici Monsieur le Hippy, qui habite sur la plage*,' the tour guide announced to his group.

Father Jock and I had a chat about the christening and what I had to do, but the conversation kept working its way back to Andrew and Father Jock always asked about his progress after that evening.

'How's that hippy brother of yours?' he would say, and I would regale him with Andrew's latest exploits in some far-off corner of the world.

Father Jock asked humorously, but I often wondered if a little part of him was envious of Andrew's adventures in foreign lands. He listened avidly when I told him Andrew loved the Indian people and had lived for a few weeks in Calcutta Station.

'He met a young man there who had lived all his life at that station,' I said.

'Is that so?' said Father Jock, and he seemed genuinely fascinated by the ways and lives of others.

He had an enquiring mind and loved reading. Usually you would see him with his nose stuck in the Bible or *The*

Lives of the Saints, but that night as he left, he noticed a pile of western novels in our flat.

'Do you think I could borrow a couple of those, Bernadette?' he asked.

'Of course you can, Father.'

I was rather tickled by Father Jock's eclectic reading tastes and mentioned it to one of the other priests.

'Oh, we all know about Father Jock's reading!' he said, chuckling. 'He puts a cover from religious books over his novels and pretends to be reading holy stuff. Nobody reads the Bible that avidly! He goes up to the choir loft with a fag and a book for a bit of peace and quiet.'

I liked Father Jock even more after that. Next time I saw him with his head stuck in *The Life of Christ*, I chuckled to myself. I knew it was probably *Gunfight at the OK Corral*.

After the Christmas holidays I asked Sam if he got his windmill, the one that he saw in the toyshop that lit up and rotated.

'No,' he replied. 'I got one of them windmill things you blow.'

He wasn't saying much, but I could tell how deeply Sam's disappointment cut. I considered buying him one myself, but I didn't want to upset his parents.

'Santa must have misunderstood what you meant,' I said. 'What did you do with the windmill, Sam?'

'I jumped on it and broke it,' he said.

It was brought home to me in so many small ways how different these children's lives were from children in more affluent parts of the city. When it came to parents' evening, for example, I asked one little boy in my class if his mum and dad would be coming to see me. Perhaps they would like to see the work he had been doing this term and have a look at his nice drawings up on the walls?

'Me mum might,' he said speculatively, 'but me dad's out on the rob of a night.' You would think he was telling me about his dad's shift down the factory.

What chance did they have? Education – that was their chance.

As the spring term wore on, it was time for the Top Juniors to sit the Eleven Plus. Although I didn't teach the older children, I always had a lot of sympathy with them at the time of the Eleven Plus exam. This was such a critical point for them. That exam shaped their entire future, yet they were little more than babies.

A friend of mine taught the Eleven Plus class for a few years and on the day before the exam she once said to her class, 'Now, no more revising. Just have a warm bath and go to bed early.'

The next day, after the exam, one little boy came up to her.

'Do we have to have another bath tonight?' he said. That was the most important question in his mind, but I did notice that it was harder to make little boys understand the significance of the test. Little girls seemed to know exactly what the score was.

The Eleven Plus exam grew out of the 1944 Butler Education Act. Like slum clearances, it looked, on paper, like it should have been a good idea. The Act laid down the principle of free education for children from age five to fifteen and the Eleven Plus was supposed to determine what kind of education each child would be best suited to. It was a tripartite system with three different kinds of schools on offer. For the academic children, there would be grammar schools; for children who might be more suited to taking up an apprenticeship, there would be secondary moderns; and finally, there would be technical schools or colleges.

It should have been about allocating the right kind of education to the right child, but human nature being what it is, the Eleven Plus very quickly became something else. Instead of being about need and ability, it became about 'passing' and 'failing'. The different types of education that were on offer should have been equally resourced, but it became obvious that the technical schools were not going to appear on the scale envisaged. Fierce competition erupted over the grammar-school places and to be allocated anything less was seen as being thrown on the scrapheap.

My big thing in education had always been that each child has a special talent, but instead of different talents being equally valued, technical and craft abilities were soon dismissed as second rate. The whole system became very divisive and it was only in 1965, when the Labour MP Tony Crosland introduced comprehensive schools, that things began to change. Grammar schools remained, though, and the Eleven Plus was never actually formally abolished. Some areas still make children sit the test today.

I was in early the day the Eleven Plus results came out that year. The children's parents had all received results letters in the morning post, so when the eleven-year-olds arrived at school, there was much excitement. But not for everyone. Some of the children were the older siblings of children in my class and that morning I saw Sam's brother, Joe, mooching about in the yard, alone.

'What school are you off to, Joe?' I asked.

'I dunno, miss,' he replied. 'I failed.'

How awful to 'fail' at eleven, and what a waste of the potential so many of these children had. I knew that if I'd decided to teach older children, it would have been the ones who hadn't made it that my heart would have gone out to. If you didn't get to the right school, the world probably wasn't going to work out for you – and I always wanted the world to work out for children.

One year I was an invigilator for the Eleven Plus. The test used to have ninety questions, but that year they changed it to a hundred and the extra questions were on the back of the sheet. You weren't supposed to say anything about turning the paper over. The theory was that intelligent children would look by themselves. This seemed unfair to me: if you have been trained to answer ninety questions, then you are not going to think to turn over the paper, are you? That wasn't a test of intelligence in my book and I had no hesitation in quietly turning the exam sheet over for the ones who hadn't noticed. I can't imagine what trouble I'd get into nowadays for doing that!

I used to get bored stiff invigilating and sometimes, as I walked round, if I noticed a child had made a silly mistake, I'd point and frown. I didn't think it was cheating because I knew that child could do it. Was I going to condemn them to a future where the world didn't work out just because they made a silly mistake? Not me! The system was against these kids in so many ways. I was only levelling out the playing field. The truth is, I was always on their side.

I didn't want the same to happen to Sam as had happened to Joe. Sam was bright enough, but he had a few problems with his reading and I wanted to make sure he didn't fall behind. The early stages could be so critical, especially in establishing children's self-confidence and self-belief. I asked Sam's mum if I could call round to see her to have a chat. She agreed and I went looking for the address one day after school. When I eventually found the house, it was neat with a small, well-kept garden, but there was a nasty-looking Alsatian sitting growling outside. It wasn't the most welcoming sight, but I forced myself up the path and rang the doorbell, hoping the dog wouldn't make a lunge at me. A very pleasant lady opened the door and welcomed me in, and the dog ran in ahead and settled itself in front of the gas fire.

Inside, the house seemed quite clean and tidy, so I happily accepted a cup of coffee. Just as I was about to put the cup to my lips, however, the dog stood up, cocked his leg and peed down the side of the armchair. I froze, waiting for Sam's mum to do something, but she never moved a muscle.

Trying to put this embarrassing incident behind me, I had a very fruitful discussion with Sam's mum and explained how she could help at home by listening to him read and encouraging him to look at books with her. It could make all the difference, I explained, to Sam's progress. I think she was pleased that I had taken an interest and she agreed to help all she could. I said my farewells and we shook hands warmly before I headed for the door. As she led the way out, the dog suddenly jumped up and raced to the hall ahead of her. Just as she reached the front door, I was horrified to see the dog squat down to relieve itself, leaving the most enormous mess sitting on the carpet in the hall. Again, Sam's mum never said a word.

What a strange way to behave, I thought, somewhat disturbed. No wonder Sam is a bit quiet and intense. I couldn't wait to get out. Stepping over the mess, I said a hasty farewell and scuttled off down the path.

Just then, Sam's mum's voice floated out after me. 'Hey, miss,' she shouted. 'Aren't yer taking yer dog with yer?'

The christening for my friend's baby was planned for a Sunday morning and the night before Jaime and I went for a quick drink. As we came out of the pub, though, we could smell smoke and I could see flames billowing into the air in the distance.

'It's the church!' I said. I could see that the roof was alight and heard the wail of sirens.

I couldn't go home yet. I ran round the corner and down to the church, where a crowd had gathered.

'Where's Father Jock?' I gasped.

'It's all right, Bernadette. I'm here,' said a voice behind me. Father Jock was in his black suit and white clerical collar, and was looking a bit shocked.

'Thank God for that,' I said, and instinctively hugged him, taking him by surprise.

The roof was badly burned and unfortunately the christening was cancelled, but luckily the fire brigade managed to restrict the damage. Their report said that the fire was caused by a cigarette butt.

'Did you hear it started in the organ loft?' I asked Father Jock suspiciously.

'In the croft? What croft?'

'The ORGAN LOFT!'

'Oh, the organ loft.'

'I wonder how that happened,' I said. 'Who could have been smoking in the organ loft?'

'Absolutely no idea,' he replied.

It was almost Easter and it felt as if the year was flying by. Quite by chance, I bumped into someone who was going to change my life again. It was Mavis Deans, the headmistress of my old primary school, where she was still in post.

'What are you doing these days?' she asked.

When I told her I was teaching at Woodchurch, she looked thoughtful.

'You know,' she said, 'I've got a vacancy for next year and I'm looking for a young, enthusiastic teacher like you. Why don't you come and work with me? It will certainly be easier than where you are.'

Easier, perhaps, but would it be as satisfying? Then Mavis offered me one very, very big incentive.

'You can have the reception class,' she said.

My mind whirled round in circles for the next few days. I had only been at Woodchurch for a year. Was it too early to move on again? Looking out of the window of my classroom, I watched Robert scurrying deftly up the school fence in the playground, and Joseph running like the wind, whooping at the top of his voice. I loved the children I taught here. I loved their energy and their resilience. They didn't have much, but usually they managed to be happy. I also loved that I could make a difference to them. You are never more conscious of the importance of education than when you are working with deprived children who have nothing but the knowledge that you can pour into them.

At the Easter assembly, I stood at the side and looked out at the sea of faces and wondered what to do.

'Which clever child can tell me what happened on Good Friday?' Father Jock was saying.

A flurry of hands shot into the air, accompanied by cries of 'Me, Father! Me, me, me!'

One of the little ones, just five years old, had his hand up and was bursting to answer.

Father Jock pointed to him. 'Right, laddie, you,' he said. 'What happened on Good Friday?'

'I got a banana,' replied the little boy, named Gerard.

'That's right, laddie! Jesus died on the cross.'

It was like something from a Monty Python sketch and, beside me, Annie dissolved into giggles. I didn't dare look at her, but I looked at the little five-year-old, to whom a banana was the most important thing in the world, and my heart melted. The reception class? It was too good an offer to turn down.

A telegram arrived from my brother, Andrew. I frequently wrote to him with news from home and sent the letters to *poste restante* addresses, which is where travellers pick up their mail when they have no fixed address. I was always relieved to hear back from him and I knew that at the moment he was trying to reach Australia. This telegram, however, which was actually sent to Mum, was worrying. 'Help. Send £10 to *Poste Restante* Jakarta,' it said. Andrew was very independent and it was the first time he had ever asked for money. All we could do was respond to the request and wait anxiously to hear more.

15

The Reception Class

There is something very special about reception class children in their bright white socks and shiny new shoes. Shiny new lives. They are like blotting paper, just waiting to soak everything up. And they have no inhibitions. They say it as it is. They think nothing of being curious about what you are wearing under your skirt and just having a wee peek to check . . . I remember one gorgeous little boy peering over the top of his NHS specs at me after a few weeks in school and saying, 'I like that jumper you've got on.'

'Thank you,' I replied.

'I don't like that nuther jumper.'

'Which other jumper?'

'You know, *that* jumper.'

'Oh, *that* jumper,' I said sagely. I always think children give little clues about what they will one day do with their lives. Perhaps that little boy became a fashion designer.

My new school, Our Lady's Primary School, was a very different world from my first two. The building itself was reasonably modern, not an assortment of rain-soaked old huts with steaming fires and the stale smell of urine permeating everything. The staffroom and the head's office had once been a convent. In the 1940s the nuns had built an extension on the back and partitioned off three classrooms as a little prep school. Eventually, the nuns sold it to the parish and a new school was built on the side of the original, with the extension being retained as the dining room. The school remained Catholic, however, just as Woodchurch was.

Another new start. I was getting an old hand at first days by now, having worked at three schools in as many years, but I was still very excited and couldn't wait to meet my new charges. Sadly, some of them weren't quite as eager to get started as I was! I had never realised, until my first term as a reception-class teacher, just how traumatic starting school can be for some children. It really was like trying to separate defenceless cubs from protective lionesses! The bond between mother and child is so intense at that stage and it can be very touching to observe.

Peter was a dark-haired little boy with beautiful soft eyes, like a fawn. He stuck to his mother's knee in the cloakroom as if there was superglue on the seat of his trousers, and nothing I said could convince him to be parted from her. I knelt down beside him.

'Do you like painting, Peter?'

His eyes swivelled round; he peered out from his mother's jumper and nodded.

'Well, perhaps you would like to come with me and have a go with all my lovely paints?'

I held out my hand, but Peter shook his head fearfully and suddenly the fawn had rushed back to hide in the undergrowth. I told him what a wonderful time we could have with all my storybooks and toys, but it fell on deaf ears. Peter's arms were like a vice round his mum's neck and I could see that his fear was beginning to upset her.

Things were getting desperate. Then Peter's mum, recovering herself slightly, tried to explain things to him.

'When Mummy was a little girl, she had to go to school,' she said gently.

Peter moved his head and looked up at her.

So far, so good, I thought.

'When Daddy was a little boy, he had to go to school until he was a big boy,' she continued.

With a big sniff, Peter climbed down from his mother's knee and walked towards me, lip trembling. Then he turned back to his mum with liquid eyes. 'Will you come back for me when I'm a big boy?' he asked.

I don't know whose eyes filled up quicker, his mum's or mine!

After a few weeks of settling in, the children's confidence tended to return. They were so unselfconscious and I loved the way they considered themselves kings and queens of their own little world.

One day Mrs Deans, the head teacher, came in to introduce herself and talk to my class. She walked up and down between the rows of desks, looking thoughtful.

'Who's the boss in here?' she asked.

Almost every hand shot up into the air.

'Me, me, me!' they all chorused.

Even Peter was comfortable enough now to shout out! I loved that, the instinctive sense of themselves the children had before the system taught them to conform, for just a short while later, when Mrs Deans asked the same question, the children had a different answer.

'Mrs Cubells!' they shouted.

I felt a bit sad, actually, as though a little spark had been stamped out by school already. I suppose that's the way it has to be, though. As a teacher you have to have discipline, and anyway, we can't all go through life saying exactly what we want. Much as we'd like to!

The children became more independent of their mothers, knew where to hang their coats and how to tie their laces, but they also lost their ability to simply say whatever came into their heads. The way children see the world is very special and they often get straight to the heart of things: 'My granddad is very old,' one little boy in my new class told me, 'but when he was new, he was a little boy.'

The way you talk to children is so important. They don't like sarcasm and I tried never to use it. Firstly, it confuses them, and then it makes them feel silly when they realise they haven't got the joke. They don't much like sayings and expressions either, unless they are meant literally. Mrs Deans had a habit of saying, 'Act your age, not your shoe size.'

'What does she mean?' Peter asked me one day. 'Why does Mrs Deans always say that to people?'

'What age are you?' I said.

'Five.'

'And what size shoes do you take?'

'Ten.'

'Never mind,' I said. 'I don't know what she means either!'

Then there was Reg Mandelson, our deputy head, with whom I was to become good friends. He was an eccentric, witty character, with an at times outrageous sense of humour, but his humour would often go right over the children's heads. He could be very funny, but I sometimes thought he would have been better suited to a secondary rather than a primary school. I recall talking to him in the playground one day when a little girl in my new primary-one class ran up to me. She was very cute and had lovely big fat plaits.

'What's your name?' asked Reg.

'Jennifer Jones,' she replied shyly.

'I've seen all your films,' he said.

Jennifer looked at him in bafflement.

'This is Mr Mandelson,' I whispered to Jennifer, 'and we don't take any notice of him!'

My morning in the primary-one class started in the same way each day. Each child would take a lump of plasticine out of the container and roll it into a snake. Then they cut bits off and tried to form the letters of their name, placing them over the name cards that I had made for them, just as I used to do with Daniel at Huyton. This proved to be highly successful for most children, and within a few days they could recognise their names when I held up the cards.

One morning, during one of these plasticine sessions, a little boy called Christopher beckoned me over.

'I can't fit any more of my name on my card,' he wailed.

When I looked over his shoulder, I saw that he had managed as far as 'Christ'. Poor thing!

'Never mind, Christopher,' I said. 'That will do just right!'

As I moved away from Christopher, I caught sight of Jack, who sat close by. Jack seemed lost in thought and was rolling his plasticine aimlessly without making any shapes.

'All right, Jack?'

Jack nodded but kept his eyes cast down. He was a delightful boy with a little snub nose covered in freckles, and a really lovely sense of mischief, so something was obviously wrong today. I watched him carefully for the rest of the day and noticed that he was very reserved, not his usual sunny self at all. When his mum came to pick him up, I had a quiet word.

'Is everything all right with Jack?' I asked. 'He seems very subdued and I wondered if anything could be the matter.'

'We're moving house,' his mum told me. 'Perhaps he's just excited.'

'Oh, I do hope I'm not going to lose Jack from my class,' I said.

She smiled. 'No, we're not going far. We're just moving to a bigger house nearby, so Jack will still come to this school.'

I was relieved, as I recalled how disrupted I had felt as a child when I'd been moved from my primary school and sent to the convent boarding school.

'I'm glad,' I said. 'He's such a pleasure to teach.'

His mum frowned thoughtfully. 'You know, he has wet the bed a couple of times recently, which is very unusual for him, but I've just assumed that it was a bit of nerves about moving. I'll keep an eye on him.'

I did too, but far from getting better, each day seemed to see Jack a little lower than the last. He often looked sad and he didn't even want to play with the other children much. One day, when the others were racing out for playtime, Jack was last out of the door. He seemed particularly down and I called him back.

'Come and have a chat, Jack.'

He came and stood beside me at my desk, gazing balefully at the ground.

'What's the matter, Jack?' I said. 'You can tell me, can't you?'

He climbed up on my knee and I gave him a cuddle. I knew from experience how much a hug can mean to a child in distress.

Jack sniffed and sank into my arms. 'Will the new mummy and daddy like me?' he asked, fighting back tears.

'What do you mean?' I said, puzzled.

'When they buy my house, will the new mummy and daddy like me?' A big tear ran down his face and plopped onto his jumper. 'I don't want a new mummy and daddy!'

Oh my goodness me – Jack thought he was being sold with the house! I got in touch with his mum and we got to the bottom of the mystery. When the couple who were buying the family house had been shown round, his mum had said, 'This is Jack's room.' Jack had overheard and assumed it would still be his room if the couple bought the house. And since he hadn't been taken to see the new house, what else was he to think?

You say things to children sometimes just assuming they understand, but so often they don't. They take things very much at face value.

Sometimes, of course, their gullibility can be funny and you can have a little gentle amusement with their willingness to believe everything you say. That term, we took all the children in the school to Speke Hall, which is an Elizabethan house on the outskirts of Liverpool. The curators there were great fun and really good with the children. As part of the tour, we went into one of the bedrooms.

'This is called the Ghost Room,' the curator said.

The children all shivered and clutched one another, enjoying the moment of fear in much the same way adults enjoy scary films.

'Why?' they chorused.

'Well,' he said, 'years ago the lady who lived here had just had a baby when she discovered that her husband had lost all their money. She didn't want to bring up her son poor, so she took the baby in her arms and threw herself out of the window. Both of them died and some people say they have seen her ghost walking around in here. But don't worry – she only ever walks around at eleven on a Tuesday morning.'

He dropped the words like pebbles into the water and simply waited for the ripple effect, and of course one of the older children suddenly cottoned on. 'It's eleven o'clock!' he said in a panic-stricken voice as he looked at his watch. 'And it's Tuesday!'

I have never seen children move so fast.

* * *

Jaime and I had spent the early years of our marriage trying to save up a deposit for a house. We had saved £550 when we saw a lovely semi-detached house for sale for £6,250. We set our hearts on it because it was in a quiet cul de sac, just five minutes' walk from my new school. However, at the building society, they told us we needed another £75 for the deposit. It sounds nothing nowadays, but back then it was a lot of money. Jaime asked me to call in at the bank to make an appointment for us to see the manager, which I did on my way home from school. I was taken aback to be told I could see him there and then but he would be off on holiday the next day. The assistant went to double-check and a moment later the door to the manager's office opened.

'Come in, my dear,' he said.

His name was Mr Mumford and he was quite elderly, or so he seemed to me at the time.

'I was hoping to make an appointment to see you with my husband,' I explained.

'Oh well, now that you're here, you might as well just tell me what it's all about yourself,' said Mr Mumford.

Two coffees later, the money was mine and there was another £75 in our account, and thanks to Mr Mumford's loan, we bought our lovely semi. (His investment was more than rewarded since we sold the house for twice what we paid for it just two years later, when we moved to somewhere bigger with a larger garden.)

Father Jock called round to say goodbye before we left our old flat because although I had already left the school, I was now leaving his parish too.

'So where's that hippy brother of yours these days?' he asked.

'We had a telegram from him last week,' I said, handing the folded paper to him.

' "Help. Send £10 to *Poste Restante* Jakarta," ' read Father Jock. He looked up at me. 'What's that about?' he said, sounding concerned.

'He's fine now,' I reassured Father Jock. 'He'd been booked on a boat from Jakarta to Australia and the fares had suddenly doubled due to an oil crisis.'

Rest assured, Mum and I had explained to him in no uncertain terms that the wording of his message had caused us more than a little worry! Andrew's tale of his latest exploit soon had us smiling, though. Even with our contribution, my impoverished brother had had to travel third class on the boat, which meant meals were no more than a bowl of rice with a fish head, and passengers were supposed to hang over the edge of the boat if they needed the toilet! Ever resourceful, though, Andrew had managed to sneak into the indoor toilets. The important thing was that he had finally made it to Australia, and it was a journey that would change his life. When he eventually came home a few months later, he informed us all that he loved Australia so much he was going back there to live, so we had to say goodbye once again to Monsieur le Hippy.

For the moment, though, it was goodbye to dear old Father Jock.

'No more fags in the organ loft,' I cautioned, giving him a quick hug.

'Bags in the organ loft?' he said innocently. 'What would I be doing with bags in the organ loft?'

'FAGS!' I shouted.

He grinned. 'I heard you the first time,' he said.

Old fraud!

We didn't have much furniture when we moved into our new house, but friends and family were very generous and soon it was 'home'. Next door lived a lovely Jewish couple, Joe and Sylvia, who were a bit older than us and had two grown-up daughters, Alison and Helen. Joe was a rep for Outdoor Girl make-up, but at weekends he worked the clubs as a comedian with his close friend one Jimmy Tarbuck. Joe was a really funny guy, but things didn't take off for him the way they did for Jimmy.

One Sunday a Rolls-Royce pulled up next door with the registration COMIC. Guess who? Joe invited us over for coffee and between him and Jimmy, we were in stitches by the time we left. My mother was completely unimpressed when I told her. Jimmy Tarbuck might be a star now, but he had been our paper boy and apparently frequently left our papers out in the rain, then had the nerve to give her cheek when she complained. Once a scally, always a scally in my mum's eyes – Rolls-Royce or not!

There was only Mum and I left in Liverpool by this time: as a family, we were scattered all over the world. Aideen was still in the convent, and though I missed her, in those days you just accepted that if someone was a nun, you weren't going to see much of them. It was the same if family members moved abroad. Andrew was in

Australia, of course, and my sister Helena had married and decided to move to Canada. When someone emigrated in the 1960s and 1970s, it really was more or less a wave goodbye. Travel was not as easy as today and people simply didn't have the money to go to exotic places for a holiday. My younger sister, Kathleen, had also married and had moved to Wiltshire, so for different reasons, none of us saw each other as regularly as we would have liked.

It made me sad to think that my family were so far away, but despite that, it was a happy year for me with my first proper home and, at school, my first reception class, and my life has always been blessed with plenty of good friends. The staff in my new school were a friendly bunch and I struck up a rapport with Marie, the teacher next door, almost instantly. The first time I saw her she was sashaying down the corridor, a willowy, elegant figure who was immaculately dressed. One of my little ones came tearing down the corridor and ran slap bang into her.

'Sorry, Miss Cumming!' he said instantly.

Marie was very imposing, almost intimidating, and could cut children dead with just a raised eyebrow. She also had a clipped cut-glass accent, which she used to great effect. She put a restraining hand on his shoulder while he quivered like blancmange beneath her gaze.

'Anthony,' she said mildly.

'Yes, Miss Cumming?'

'Am I invisible?'

Anthony's little mouth gasped like a stranded fish. 'No, Miss Cumming.'

'Excellent, Anthony. We are both agreed. I am not invisible. Please do not behave in future as if I am.'

And she sailed forth like a ship, the corridor full of children parting like the Red Sea as she came towards them.

I would soon discover that Marie was also warm and funny and a kindred spirit. It was she who always made a fuss of the children if I sent them in to her with things they had made, like egg sandwiches decorated with the cress that we had grown in the classroom. Reg Mandelson, on the other hand, the nonconformist deputy head with the quirky sense of humour, would quite openly drop them in the bin, so I told the outraged children to miss Mr Mandelson out next time because he didn't deserve any!

I loved the infants in my reception class, and although I wanted my own children one day, I was happy to wait for another year or two. 'Are you getting broody?' people would ask me, but I was with young children all day and had great fun with them – then I got to hand them back for someone else to take over. And I was never really a tiny-baby person. Some people say they would be content to hold a baby all day long, but that was never me. I wanted them at the stage where they could talk and inter-act, when they could listen to songs and stories. No doubt when I held my own baby in my arms for the first time, I would feel differently, but I was young and happy and for the time being I was content to be a surrogate mum to forty!

16

My Little Shining Light

Strictly speaking, perhaps a teacher, like a mother, shouldn't really have favourites, but at times it's hard not to. Some children just seem to leave their mark on you and it never completely goes. Joey and Robbo and Margaret had captured my heart at Huyton, just as Robert and Joseph had at Woodchurch, and here in my new school too, though I honestly loved them all, there were a few children with whom I formed a special bond.

To this day I smile when I think of Johnny. I really could quite happily have taken him home with me. He had tight blond curls and a cherubic mouth and I called him 'My Little Shining Light' because even on cold, damp mornings he would light up the classroom with his smile.

'I'm glad it's raining,' he said to me one morning.

'Why?' I asked.

'Because when it rains at playtime, you take us into the hall to act out nursery rhymes. Can I be Humpty Dumpty today?'

He flashed me his most winning smile and I was a goner. Yes, he could be Humpty Dumpty!

To a certain extent, children are sponges, waiting to soak up whatever influences are poured into them, but

there are also little character traits, personality prefer-
ences, that seem instinctive and come almost fully
formed, even at a young age. Johnny had quite feminine
mannerisms and he was drawn to the world of dressing-
up and make-believe. He particularly loved Friday afternoons, when the class were allowed 'choosing time'.
Some of the children chose to play with sand or water or
building bricks. Some headed for the paints or for board
games, while others were content to play for hours in the
Wendy house. My Little Shining Light always headed
straight for the dressing-up box.

The box was a treasure trove of hats and shoes, dresses
and trousers, beads and bangles. Johnny never tired of
experimenting with different costumes and roles. One
Friday I noticed him trying to persuade some other little
boys to dress up so he could act out a story with them.

'What story do you want to act?' I asked him.

'I like the one where the princess falls asleep,' he
replied.

'Boys can't be princesses,' scoffed one of the other
boys.

My Little Shining Light was not about to have his
burgeoning career on the boards thwarted by gender
stereotypes. 'Well, I can,' he said firmly.

'When you're ready, let me know and I'll come and
watch you,' I promised.

Out of the corner of my eye, I saw Johnny proceed to
put on one of my mum's cast-off dresses, a hideous silver
lamé number, with high-heel shoes and equally hideous
beads.

'I can't find a crown,' he wailed.

'That's all right,' I said, quickly coming to his rescue. 'I have some tinsel in the Christmas box.'

I tied some round his head and he looked in the full-length mirror that was fastened to the wall. Pleased with the effect, he smiled at his reflection. Sadly, the play did not quite live up to the splendour of the costumes, but Johnny did what any self-respecting thespian does: blamed the other actors.

'They're not doing it properly!' he complained.

Acting, pretending, music . . . Johnny lapped it all up. I loved music time, and though I belonged to the Les Dawson school of music, I could knock out a basic tune on the piano. The children used to love skipping round to 'Skip to My Lou' when it was a wet playtime and I always kept a big box of musical instruments for them to experiment with. They'd all fight over the tambourines and I remember one teacher coming in and screwing up her face.

'What are they supposed to be playing?' she asked grumpily.

Who cares? They're enjoying it!

Whenever there was any acting to be done, Johnny would always be the first to volunteer. That Christmas my concert was to be about Father Christmas and his fairies and elves arriving at a house on Christmas Eve. To be seen to be fair, I decided to hold auditions. One rainy Friday afternoon in November, I gave all the boys a piece of paper with the opening lines to be spoken by Father Christmas.

'Now,' I told them all, 'I want you to go home and have a look at this over the weekend. Ask Mum to go into the kitchen while you go to the top of the stairs and say the words. If Mum can hear you in the kitchen, then so will all the people in the hall on the day of the concert.'

I think more than a few mums resorted to reviving their flagging festive spirit with the gin bottle that weekend. The words that I believe eventually drove most of them to drink were 'Here I come upon my sleigh, making this a happy day.'

The following Monday we all went into the hall for the auditions. Each boy, in turn, went onto the stage and delivered the all-important lines. By the time they had all trooped on and had their turn, even I was nearly driven round the bend, but there was one clear winner. My Little Shining Light not only had the loudest, clearest voice but he had also developed a gruff 'ho, ho, ho' laugh that was just right. Marie had come in halfway through and watched Johnny with me.

'I think Santa just arrived,' she said.

The children always took concerts very seriously. So did the parents, who turned up two hours in advance to get the front row, and even the staff could be driven to madness by the stress of it all. On the day of the concert everyone was ready to go apart from the primary-three class, who were missing their teacher.

'Where's Miss Simpson?' I asked.

'She went to the stockroom,' said a passing shepherd, as his tea towel slid down his head.

I left my elves round Santa's fireplace and asked Marie to keep an eye on them while I went to the stockroom to look for her. I tried the handle, but it was locked. She must have gone. I was just about to head back to the stage when I heard a muffled sniff behind the door.

'Hello? Myra?' I said, knocking gently.

No answer.

'Myra, can you open up?'

The lock turned, and when I pushed the door, Myra was sitting on a pile of boxes with a hanky in her hand.

'What's the matter?' I asked sympathetically, secretly hoping the elves wouldn't be dismantling the prop fireplace in my absence.

'I'm just fed up,' she said, wiping her eyes, 'and tired. And do you know what she's done now?'

'Who?'

'Mrs Deans.' Myra took a deep breath. 'My class were supposed to be doing a song at the front of the stage and at the last minute she's put a whole row of plants there so that you can't see their faces and now it looks like a scene from *Tarzan* with them fighting to get out of the jungle,' she said in a rush. 'We've worked so hard as well.'

I was desperately tempted to laugh at the idea of Tarzan swinging through the Christmas concert, but Myra's final words struck a chord. It *was* hard work at the end of term and I knew how easy it was to lose the plot when you got stressed.

'Never mind, Myra,' I comforted her. 'Come on out of here because everyone's waiting. All we need to do is move the plants.'

'But what's Mrs Deans going to say?'

Myra was a bit wary of Mrs Deans's sharp tongue, but I went back and roped in Marie to help me. We lined up the elves and got them to place the plants below the stage. Problem solved.

'Miss! Miss!' hissed a worried voice. A miniature elf came skidding up in felt pixie shoes, legs flailing like a newborn colt on the polished floor. 'We can't start.'

Now what? I thought wearily.

'Why not, Elsie?'

'I can't see my mum,' she said.

'Don't worry. I saw her earlier,' I lied, keeping my fingers well crossed. I knew she'd be out there some-where. 'Everyone in position,' I shouted.

I had my hands on the curtain strings when I heard Mrs Deans call, 'Who is responsible for moving my plants?'

'Too late!' I muttered, and winked at Myra as I pulled the curtains open.

The fairies had practised their 'Dance of the Hours' for days and had almost mastered it, but on the after-noon of the concert they were all so busy looking for Mum and Dad that they kept crashing into each other. From the wings, I saw the parents were absolutely convulsed, but children, like adults, do not like to have their serious efforts ridiculed, so we all tried desperately not to laugh too loud – just encouragingly.

The big moment, though, belonged to Mr Claus. With all eyes on him, my golden-haired Santa was, of course, in his element and ho-ho-hoed with gusto. Like all performers, Johnny knew how to milk applause, but when the audience started to clap, he got a bit carried away and bowed for what seemed like for ever. I thought we were going to have to drag him off there as he basked in his audience's love like a sun-worshipper in the sun's rays. Push off, elves – this is Santa's time to shine!

There were inevitably funny moments when it came to children performing on stage – the funniest ones always unscripted. The juniors' contribution to the concert was *Jolly Jack Tar*. Most of the boys were to be dressed as sailors with navy jumpers and trousers, and little white sailor collars. The story was that the sailors went round the world, meeting up with a little Dutch girl in one port, with Hawaiian dancing girls in another and so on. There were plenty of opportunities for colourful costumes and songs and dances, but the most colourful thing of all was the language. There was a suppressed guffaw from the audience when the boys sang 'I'm Jolly Jack Tar the Sailor Boy' and ended with the line 'Hear me singing, "Ship ahoy! Hurrah for the open sea."'

Behind the curtain, Marie's hand flew to her mouth as she stood beside me. 'Did they really just sing, "Shit ahoy"?' she whispered.

It was the year-two children who performed the nativity play to end the concert and that always prompted a few tears from the mums, but also some laughs. The combination of sweet innocence and comical mishaps was hard to resist. Bemused angels, who weren't sure which way up their halos went, floated aimlessly around the stage, while the shepherds peered out from under striped tea towels, which were tied round their heads with string. Does every household in Britain have one of those tea towels, just waiting in the cupboard for its big moment in a nativity play?

Unfortunately, Mary, dressed in a blue dress and white veil, kept dropping the baby Jesus. He must have had concussion by the end of the concert.

'He keeps slipping out of the blanket, miss,' wailed Mary, looking across at me and Marie in the wings.

The funniest lines were the ones the 'actors' didn't fully understand but the adult audience did. Mary's star line was when she turned to Joseph and said, 'I hope we find somewhere soon, Joseph, because I think I am having a contraction.'

'What's that, Mary?'

'Oh, it's a woman thing,' retorted Mary. 'You wouldn't understand.'

It brought the house down.

We always had to improvise as best we could with costumes. Joseph wore a brown poncho that came down to his feet. The angels had costumes of white crêpe paper with a hole cut out for the head, and a cardboard head-band with a silver star stuck on, but it was the three kings who normally had the most extravagant costumes of all. At the dress rehearsal, though, one mum had been very unimpressed by her son's costume.

'Aarh ray, that's a bit scruffy for a king,' she protested. 'I'll make him a better costume than that.'

The poor lad turned up in an outfit made up of a gold satin dress with an ermine bolero over it, while the crown was covered in so much bling he could hardly lift it, never mind wear it. Marie and I exchanged glances when we first saw it. Unfortunately, the crown went 'missing' on the day of the performance.

'Have you seen that crown, Marie?' I asked her innocently.

'No, Bernadette, I haven't seen it. Have you?'

'No, Marie, I haven't seen it either.'

'Strange, that.'

'Very strange.'

Towards the end of the nativity, by which point Mary had dropped the baby Jesus at least twenty times, the choir were just about to start singing 'We Three Kings of Orient Are' when disaster struck. The choir were sitting on the benches at the front of the stage when a terrible commotion started up behind the back curtain. A disembodied voice wailed out, 'I don't want to be a king!'

A hissed whisper followed. 'But all the mums and dads are waiting! You have to!'

The wail got louder. 'No, no, I don't want to!'

Everyone looked at one another and there were a few sniggers. Then some wag in the choir started singing solo 'We Two Kings of Orient Are', only to be hauled out by the year-two teacher and slapped across the back of the legs. It seemed a bit harsh to me, but then, I love that quirky, funny spirit in children. I wouldn't have chastised him; I would have given him a clap for ingenuity.

I had a similar feeling about one of the mums who was wrapped in a lovely fur coat but looked slightly dishevelled. At the end of the concert, as polite applause rang round the room, she stood up a little unsteadily and whooped, 'Oh, come on, you miserable lot!' she shrieked. 'They've worked so hard – give them a bloody good clap!'

I wanted to go and shake her hand, and I rather think Myra did too.

There is a postscript to My Little Shining Light's story. Whenever you uncovered a child's talent for something it was a really lovely feeling. It didn't matter what it was. My Little Shining Light had a very academic older brother, but Johnny's talent was acting and these school concerts were an opportunity for children like him to have their moment in the spotlight. One of the best things about being a reception class teacher was that you didn't lose the children afterwards; you were able to watch them grow up and keep an eye on them as they progressed through the school. I kept an eye on Johnny in particular throughout his remaining years at primary school.

When he was about eleven, and all set to move on to secondary school, he came to visit my class. Rommy, my class gerbil, had recently died and I had taken the class outside to bury him. I dug the hole, and just as I was about to place the 'coffin' in the grave, I heard a familiar voice behind me.

'Miss, I've written a poem for your gerbil. I heard he died. Can I read it aloud?'

'Of course, Johnny,' I told him. 'I'm sure the children would love to hear it.'

So he proceeded to read a lovely, thoughtful poem, entitled 'Ode to a Gerbil', which ended with the lines 'So farewell, Rommy. We're sorry you've died, but be happy in the gerbil heaven in the sky.'

Not Shakespeare, maybe, but a start for a budding actor and declared with Johnny's usual sense of occasion.

Johnny went on to the local secondary school, so I continued to watch his progress over the years and wow, could he act. Twice a year he was given the chance to shine, whether it was in Shakespeare or a light musical. He handled it all with equal aplomb.

Many years later I was in Max Spielmann, the photo shop, and was vaguely aware of a handsome young man looking at photo albums. Just as I was collecting my photos, a hand tapped me lightly on the shoulder.

'Hello, miss. Do you remember me?'

My Little Shining Light? Of course I remembered him!

'I heard you went on to become an actor,' I said. 'That doesn't surprise me. You were a very good Humpty Dumpty and, of course, Father Christmas. Are you acting at the moment?'

'I'm resting, as we say in my profession,' he said, 'but I have just been in a big show and I have an audition soon for a part in a West End musical.'

'If it would help,' I joked, 'I would offer to sleep with the director for you.'

'Well, miss,' he said with a smile, 'I think I might offer to sleep with him myself.'

I had to laugh. I had known Johnny since he was a little boy. There was no surprise to me in what he said, but I thought it was lovely that he felt comfortable enough in himself, and with me, to confirm what I had instinctively known all those years before.

17

Hissing Sid

'There is too much of this nonsense,' said Father Tom Collins, wagging a reproving finger around my classroom before he was even properly through the door.

'Well, good morning, Father Tom,' I said with exaggerated politeness.

He shot me a withering look. 'All these fluffy lambs and bunnies,' he continued. 'Where's Jesus on the cross?'

Father Tom was the new parish priest to the area. He was tall and quite distinguished-looking with a fine head of thick, wavy grey hair. I believe some of the older ladies in his congregation thought he was a bit of a dish; he was always getting invitations to dinner. The children of the parish were less fond of him and I found myself – as usual – on their side. Secretly, the altar boys called him 'Hissing Sid' because of the way he emphasised 's' when he said, 'Thisss issss my body,' during the Mass.

Although there would sometimes be sparks when Father Tom and I clashed over the years, I did appreciate his kind side. At the end of every term he would arrive in the staff-room with a couple of bottles of wine and a box of cakes, which we all devoured hungrily at afternoon playtime. At the end of one term he arrived empty-handed and Reg said, 'What, no cakes?' in such a tone of disappointment that Father Tom disappeared immediately. He took himself off to the shops and came back just in time for us to wolf down his delicious offerings before the bell went. If only he had always been that sweet!

My religious topic that term was 'New Life' and it was one I really enjoyed teaching the children. I took them to Croxteth Country Park to see the baby animals and we planted various seeds and watched them grow. I had a lovely classroom assistant called Janet who was very artistic and she did some wonderful artwork with the class. The friezes were really striking, with one devoted to baby animals and another to brightly coloured flowers. Most people were impressed when they walked into the room and saw them. But not Hissing Sid.

'Look,' I said, trying to be reasonable, 'these children are just five and six years old. Many of them only got to know Jesus a few months ago at Christmas when he was a baby in the manger. How do you expect them to understand that a few months later he's now thirty-three and being nailed to a cross?'

'You're the teacher,' he retorted. 'It's your job to make them understand.'

'Yes, I'm the teacher, and I think you'll find the crucifixion is not in my syllabus.'

Behind me, the class were beginning to get a bit restless.

'Now, is there anything else?' I said to Father Tom pointedly. 'Because the children are waiting for me.'

'I'm going to take this further,' he warned, and flounced out of the door.

'You do that,' I muttered to the closed door. Not for the first time, I felt a pang for Father Jock back at Woodchurch. I missed him.

'Miss?' said a little voice.

I looked round. It was Johnny, wide-eyed.

'Please, miss,' he said, 'were you and Father Tom cross?'

Trust Johnny, my little actor, to hone in on any drama! The rest of the class hadn't noticed anything amiss. I smiled.

'No, no, Johnny,' I said. 'We were just having a grown-ups' chat.'

Hissing Sid had probably gone off to see the head, I thought. Mrs Deans had left the term before for a new school and there was a man in charge now, Mr Connolly. Mrs Deans had wanted me to go to the new school with her, but I had been through enough changes with three schools in as many years and needed some stability. I opted to stay.

A few minutes later there was a knock at the door and one of the senior girls came in.

'Excuse me, but the headmaster says can he have a copy of your religious syllabus, please?' she said.

Here we go! I thought.

'Tell him I'll bring it at playtime.'

A few minutes later the girl came back.

'He says can he have it now, please?'

'Right,' I said to Janet, 'will you keep an eye on this lot for me while I go and sort this out?'

I marched down to the head's office. I am quite a calm person and really not prone to displays of temper. It takes a lot to make me angry, but I must admit that by the time I got to the head's office I was absolutely livid! How dare Hissing Sid think he could come in and criticise my work with the children and demand that I do things that weren't even in my syllabus? I gave one short, sharp knock at the head's door and then opened it without waiting for an answer. Mr Connolly looked startled as I dropped the syllabus down on his desk.

'Can you show me,' I said pointedly, 'where it says anything about Jesus dying on the cross in there?'

There was silence and then I saw his horrified gaze shift to behind the door. I swung round and there was Father Tom, sitting on a chair behind the door.

'Good morning – again – Father Tom,' I said, without missing a beat. I turned back to the head. 'If the syllabus is to change, perhaps you would like to discuss that with me later.'

I went out closing the door a little more loudly than usual.

I never did have that discussion with Mr Connolly, but Hissing Sid never forgave me.

Catholic schools usually have lots of visual reminders of religion, like statues, crucifixes and paintings. There was one statue that I particularly disliked. It stood on a table outside the assembly hall and it was of the Sacred Heart: an adult Jesus with his bleeding heart visible on the outside of his chest. Bad enough, you might think, but to add to that, there was a sword piercing his heart, which attracted a great deal of curiosity.

'Why has he got bleed on him?' the children often asked as we went into assembly.

Why indeed.

Assembly seemed to drone on for ever sometimes. It was always difficult to keep my lot from fidgeting.

'Billy,' I hissed, 'come here!'

Billy propelled himself along the floor on his bottom to where I was sitting at the side on a chair and looked up innocently.

'Billy, why are you picking Michael's nose?' I whispered.

'Because he asked me to, miss,' he whispered back.

There's no good answer to that!

'Stay here beside me and be a good boy,' I said, trying not to laugh.

Finally the endless sermon was over.

'Now,' said Mr Connolly, 'before we go, does anyone have any news they want to tell us?'

'Me, sir! Me!' One of the little primary-two girls shot her hand into the air, clearly bursting with news.

'Yes, Maria. What would you like to tell us?'

'My mum's having a baby and she's forty-four and we're not to tell anyone,' said Maria excitedly.

The staff shot amused looks at one another. There might as well have been an announcement in the *Liverpool Echo*.

Back in the classroom, I gathered the class round me to give them some news of my own.

'Who remembers what Maria's news was at assembly?' I asked.

'Her mum's having a baby!' they all shouted.

'Well, I have some news as well,' I smiled. 'I'm going to have a baby too!'

The children digested this for a moment. Rachel, a serious little girl who wore her hair in bunches with big polka-dotted red ribbons, was listening particularly carefully, I noticed.

'When it comes out,' I promised, 'I'll bring the baby in for "show and tell".'

Rachel, who had a very cute lisp, put her hand up. 'Will he be a baby Jethuth?' she asked.

I would have loved to have said yes, but I thought one baby Jesus in the world was quite enough!

It was 1972 by this time and I was twenty-eight: time, I had decided, to take the plunge and have my own family. I was glad I'd waited but absolutely thrilled at the prospect of becoming a mother. We'd recently moved to a larger home too, so it felt like the stars were aligned. The children in my class were unfazed by any changes to our routine. I did get morning sickness and once, I just made it to the sink in my classroom in time. None of them batted an eyelid. Not one even asked a question. They just looked at me as if to say, 'Oh, there's Miss throwing up,' and then got on with what they were doing!

I had to have some time off to attend the maternity hospital and as soon as I got there, I would be asked to go and provide a urine sample. I decided to take a sample with me and one time, the only container I could find was a miniature whisky bottle. I used to travel there on the bus, but when I got to the hospital and opened my bag, the bottle had disappeared. The thief must have thought it a particularly bad vintage!

One afternoon as we drew towards Easter, there was a knock on my classroom door.

'Father Tom says could all classes now come to the hall for the Zeffirelli slide show,' said a boy.

'I don't think the reception class go to that,' I said.

The slides were of Franco Zeffirelli's paintings of Jesus dying on the cross, with dirge-like music in the background. I didn't really want my class being disturbed by such stark images. I thought they were completely inappropriate for little ones.

A few moments later, however, the boy was back.

'Father Tom says *every* class has to go.'

I sighed and lined my class up.

Sometimes children could get quite emotional about religious stories. A teacher friend of mine told me how she was reading the story of the Passion of Christ to her senior class and eventually she got to the bit where Jesus' hands and feet were nailed to the wood.

'Then he lifted his eyes to Heaven and died,' she said.

One little boy had tears in his eyes as he listened. 'The bastards!' he shouted.

She didn't have the heart to tell him off for his language.

We all filed into the hall past Father Tom and of course the reception class had to go right at the front. The slide show began. Fortunately, on this occasion, most of my class seemed oblivious to the darkness of the Zeffirelli images and didn't react until the end. Inexplicably, a picture of a little chick had been included, the last image to flash up on the screen.

'Ahhhh!' said all the children in my class. 'Isn't that lovely?'

'Yes,' I said in a very loud voice. 'A lovely little chick for our "New Life" project. Thank you for that, Father.'

Father Tom's face was a picture, I can tell you!

We lined up again and were about to troop back past the Sacred Heart statue. As we walked to the door, I felt a little hand slip into mine and I looked down. It was Rachel. I smiled. Those Minnie Mouse polka-dotted ribbons always seemed so incongruous somehow on a little girl with such a serious demeanour.

'Miss,' she said, 'why did they kill that baby Jethuth? Was it because he dropped the cross?'

I truly didn't know how to answer the question and let's blame the cocktail of hormones my pregnancy was swirling round my system because what I did next was completely out of character. On the way out, I had a sudden rush of blood to the head. I was fed up of all this gore. Outside the assembly hall, I 'tripped' and goodness me, what did I stumble into? Only the Sacred Heart statue! It fell to the floor and shattered into hundreds of pieces, the blood now little specks of red among the white plaster splinters.

Hissing Sid was standing at the back of the hall, and as I righted myself, I caught his horrified gaze.

'Silly me,' I said to my little ones, who were wide-eyed at the mess. 'Wasn't that clumsy?'

Unfortunately, the top juniors were also watching. They say that nothing goes by the Lord, but there's not much escapes eleven-year-olds either. Rows of eyes fixed intently on me.

'She did that on purpose,' I heard one of them say.

Top of the class!

At Christmas and Easter I often made decorations with the children that they could take home. That Christmas, we made a candle decoration, which probably flaked all over the dinner table. The children brought in a round margarine tub and painted it a nice bright red – hence the flaking. Then we mixed white Daz in it. Before it set, we put in a candle and a pine cone. Sometimes I used silver spray paint on the pine cone, but I decided I'd better do this out in the corridor after Johnny, who was standing beside me, sniffed the air and said, 'Ooh, I like that smell!'

I went outside the door and was so engrossed I didn't hear anyone approach behind me. I had almost finished spraying when a hand grabbed me on the shoulder.

'Well now, I've found the culprit,' said a familiar voice.

I wheeled round. Hissing Sid!

'Pardon me?'

'I thought it might be you,' he said darkly, disappearing off down the corridor without saying anything more.

I shrugged, but it puzzled me and I later mentioned it in the staffroom. What was he on about?

'You obviously didn't go to church yesterday,' murmured Reg.

Someone had used silver spray paint to write obscenities all along the church wall. Apparently, it said, 'Priests wank!'

We might not have seen eye to eye, but I couldn't believe Hissing Sid was holding me accountable. I went home and told Jaime, torn between indignation and laughter. Did Hissing Sid seriously think I was out in my balaclava with my spray paint, decorating the church wall? Well! And a Happy Christmas to you too, Father Tom!

18

Great Expectations

'Pregnant lady coming through!' shouted my friend Bette.

Along with some other friends, we were at a classical concert at the Liverpool Philharmonic, and at the interval there was the usual interminable queue for the ladies' almost snaking out of the door. By the time the queue went down, I reckoned I would need more than a miniature whisky bottle, and Bette, fully understanding the pressure a growing baby can put on a girl's bladder, had taken matters into her own hands and pulled me into the gents'.

She shoved me through a door and locked us both into a cubicle. I can't tell you if anybody raised an eyebrow because I didn't dare look anyone in the eye – or in the anywhere else – on the way out. The two of us just scarpered.

Bette was a teacher friend from a neighbouring school and a great character. She was very colourful and great fun, with an energetic – and at times scatty – approach to life. (It was the same Bette who told the 'spiritual ejaculation' story at a dinner party but omitted the key word!) When she'd met us outside, I'd hooted with laughter when she'd told me that on her way to the concert, she had seen a sign for an AA conference at a hotel down the road. She had stopped by and asked to speak to one of the organisers.

'I just want to say thank you,' she had said, 'for all the times that I've broken down and you've come out to rescue me.'

'That's very nice of you,' said the smart young man in a suit, 'but this is actually an Alcoholics Anonymous conference.'

I had asked Bette to join me and a few friends, including Marie, Reg, Tweet and Maggie Gee, at the concert. It was a treat to mark the start of my maternity leave – though to be honest, I would have gone on working longer if it had been left to me. I was entitled to eighteen weeks' leave – eleven weeks before the birth and just seven after – and while I would actually have preferred the time off after the birth, I didn't have a choice. Oh, how I envy teachers nowadays! Having said that, by the time of my due date, it was just as well I was off work because I could hardly move – or get behind the wheel of a car.

Two weeks before the birth, I drove to Tesco. Later, our car would become the typical family saloon every parent resorts to, the kind that gets covered in mud, sticky fingerprints and ground-in chocolate buttons. I once saw a sign for half-price valeting and was shamed into accepting the special offer when I realised the car had never even been washed . . . A young man took the keys, walked round the car, then looked at me.

'Hey, love,' he said, with typical Scouse quick-wittedness, 'are you from *Challenge Anneka*?'

But when I was pregnant, there was still a little pride left. I was driving a Triumph Spitfire sports car that would later become no more than a wistful memory. Did I dream it? It was quite low on the road, and when I parked, I just couldn't get the momentum to lift myself out of the car. I tried pulling on top of the driver's door while attempting to lever myself out . . . No good. Then a young man passed by.

'Excuse me,' I called out, 'could you come here a minute, please?'

He looked a bit nervous but came over to the car.

'Could you help me, please?' I asked.

He took one look at my bump and said, 'Sorry, love. I haven't done first aid or nuthin'.'

'Oh, no, I'm not giving birth,' I assured him. 'I just want out of this damn car!'

He huffed, I puffed, and finally I was out. I resolved not to drive again while pregnant. I couldn't wait to see my newborn baby. I also couldn't wait to see my feet again.

In a way, little Rachel was right. My first born *was* like a baby Jesus – or 'Jethuth', as she would say – in that he was a beautiful little boy. It might have been tempting to name him after the Saviour just to watch Hissing Sid splutter when I announced I was the mother of Jesus, but I resisted temptation and named him Simon. The neighbours in our street said he broke the jinx because he was the first boy in recent memory to be born to a family living in that road. We had four girls living in the house attached to ours, two more over the road and a further two on the corner. When Simon was a few weeks old, there was a knock on the door, and when I answered, there were ten girls standing on my doorstep.

'Can we take the baby out for a walk?' they asked, in chorus.

I was delighted as I could have a quick, and much-needed, sleep on the sofa!

Despite being exhausted, Jaime and I adored our gorgeous baby and revelled in our new roles as parents. Even so, while I wished I had a little more leave after the birth than I got, and would have loved more time with Simon, there was no question mark in my head about returning. Financially, leaving teaching wasn't an option. In any case, I wanted to get back to the chalk face for one simple and important reason: I missed all the children in my class.

Life after Simon was born developed a routine very quickly. He started at nursery at just seven weeks old, but he barely slept, so I often went out to work like a zombie. I missed him greatly during the day, but I certainly saw plenty of him at night! The nursery was close to my school and – inevitably, somehow, given the pattern of my life – was run by nuns. I just couldn't seem to escape from them! The nursery had previously been a home for unmarried mothers with a laundry attached, but it had been shut down and made into a nursery. When I asked why, I was told the girls who came there had become too much of a handful.

'Sure, one of them,' the Reverend Mother told me, 'just as she was leaving, said, "Bye, Sister. See you in nine months." The sad thing was, she meant it.'

Then there was the girl who, when her baby was delivered, said, 'Oh God, Sister, I didn't realise it would be black!'

The nursery was a godsend for me and its past as a laundry was very handy. The machinery was all still there and it meant that everything was washed and dried for you and you never had to take home dirty nappies. An added bonus was that some of the young girls who worked there were willing to do babysitting for you. There was a lovely young nurse called Valerie who sometimes looked after Simon if we wanted to go out. Poor Valerie. I asked her to babysit one Saturday and for once, she couldn't.

'I'm made up,' she told me excitedly. 'Jason's mum has given me tickets to see Gilbert O'Sullivan on Saturday. I love him and me and my mate can't wait.'

The following Monday morning I asked her if she'd had a lovely time.

'He never came on,' she said, the disappointment writ large across her face. 'There were, like, these Japanese people singing and bowing their 'eads, but Gilbert never came on.'

What Jason's mum thought a teenage girl wanted with Gilbert and Sullivan opera tickets I really don't know.

I arrived back from maternity leave in the spring, when the cherry blossom was blooming and pink and white flowers rained down softly on the lawns. May is a month that is dedicated to Our Lady in the Catholic Church and there were lots of processions and hymn-singing sessions at school, but the biggest day of the spring and summer terms by far was first Holy Communion day. Catholics believe that when the priest consecrates the bread and wine during the Mass, it becomes God's body and blood. It's called transubstantiation and is a core belief of the Catholic faith. First Communion normally happens when children are around seven or eight and this is the day when they are allowed to receive the conse-crated host for the very first time. There's a big build-up to the ceremony with lots of preparation and the whole thing becomes a Very Big Deal Indeed.

Mums were stood at the school gates discussing all the most important bits of the ceremony when I came back from maternity leave: white dresses, shoes, headdresses and veils. God didn't get much of a look-in, really.

'I haven't got our Lizzie's Communion dress yet,' said one of the mums as I walked past. 'I need to get a move on, but she can't make up her mind which she likes best.'

'Well,' said another, 'I've gone for a long dress rather than short, with lots of sequins and some crystal beads sewn into it. I wanted something a bit special, like. We'll probably never get to see 'er in a white wedding dress 'cos she'll no doubt be living over the brush with some lad. So we're making this 'er big day.'

Though the children I taught weren't old enough for taking Holy Communion, the whole school got involved in the event and I always turned out to see the children on their big day. Part of Communion preparation is when the children are taken for their first confession and confess their 'sins' to the priest. I had a bit of difficulty believing seven-year-olds had much in the way of heinous crimes to confess, but it's meant to cleanse your soul so that you receive Communion in a 'state of grace'. Nevertheless, going into a dark confessional box and confessing all your naughty deeds to an anonymous shape behind a grille is really daunting for children. I certainly hated it when I was at school. What should you say? My 'confession' usually consisted of the same tired – but safe – list of misdemeanours.

My mother once told me that she had asked her own mum what to say in confession. 'Just say, "I cursed, I boxed, I called names,"' her mother told her.

My mother was still repeating it, parrot fashion, many years later until it suddenly dawned on her what she was actually saying. I refused to carry on the family tradition. My own version was 'I lied and was disobedient.' The response would be 'Three Hail Marys for your penance, my child, and do not sin again.' We always did, though! At the convent, Breda used to egg us all on to 'confess' to something awful, like a murder, just to liven things up, but none of us ever dared.

I'm sure some of the priests used to nod off with the boredom and one or two certainly did the crossword. Bette taught the Communion class for years and she once had to rescue a little boy who disappeared for ages into the confessional box.

'Are you all right?' she called.

The little boy finally emerged. 'I don't think Father knows I'm in there,' he said, looking confused.

Communion day that year was blessed with early summer sunshine, the air warm and smelling of freshly mown grass. The children lined up outside the church to process in, the light dappling through the trees and picking up the sparkle in the girls' silky dresses so that some looked almost studded with diamonds. Frilled white socks and round-toed satin shoes . . . apple cheeks and shining hair . . . for that afternoon they looked the picture of childhood innocence and the sight always brought a lump to my throat.

Little boys who normally had dirty knees and grubby jumpers, and fingernails caked with grime, appeared in grey trousers and white shirts with red ties, faces scrubbed and hair slicked down, hands joined solemnly together in prayer. Occasionally we did get some poor lad turning up in an all-white suit looking mortified, but it was usually the girls who were more extravagant. Even the naughtiest of children looked perfectly saintly in this setting, and it was like a little angelic procession as the children walked into church singing, 'O Mary, we crown thee with bottoms today. Queen of the angels and Queen of the May.'

I was walking with Marie, and we looked sideways at each other, shoulders shaking. The more conventional version is 'crown thee with blossoms today', but crowning with posteriors was a colourful variation, typical of the mistakes children make. They often got religious words mixed up, no doubt because they didn't have a clue what it was all about. I particularly enjoyed when we sang the hymn 'Our God Reigns', a hymn with a very rousing tune, and the children all innocently sang, 'Ah, God's brains,' with gusto. And sad as it was when somebody died and we said the 'Prayer of the Departed', which contained the line 'Let perpetual light shine upon them', I often felt a little better by the time the children had prayed intently for 'the petrol light' to shine on the dear deceased.

'Oh God,' muttered Marie, as we walked towards the church.

'What?'

'It's Ben,' she said, nodding across the road. 'I should never have told him where I was going! He threatened to turn up, but I didn't believe him.'

Marie was going out with a very nice Jewish chap at the time and I glanced across to see him and a group of his friends standing grinning at her.

'Miss,' a little girl hissed behind me.

I turned round.

'Why is Miss Cumming hiding her face with her hymn sheet?'

The less endearing side of the day was when it all got a bit competitive. Outside the church was a limousine, which one little girl had made her entrance in, like a mini celebrity. She was dressed in a full veil with a very elaborate tiara and her dad had turned up two hours before, armed with a video camera, to bag the front pew. The children filed into the front rows and the rest of us shuffled in the back. Sunlight flooded through the stained glass, the rays bouncing off the children, who for once sat primly, waiting for the Mass to begin.

As parish priest, it was Father Tom who took the ceremony. He was never one to underplay a moment, and when we reached the Communion stage, he said a few words to the children about what a very important occasion this was. As usual, he didn't adapt his language much for his childish audience, but addressed them as mini adults.

'You have all been to confession,' he said, rather portentously, 'and so your souls are in a state of grace for meeting Almighty God. This should be one of the happiest moments of your life and you should remember it always. You must carry Jesus with you, in your heart and in your soul, reverently and solemnly, for the rest of your life.'

The children filed up to the front and Father Tom took a host, held it up and handed it to the first child before him, who happened to be the little girl from the limousine. Just as she took it, her father in the front pew zapped a remote control and her tiara lit up like Blackpool illuminations. Father Tom nearly had a heart attack and I thought he was going to drop the hosts. A ripple went round the church and a lot of heads suddenly bowed as if in prayer. I guess you can buy everything but good taste!

After the big day we often got the children to write about their experiences and their memories and we had a lovely 'First Communion Remembrance' section on our staffroom noticeboard, with all the stories the children had written about their special day. 'Yesterday I made my first Communion,' one little boy wrote. 'We had jelly and ice cream and God's body.' We kept that story pinned to the noticeboard for years, much to the annoyance of Father Tom. It never failed to amuse me, but then, anything that gave Father Tom apoplexy usually did.

When Simon was a few months old, I decided it was time to meet up with all my old friends. By this time Barbara Mc had married and moved away from the area, and sadly, we had all gradually lost touch with her. We were now down to the Three Buddies.

After training college, Jellybean had begun teaching in private prep schools and was giving music lessons from her home. She was about to move to Bristol, where her husband, Rob, was to study for a PhD. In fact, when she did finally move, we were all invited down for the weekend and were told to bring any colour of paint and a brush with us. Jellybean had an organ that she used to play at all hours – I'm sure the neighbours loved her – and during our visit she played to us while we decorated the walls in a rainbow assortment of colours. It was quite a sight when we'd finished!

While I had moved back to Liverpool to my new school, Annie was still living in Birkenhead near the old one in Woodchurch. For a while after Simon was born, I would drive back to Birkenhead and the three of us would meet up on a Wednesday night. Birkenhead is on the west bank of the River Mersey, so it's more or less opposite Liverpool. I would drive into town, through the Mersey Tunnel, and then it was another fifteen minutes on the other side to Annie's house. It really wasn't an arduous journey, but from Jaime's reaction each week, you would have thought that I was trying to drive single-handed across the Kalahari Desert.

Every Wednesday when I arrived at Annie's, I would be greeted with the same message: 'Jaime's been on the phone. Can you ring him straight away, please?'

The first few times, I rang in a panic. I was like any new mum: completely besotted with my new baby and overanxious about his safety when I wasn't around.

'Is Simon all right?'

'Yes,' he would say. 'I just wanted to make sure you arrived OK.'

Annie, Jellybean and I would all head off to a pub for chicken or scampi in a basket and a glass of wine. It was so lovely to catch up and have just one night of girly company without a baby howling in my ear! Afterwards I'd go back to Annie's house for a coffee before setting off home again. Every time we arrived back at Annie's, there would be another message waiting for me.

'He's just phoned again.'

I would ring again and ask the same question.

'Is Simon all right?'

'Fine. I just want to make sure you haven't had too much to drink before you drive home.'

'But you know I only ever have one glass of wine.'

It was like the boy who cried wolf. After a while I got used to it and stopped worrying that there was some crisis at home.

'He really cares about you, doesn't he?' said Annie curiously.

I knew he did, just as I cared about him, but I also knew that wasn't the purpose of the calls. I never liked to admit it to my friends back then, but secretly, I knew the way Jaime's mind worked. He was checking up on me. Many years later he admitted that as I drove off on a Wednesday, in his mind I was having an affair. With a tiny baby to look after, chance would have been a fine thing! In any case, I didn't want one and I didn't understand this side of Jaime. I trusted him and I didn't understand why he didn't trust me. At that time I really couldn't have loved anyone more.

19

Special Children

Parting with a class each year was often poignant because by the time they left me, I felt close to the children and had formed special bonds. Each time, I felt there would never be another class quite like it, but then a new batch of children would come in: new personalities, new joys – and new problems too.

Andrew Robertson came into my class in the mid-1970s. He was the youngest in his family, the little dot at the end of his family's sentence. He was a beautiful child, angelic with his blond hair and big blue eyes. Actually, all four children in his family were very handsome, and the older ones doted on their little brother. Some psychologists argue that a child's place in the family is important in the development of their personality and I think that being the youngest certainly affected Andrew. It just took us a while to work that out.

At Huyton, I had dealt with Daniel, who I am sure these days would be diagnosed as dyslexic. Daniel had trouble with the written word, but Andrew's problems were different: it was the spoken word he struggled with. In fact, at times his speech was simply impossible to decipher. It sounded as if he was talking gobbledegook. To make matters worse, he didn't speak in complete sentences.

'Tell Mummy what we have been doing in class today, Andrew,' I would say, when his mum, Jill, came to pick him up, but he would reply with just a single word.

'Books,' he'd say. Or, 'Story.' Or, 'Toys.'

'Yes, but what did we do with the toys, Andrew?' I would prod.

'Play toys.'

He communicated on the level of a two-year-old, yet I knew Andrew was perfectly intelligent. We could sit and play number games quite happily, and while he didn't have much to say, he could match up numbers and respond normally to instructions. There was plenty going on inside his head; he just didn't know how to let other people see in there. Perhaps I particularly empathised because Andrew had the same name as my brother and that made me think back to childhood, when my Andrew was locked inside his own head with hearing problems. Nobody had reached out to him for such a long time. My brother was very much in my thoughts at this time because he had just written to tell us he was getting married and had enclosed pictures of a beautiful Sri Lankan girl.

'I think maybe we should get a little help for Andrew,' I said to his mum, Jill.

She looked at me a bit fearfully and I could tell my words upset her.

'Don't worry,' I tried to reassure her. 'I'm sure it's not a major problem, but perhaps we need to find out why Andrew isn't talking quite as much as the other children.'

We had a very good child psychologist to whom we could refer children if we had any particular concerns about their behaviour or development. In Andrew's case, a speech therapist was brought in to help. Miss Taylor arrived in my class shortly after to assess him. She was a neat, ordered young woman with a short black bob and black-rimmed glasses that she had a tendency to look archly over the top of. She was very organised, but although her manner was efficient, it was a little brisk. Andrew seemed slightly intimidated by her.

'Thank you, Andrew,' she said, at the end of her chat with him, as if she was dismissing a business colleague at the close of a meeting rather than a little five-year-old boy.

The bell rang for playtime and the children ran out happily. Miss Taylor continued sitting at the small desk, writing some notes while I waited for her. Finally, she looked up at me and her glasses slid slightly down her nose. 'He needs to go to a special school,' she said abruptly.

Just like that!

I was alarmed by her conviction. She had only met Andrew once.

'Maybe we should try other things first and see how it goes,' I replied slowly. 'Let's just wait and monitor his progress, because I'd really like to keep him here if it's possible.'

Miss Taylor shrugged. 'We can try, but I think he'll have to go in the end. We should probably begin the process of discussing it with Andrew's parents.' She closed over her folder and zipped it away in her bag, smiled coolly and was gone, leaving only a faint whiff of her crisp, citrusy perfume behind. I looked at the closed door after her departure and sighed.

The special school she had in mind was on the other side of the city and would have been very disruptive for Andrew's family. I could tell Jill was distraught when it was mentioned. Her eyes filled and for a moment she couldn't speak. No parent wants to be told their child isn't normal and Jill was desperate for Andrew to remain at our school with the other kids, especially as it was where his siblings attended. Had it been best for Andrew to go elsewhere, I would have had no hesitation in trying to gently persuade her and support her through the process, but something told me that despite Miss Taylor's dismissal of other options, Andrew's problems were not insurmountable. His speech was sitting behind a closed door, just waiting to be unlocked. Like Alice trying to find her way through the confusing array of doors in Wonderland, all I needed to do to unlock his potential was find the right key.

Some teachers change when they become mothers, as parenthood gives you a little more insight into, and empathy with, children. Simon's birth changed my personal life and I loved being a mum, but I didn't actually feel I was a very different teacher now that I was a mum myself because I had always felt such a strong bond with children anyway. I might have been less naïve and have given up on thinking I was the saviour who was instantly going to change their lives, but I did always retain my desire to make a difference. Looking back, perhaps what becoming a mother *did* do was give me more sympathy for parents than I once had, an insight into how they felt about their children and how much they worried about their futures.

I understood Jill. 'Imagine,' I said to Jaime when I talked it over at home, 'if someone told us Simon was "different" in some way. How would we feel?'

Parents want to protect, and sometimes the hardest threats to deal with are not to your child's physical safety but to their emotional well-being. A fall from a swing is much more easily mended than being labelled 'different'. The hard truth is, though, that sometimes your instincts as a parent and as a teacher can conflict. As a parent, you want what's best for your child, but you also want them to be 'normal'. As a teacher, you know that sometimes what's best is accepting a child has special needs, different from other children.

I really believed in special education. That wasn't the issue. I just didn't believe it was what Andrew needed. As students, we had to spend part of our holidays on special-school placements, so I knew what great work went on in the different special schools available. I spent several weeks in the blind school and then went to the deaf school, and the work that those places did was remarkable. I remember watching the blind children whirling into the cloakroom to get changed for PE, running their hands along the Braille nametags to find their space, feeling their way through the world.

They were fearless in the lesson itself and I gasped watching them.

'They don't know how high up they are,' said the teacher.

The sad thing is that many of the special schools we had in Liverpool had now closed. By the 1970s the official explanation was 'integration', a move to include all children with special needs in mainstream schools where possible. It would be hard to argue with the theory. Like the 'Care in the Community' initiative for mental-health patients, it sounds both kind and inclusive. As in so many things, however, the theory never quite matched the reality. I felt uneasy as I watched school buildings being sold off and special-needs children being put in schools where the more able children often bullied them. Inevitably, they had to sit through lessons that had no relevance to their lives or futures.

A little neighbour of mine, Jordan, was a good example. Jordan had Down's syndrome and sometimes I looked after him for his mum. When he finished primary school, he should have gone to a lovely special school where a friend of mine taught, a big old house in Liverpool with extensive grounds where the children helped look after animals. Here, the emphasis was on life skills, teaching the children how to care for and look after themselves. They were brought into school by taxi in the mornings because they came from different areas, and their first task of the day was to take turns to put the kettle on for coffee. Everything was practical and geared to the children's needs. Maths was taught by going shopping, spending the right money and getting the correct change. English focused on communicating appropriately and effectively with the shop assistant.

The school had a wonderful relationship with their local Tesco supermarket. The school would ring up and say they were bringing a group of children down in the minibus. Each would have the same shopping list of ingredients for something they were going to make, and each would be given the same amount of money. They would collect the items on their list and then go through the till, getting used to handling money and waiting for their change. Then they would get back on the bus and their teacher would return to get a refund for all but one of the sets of ingredients. Back at school, they would use the ingredients to cook a dish together. Other children take such simple things for granted, but for the children in the special school, shopping and money-handling were skills that needed to be taught again and again. Sometimes education is not about passing exams; it's about helping children to achieve everything they realistically can – whatever level that may be at.

Jordan never did get the chance to go to that school. Instead, he ended up at the back of a class in mainstream school, studying subjects like French with a 'minder' to interpret for him. You can sit someone in any class you want, but you can't make them part of something that they don't fit into. Down's syndrome children often have very affectionate natures and Jordan was a lovely boy, but to the other children, he was an outsider.

'They say I'm a Mong,' he told his mum when he came home from school one day.

When I heard that, I couldn't help feeling that the education system had let Jordan down. We should have taken better care of him than that.

In fact, there were many children in the past whom we let down simply because we didn't know how to help them. A lot more is known now, but just as none of us had heard of dyslexia and dismissed such children as 'slow learners', neither did we know about other communication disabilities, such as those on the autistic spectrum. Asperger's syndrome is one such condition, and is particularly confusing because children who have it are often of at least average, and often above average, intelligence. They don't usually have a problem with speech, but they do have difficulties understanding and processing language. They take everything you say literally.

Looking back, there was another little boy in Andrew's class that year, Sammy, who I am now convinced had Asperger's. One day I had to leave my class for a minute to get something from the teacher next door.

'I'll only be a minute,' I told the children. 'And remember,' I warned, 'I have eyes in the back of my head, so I will know what's going on in here!'

I was back quickly and forgot all about it, but half an hour later I was doing something at my desk when I felt a little hand going up through the back of my hair. I looked down to see Sammy, his hand now entangled in my hair, and smiled.

'Hello!' I exclaimed.

'I want to see the eyes,' whispered Sammy. 'The eyes in the back of your head. Can I look?'

I had to explain that I didn't really have an extra pair of eyes and it was just an expression, but I wish I'd understood about Asperger's back then. Perhaps I could have helped Sammy more while he was in my class that year.

There is a difference between children who have difficulties that mean they just need a little extra support and those who need more extensive help. I don't believe in keeping people in institutions they don't need to be in, but we have to be honest. Some mainstream schools have excellent special-education departments, but if my own child had complex special needs, I know I would want them to be taught in a school that was specially designed to help them. The special school Jordan should have gone to was sold off, like so many others. It was in a beautiful area and they pulled it down and built twenty houses that sold for God knows how much. But of course it wasn't about money. It was never about money. Or so they said.

Every child is a special child. They all have their own needs that we have to respond to. While Andrew's speech difficulties seemed severe, I wasn't convinced they were intractable, or long-lasting, or best addressed in a special school. I thought that with a little help, he would do just fine where he was. All I had to do was persuade those making the decisions to probe a little deeper into the cause of his difficulties, and not make too quick a judgement.

He had been referred to a Dr Rosenbloom at the Child Development Centre in Alder Hey Hospital and I asked if I could go to the next meeting. I liked Dr Rosenbloom as soon as I met him. He was warm and approachable, and unlike Miss Taylor, I didn't feel he was threatened by someone questioning his judgement.

'Could you just leave this with me for four weeks?' I asked him.

Dr Rosenbloom agreed to give me the time and said he would delay his decision for a month. Four weeks. It wasn't long, but I was determined to try to prove my point. Something about Andrew had struck me. He didn't need to talk. As the youngest in the family, he just needed to start a sentence and someone would finish it for him.

'Juice,' was all he had to say.

'Mum, Andrew would like some juice. Would you like orange, Andrew?'

Nod.

I spoke to Marie and some of the other teachers about the problem. With their agreement, I was going to send Andrew into their classes frequently over the next few weeks.

'He will have a blank sheet of paper in his hand and he is going to say something to you,' I explained. 'Will you write down what you think he said and send the paper back?'

Before he went, I would tell Andrew the message and practise it with him. For instance, I would tell him, 'I want you to say, "Please can I have a red pencil?" Now say it after me.'

Andrew practised whatever message I gave him and slowly his speech became more distinct. I worked hard to force him into using the language that was untapped inside his head. I could see this approach was making a difference, but progress was slow.

'He's definitely improving,' Jill told me. I knew that was true, but I also knew that, understandably, Jill was saying what she *wanted* to be true. I wasn't sure. Would the changes be fast enough and significant enough to influence the next Alder Hey meeting?

We had been told this was the final meeting and Jill was very nervous as we went in. Miss Taylor, dressed in a straight charcoal-grey skirt and frilly white blouse looked the picture of professionalism, but there was no sense of any emotional connection to the outcome of the meeting. She nodded hello at us, but I wished she would smile at Jill and reassure her that we had Andrew's best interests at heart and would do everything we could to help him. That's all any mother wants to hear. After all, this was a very big moment for her. This hour was going to decide her son's future.

Andrew was told to sit down at a little desk with the speech therapist, while Dr Rosenbloom observed his interaction with her.

'Right, Andrew,' said Miss Taylor, 'I have a ball in my hand. Where is it now?' She placed the ball on the table and waited.

Andrew looked at her and I held my breath. Jill took hold of my hand.

'It's on the table,' he said.

What a moment! I could feel Jill's emotion as she gripped my fingers and I squeezed her hand back.

'And now?'

'It's under the table.'

By this time I was nearly crying behind my glasses. Andrew's interaction was obviously still quite limited, but it had significantly improved. As the minutes ticked by, it was clear from his responses to Miss Taylor that there was no need to do anything radical yet.

Afterwards Dr Rosenbloom smiled at me. 'He's fine.'

'I know he's fine,' I said, returning his smile.

Outside, Jill was crying with relief.

'Thank you so much,' she said, as she hugged me. It was one of those moments that I had come into teaching for. I had helped a little boy to grow and develop, and the pleasure and satisfaction that gave me was beyond riches. Had I been a well-paid accountant, or a successful property developer, I would never have known a moment like this one, and I would have been so much the poorer for it.

It took many months for Andrew to speak completely normally, but I knew that all he required now was time.

'You don't need to cry any more,' I said as I hugged Jill back. 'Andrew is going to be OK.'

And he was.

20

'The Milky Bar Kid Is Strong and Tough . . .'

When Simon was four, much to my delight I fell pregnant again.

'I'm going to have a brother,' Simon announced in response when I told him.

'Or maybe a lovely little sister?' I said brightly, trying to make it sound equally appealing.

Simon frowned at me. 'No, a brother,' he said adamantly.

Even when it came to my own child, it never failed to make me smile how simply children could see the world and how confident they could be in their own opinions!

By now Simon was at a small local prep school and I was picking him up each day. I remember collecting him from school one day when I was heavily pregnant.

'Come on, then,' I said, wrapping his scarf round his neck. 'Let's get home and maybe we can watch some telly for half an hour before tea.'

Frankly, it was all I had the energy for.

To the right of me, I caught the eye of a tall woman with dark, shoulder-length hair who was fastening up her twins' jackets. We had nodded at each other in passing often enough but had never spoken properly.

'Hello,' she said. 'I'm AnnMarie.'

'I'm Bernadette,' I said, reaching out to shake her hand.

Simon looked up at her. 'I'm going to have a brother,' he said. This was long before mothers could opt to know the sex of their baby, so AnnMarie laughed when she heard Simon's self-assured announcement.

'Are you?' she said, eyes widening. 'Are you sure? Maybe it will be a sister.'

'No,' said Simon, quite definitely. 'I'm having a brother.'

'Well, that will be lovely,' said AnnMarie. 'I hope you get what you want.' She turned to me and nodded at my 'bump'. 'How are you keeping?' she asked.

'I'm knackered!' I replied honestly.

'Well,' said AnnMarie, 'maybe I could bring Simon home every day for you until you have the baby?'

I was so grateful! I was even more grateful for the close friendship that developed with AnnMarie from such a simple conversation. Later I was able to do exactly the same for her when she started teacher-training college, but at this time Simon's fifth birthday was fast approaching and I told her I wasn't sure what to do about his party because his birthday clashed with my due date.

'Have it early,' said AnnMarie. 'Children know nothing about dates and care even less. I know a great children's entertainer you could hire to make the whole thing easy. He does magic, plays the banjo, models animals from balloons . . . Honestly, he's fantastic.'

Uncle Jim, as the entertainer was called, was a policeman during the day and turned up straight from work in his uniform. He was as wonderful as AnnMarie had said, and since I was hardly in a fit state for running around, it was a relief to have someone who could keep the children amused.

AnnMarie and I sat in the kitchen, listening to the whoops and squeals from next door while Uncle Jim did his tricks. I had just made us both a cup of tea when a little girl with flushed cheeks and a swish pink party frock appeared at the door with an empty glass.

'Uncle Jim says can he have some magic lemonade, please?'

'Yes, of course, Emily,' I said, reaching for the bottle. I poured some into the glass and off she went.

Two minutes later Emily was back.

'Uncle Jim says can he have the *magic* lemonade, please?'

I went next door to speak to him myself. 'Sorry,' I said, 'but what sort of lemonade is it you want?'

'Scotch lemonade,' he whispered with a wink.

'Oh, I see,' I said. 'I thought you were going to magic it into something.'

'I'm not Jesus, love,' he said.

I poured him a generous glass, but it wasn't long before he came out for seconds.

'Come and see this,' he said.

I walked into the room and all the children were sitting in complete silence with their eyes closed. In the middle of the room was a Jack-in-the-box.

Uncle Jim stood at the doorway sipping his Scotch and every now and then he would shout out, 'Has he come out yet?'

'No, Uncle Jim,' chorused the children.

'Well, someone's peeping, then,' said Uncle Jim, knocking back another half-glass.

The children all began nudging one another.

'It's you – close your eyes.'

'It is not me!'

'Alice, is it you?'

'I did this for ten minutes once,' said Uncle Jim, leaning against the wall and holding out his glass for more whisky.

Eventually, he went back – a little unsteadily – and triggered the box. Out jumped Jack and the room erupted.

Hmm, I thought. They don't teach that one at college! But I could see the potential of that ten-minute silence. From now on it would certainly be in *my* box of tricks. Minus the Scotch, of course!

As it turned out, Simon's prediction of a baby brother was completely wrong and my little dark-haired girl was born the day after Simon's birthday. I called her Anna. She was utterly beautiful, but the district nurse was concerned when she visited me at home.

'I think this baby is jaundiced,' she said.

The doctor came out, took one look at her and sent her to Alder Hey Hospital. She was put in an incubator under an ultraviolet light, sunglasses on her yellow face.

There is nothing more vulnerable than a tiny baby in an incubator and it stabbed at my heart just to look at her. Her little screwed-up face was the colour of the sun, and her scrawny limbs would suddenly jerk as she slept, as if something had given her a fright. I caught my breath each time she did it.

It was around then that the rules were relaxed at Aideen's convent and she was allowed to come over from Ireland to help me. Aideen was by now a more senior nun and she had exciting news of her own to tell me: she was to be made head of the convent school we had attended as children! Shock and horror!

'Just as well I never burned the place down as I'd wanted to when we were at school,' I told her ruefully.

Aideen kindly looked after Simon for me while I stayed at the hospital. Perhaps he was disappointed that he didn't get the baby brother he was longing for, but as far as he was concerned, Anna was a little nuisance who had disrupted everything.

'Have you come to be my new mummy?' he asked Aideen, as she tucked him into bed one night.

At the time he was desperate for a new toy, an action man whose muscles would inflate if you pressed his chest. I got Jaime to buy one and give it to me, and when Simon came to the hospital with Aideen to see me, I brought the action man out and handed it to him.

'Guess what your little sister bought for you to say hello?' I said.

Simon's face lit up and I could see he was thinking that maybe sisters weren't such a bad deal after all. He tiptoed over to the incubator and peered in, almost in awe of the sleeping contents.

'Hello!' he said, clutching his action man in one hand and waving his other hand gently at the dozing figure.

From that point on he loved his baby sister and we had no problems. Amazing what a little bit of bribing can do!

Once again maternity leave flashed by quickly and it felt like no time before I was back in school. I was happy being with the children at home, but I loved my job too. I was always careful to have special times set aside at home for Simon and Anna once I returned to work so they knew just how much I loved them. I used to get Simon to help me with Anna's bathtime so that he felt included, and I always had storytime with him before bed.

'I love you this much,' I used to say as he got his pyjamas on, opening my arms wide.

Simon always tried to open his arms wider. 'I love you this much!'

I'd open mine wider again. 'But I love you this much.'

Simon looked, then stood on tiptoe and reached for the ceiling. 'I love you all the way up the sky and back again!' he declared.

I wasn't unhappy about going back to school – I had managed last time with Simon and was sure I would manage this time – but it took some planning to be that organised again. When you have a small baby, you find yourself still in your dressing gown at ten o'clock some mornings. I had been back only a few weeks and was still finding my feet when Marie came into the staffroom one playtime. As usual, she was dressed very elegantly. Her charcoal skirt fitted tightly over her hips before flaring out slightly into a sexy little flounce over the knee. Her scarf, in swirling tones of greys and blacks, looked very chic draped loosely round her neck and caught the colour of the skirt perfectly.

'Have you heard?' she asked, as she poured herself a coffee.

'What?'

'Reg says the HMI have notified Mr Connolly that we're getting a full inspection.'

I groaned. 'When?'

'A few weeks,' said Reg, who had come in behind her. I saw Reg register Marie's outfit and took the opportunity for mischief.

'Nice skirt, Marie,' I said before grinning at Reg. 'Isn't it, Reg?'

'How would I know?' he muttered.

'Of course, you need the legs for it,' I said. 'Don't you, Reg?'

'If you say so,' said Reg, flicking his newspaper up in front of his face.

Marie laughed silently but shook her head at me and mouthed, 'Stop it!'

'Oh, put your paper down, Reg,' I said, 'and tell us about these inspectors!'

On the whole, I was comfortable in the classroom and didn't mind who was there, but nobody likes being put on the spot and it was only natural that there should be a bit of anxiety about the inspectors arriving. I always resolved just to be myself and not to put on a special show, but it was inevitable that a little more thought and effort went into lesson plans when inspectors were around!

When Ms Williams walked into my room – that 'ms' was very clearly enunciated – the first thing I noticed was that she didn't return my smile. Nor did she smile at the children. In fact, she seemed to have no interest at all in engaging with them, and that always surprised me. I could never understand how an adult could come into an infant room and not find themselves drawn into conversation. Children are such funny, curious little creatures. 'What's that in your bag?' 'Why are you wearing those funny earrings?' 'Do you like my new shoes?' It's impossible not to get involved with them. Nevertheless Ms Williams sat at the back exuding all the warmth of a rainy day in November.

Unfortunately, it got worse as my lesson wore on. Ms Williams sighed. She raised her eyebrows. She folded her arms. It wasn't going well. I was teaching reading, something I had always had good results in. The reading scheme we used at the time was Janet and John, a hallmark of many adults' primary-school experience. It wasn't what I had chosen – it was what I was given. It was used all over Britain and had been devised in the 1950s.

'Would you like to see my reading book?' one of the children asked Ms Williams. 'This picture is my favourite because I like Janet's dress in this one.'

Ms Williams's lips flickered into an attempt at a half-smile that was more of a grimace, but she said nothing.

The reading scheme was certainly showing its age by the 1970s and I could understand why it was often criticised. Janet and John were like Enid Blyton children: white, middle class and in danger of saying, 'Mummy, you're a brick,' at any moment. The stories relied heavily on situations that had become tired old clichés: Janet was always in the kitchen making cakes with Mummy, while John was in overalls fixing the car with Daddy. Even if Janet was allowed to do something active, like climb a tree, her brother John would have shimmied up to the top in a trice while Janet clung timidly to some lower branch.

Nevertheless, while the materials were perhaps a bit jaded, I didn't believe my methods were. I was very committed to teaching phonics and will never understand why, for a brief period, it went out of fashion. Teaching children phonics simply means teaching them the sounds that different combinations of letters make. Sounds are the building blocks that make up words, and as far as I was concerned, children needed to know 'a' was for apple and 'b' was for ball. Once they could sound out words, their reading progress was usually very rapid. Trying to learn to read without knowing the sounds of letters always seemed to me to be a bit like trying to do sums without knowing any numbers.

Ms Williams was from the Inner London Education Authority and she thought our school was hopelessly old-fashioned. She wasn't particularly young – in fact, she was middle-aged – but she had at her fingertips all the jargon that so characterised the 1970s. We once got a directive from Liverpool Council saying that we should no longer refer to 'blackboards' in our classrooms; we were to call them 'chalkboards'. I could imagine Ms Williams sending that kind of directive. She looked around my class library with disdain, then sauntered to the front of the room, clicking her kitten heels on the floor and pulling her cardigan round her with a languid air of boredom.

'That was very old-fashioned, wasn't it?' she said to me later.

'Do you think so?' I replied, refusing to rise to the bait. 'I find teaching phonics really works.'

'Of course, you're in Janet and John Land up here,' she said dismissively.

I had to smile at the implication that Liverpool was one big middle-class leafy suburb compared to London. I think my old friend Joey with his sanitary-towel earmuffs, and Robbo with his self-ventilating shorts, might just have had something to say about that!

After her visit I asked Mr Connolly what the verdict had been.

'We're in Cloud Cuckoo Land,' he said.

In truth, most teachers feel it's those who are out of the classroom for too long who get unrealistic expectations. Not long after Ms Williams's visit, it was announced that the staff in teacher-training colleges were being encouraged to go back into classrooms for a refresher course. In other words, reacquaint themselves with real children. One of them arranged to come to our school and was allocated to Marie's class of ten-year-olds.

I gulped as he walked towards me in the staffroom: he was dressed as a cowboy. There's a fine line between piquing children's curiosity and inviting their derision, and dressing as a cowboy probably crossed it. The effect was doubly ridiculous because he was standing beside someone as sophisticated as Marie. She shot me a look, opening her eyes into a wild stare at me as she introduced him. He couldn't see, because he was standing beside her and was looking at me, but her crazed face almost made me giggle out loud. She could be very naughty like that.

'Would you like me to stay in the class with you?' she asked the cowboy politely.

'Oh, no, no,' he replied confidently. 'I've lectured to two hundred students at a time, you know.'

Not dressed as the Milky Bar Kid he hadn't.

Marie went off to have a cup of coffee while he took the class. When she came back, she knew before she had even reached the room that there was trouble at the OK Corral: there were twelve children standing in the corridor.

'What are you doing out here?' she demanded.

'He put us out, miss.'

'What for?'

'Dunno, miss.'

Which was, no doubt, not strictly true. Even so, whatever it was for, the last thing you do with children who are causing trouble is put them all together in a corridor without adult supervision and with nothing to do but create havoc. Marie threw open the door rather dramatically and leaned against the doorframe.

'Excuse me,' she said in her crystal-clear tones, 'is there a reason why half my class are lining the corridor?'

'They weren't paying attention.'

'And do you have any idea why that might be so?' she enquired, with beautifully modulated haughtiness.

The implication was obvious. The cowboy mustered all the dignity he could – which wasn't much given he was dressed in a Stetson and chaps at the time – and repeated, rather stiffly, his mantra about having lectured to two hundred students.

'Shame you can't keep your lasso round a mere thirty-five ten-year-olds, then,' muttered Marie.

21

Goodbye, Miss; Hello, Mum

Another summer had flown by and it was the first day of the new school year. We had spent the summer in Spain, as we always did, and the children were nutmeg brown. I think Simon and Anna benefited in many ways from their father's Spanish nationality and it gave them a broader outlook on life to have a mixed cultural background. It was an arduous thousand-mile drive to get there, though, and I must admit that I wouldn't have minded a change one year, but we had some lovely holidays, and there were always plenty of empty beach apartments belonging to Jaime's family that we could stay in for free. In the summer the Spanish head for the cooler mountains. It's only the mad Brits who bake themselves to a red crisp on the beach and emerge from the sea like scalded lobsters from a bubbling pan.

Sometimes Jaime and I would sit on the balcony with a glass of wine while the children played on the beach below. We had quite a laugh watching the comings and goings at the doctor's surgery in the next block. There would often be a queue snaking out through the door to see the doctor, and they had a very bizarre system in which people lined up to get prescriptions at the end of the day. The nurse would come out and shout out not the person's name, but their ailment, and Jaime would do an impromptu translation for me as we watched. He could be very funny. 'Tonsillitis!' he would shout. 'Bronchitis!' Then his voice would lower for the embarrassing ones. 'Haemorrhoids,' he'd hiss, in an exaggerated whisper.

The children were very close to Jaime and loved the way he was willing to act the buffoon. They used to come into our room and climb into bed with us on a Saturday morning and he was very good with them and always made them chuckle. There were periods when Jaime and I had really lovely times together, so it would be a shock when suddenly the darkness would fall and Jaime started to shout and fire out questions at me. 'Who were you talking to?' 'Were you laughing at me?' 'Are you having an affair?' I sometimes wondered where funny, silly Jaime went to when the other Jaime arrived. I wished I could keep the lovely Jaime who made me laugh uproariously.

We had a neighbour across the way from us at that time who was called Lady Alice. One morning Jaime got out of bed naked and went to draw the curtains.

'For heaven's sake, put some clothes on!' I scolded. 'Lady Alice will be getting an eyeful!'

It was enough to bring out Jaime's mischievous side. He danced and pranced ridiculously in front of the window, shouting, 'Good morning, Lady Alice!' while I collapsed on the bed helpless with laughter at his antics.

I loved the holidays, but I never minded going back to work and always enjoyed that first day when I got to meet a whole new group of children who would be 'mine' for the next year. It was like being handed a lovely big bag of pick 'n' mix or a goody bag that was full of surprises! Today I had already spotted a quaint little thing who I guessed would become a favourite character. Maureen was a very bright girl, I could see that immediately. Highly articulate, her vocabulary was advanced and she prattled on relentlessly and cheerfully. I often found her at my side trying to help with something and she was very sensible for her age. Like a little old lady in a five-year-old's pinafore.

Maureen was noticeably old-fashioned – that was part of her charm. Her hair had that pudding-bowl shape that had been so popular in the 1950s, and she wore skirts that were too long for her, with tights wrinkled round her ankles like Nora Batty's. Her mum brought her the first day and it was clear Maureen was a chip off the old block, a mini version of her mum, who had a penchant for flat shoes and voluminous skirts with big, bold floral patterns. All the rage in fashion again nowadays, of course, but dreadfully dated in the 1970s!

'Please do send Maureen's reading book home with her when she gets it,' her mum said, blinking owlishly beneath her heavy glasses. 'I'll make sure to work with her at home.'

'Well, thank you. That's wonderful,' I said warmly. 'It's lovely when parents are keen to help – though I think it might be a little while yet before Maureen has a reading book.'

They are barely through the door! I thought, never failing to marvel at what different attitudes parents had. Nevertheless, it was a good sign and I didn't want to discourage her.

After that Maureen's mum was forever up at my class, with questions about Maureen's number work, or offers to help with the Parent Teacher Association, and one time she very kindly brought up a box of fairy cakes she had made for a class party. I always imagined Maureen and her mum wearing floral pinnies, their sleeves rolled up and noses smudged with flour, happily baking their own bread in a kitchen with an Aga and a whistling kettle. It was only later I discovered how deceptive appearances can be!

It was remarkable how different Simon and Anna were as they grew up. Simon rapidly turned into a clone of his dad, with very dark Spanish looks and a Roman nose, but while Jaime was volatile, Simon was incredibly laid-back. In fact, he was very good at calming down Anna, who used to flounce around outrageously as a little girl.

Anna was very funny but extremely strong-willed, and if she was in a temper, she would simply swipe things off the table. My mother frightened the living daylights out of me all my life, but she met her match in my daughter. Mum retained her matriarchal approach to children and could be quite stern, but she didn't frighten Anna in the least! One day, when Anna was about three or four, my mother called in for something. Anna was being a bit naughty that day and Mum wasn't impressed. She looked at her little grand-daughter reprovingly and wagged a finger at her.

'Just you watch it, madam!' said my mum.

It would have been enough to make most young children dissolve – but not Anna. She marched right over to my mother and looked up boldly at her. Her feet were planted squarely on the ground and she had one hand on her hip.

'Just you watch it own self!' she retorted.

The words might have got a bit twisted, but I think the meaning was clear! Even when what she wanted to say was beyond her vocabulary, she usually managed to improvise.

'And . . . and . . . YOU . . .' Anna stuttered at my mum one day, when mum had annoyed her, '. . . you will die!'

I think the phrase she was searching for was 'drop dead'!

I could never have spoken to my mother like that, even as an adult, and I was torn between horror and a sneaky admiration for Anna's fearlessness. She was some girl. When she was at nursery, I brought her into school for an odd afternoon, and even then, I really had to keep an eye on her. One day as I was showing the children out, I heard one of them talking to her mum.

'See that baby the teacher brings in,' said the child indignantly, 'she pushes us and won't let us in the Wendy house!'

When Anna started at school, I even taught her in my class for a term, but that was a disaster. It was just too difficult to be 'Miss' and 'Mum' at the same time. Poor Anna couldn't quite handle the distinctions either. One night at dinner she actually put her hand up.

'Miss,' she said, 'please may I go to the toilet?'

One day in class I told all the children to come and sit down and the only one who disobeyed me was my own daughter.

'Anna, come here,' I said.

'No!' she retorted. 'I'm playing!'

Wait till I get you home, I thought.

Let's just say it wasn't long after that I decided that trying to teach your own child and manage thirty-nine other little characters was more than anyone could handle and Anna was moved to another nursery class at the school.

It was purely for convenience that Anna and Simon had started at the school I taught in. I always said I would send them to different schools, but in the end the idea of all going in the one direction in the morning was just too tempting and all my resolutions flew out of the window.

Simon eventually ended up in Marie's class and it amused me one day when he said, 'Miss Cumming has nice legs.'

Does she now? I thought. Ten years old and he had already noticed!

'Here,' Marie said in the staffroom one day, as we both sat marking. 'You've got trouble ahead!' She handed me an essay of Simon's.

'By the time I am twenty-five, I will own a bright red Ferrari,' Simon had written. 'They are the best cars in the world.'

'In his dreams!' I said, handing it back.

There were times when it was hard for them to be Teacher's son or daughter, as I realised over dinner one evening when Simon had a quiet word.

'Can I ask you not to do what you did today again, please, Mum?' he pleaded.

My fork was halfway to my mouth and I stopped, startled. What on earth had I done? 'What was that, then?' I asked.

'Everybody saw you talking to me,' complained Simon, through a mouthful of spaghetti Bolognese.

Jaime and I exchanged bemused glances.

I thought back to the day at work. Simon had forgotten his swimming stuff and I had gone over to him in the playground to give it to him. He had taken it from me without a word. Could that be what he was talking about?

'But I was just giving you your swimming things!'

'Well, I don't want anyone to know you're my mum,' he said stubbornly.

'Simon, my name is Cubells . . . Your name is Cubells . . . How do you suggest we hide this connection?'

Simon, though, did his very best to pretend we weren't related and would turn away from me in the corridor, pretending he hadn't seen me, if I walked by. Just as well I didn't have a thin skin!

'Is my dad a Catholic?' asked Simon a few days later.

I was washing dishes at the sink but paused, my hands immersed in the warm, soapy water. What a strange question!

Simon had just come in from serving at Saturday-morning Mass. He had reached the stage where he had decided he wanted to be an altar boy, though frankly it would turn out to be a short-lived career. All it took was one comment from Anna and his vocation was in tatters.

'When I am a big girl, I am going to wear a red dress and go on the stage at church like Simon,' she said. Simon never went back.

For the moment, though, he was in training and I suddenly realised the reason for his question: Hissing Sid!

'Why do you want to know?' I asked suspiciously.

'Father Tom asked.'

Oh, did he now! I finished the dishes and dried my hands, then quietly went and got my jacket.

'Won't be a minute,' I told Jaime. 'I'm going to speak to Hissing Sid.'

'What about?'

'Tell you when I get back!'

I walked up to the monastery, which was only a few minutes away. I suppose the conversation with Simon about not wanting people to know I was his mum was still in my mind. It made it seem even worse that Father Tom was using him to find out about me and Jaime – because that's what this was about. He knew we weren't the most conventional Catholics and was trying to get evidence. I think if it had just been about me, I wouldn't have bothered saying anything, but when children are involved, I tend to get a bit like a tigress defending her cubs.

I rang the bell.

'Why did you want to know if my husband is a Catholic?' I said, when Father Tom answered.

'I didn't.'

'Yes you did. You asked Simon. Please don't use my children to find out about me.'

'All I said was, "When your father was in Spain, did he go to a Catholic church?" ' said Father Tom. He sounded a bit defensive, but then he gathered himself and went on the attack. 'And while we're on the subject,' he said, 'we don't see much of *you* here on a Sunday.'

'So,' I said, my hackles rising, 'you assume that because I don't go to *your* church, I don't go anywhere. That is a very arrogant assumption.'

And with that, I marched back down the path.

Actually, I didn't go to church anywhere, but I wasn't telling him that!

Really, Father Tom could be so bullish. Usually I managed to keep my cool with him and rise above it, but just occasionally I confess my patience got the better of me! He was very proud of his singing voice and always behaved like a frustrated Pavarotti, dragging out the words of the hymns. One term a new member of staff joined us. Her name was Frances Aston, and she offered to help out with the music for our monthly children's Mass. She was a wonderful musician and at her first Mass, she was up in the choir loft, playing the organ and directing the choir. At the end Father Tom approached me.

'Will you tell that new teacher that the tempo for the last hymn was too quick?' he said. It was typical of him.

'As she has a degree in music, perhaps you'd like to tell her yourself,' I smiled.

Not long after that Simon came home from serving on the altar with some news.

'Father Tom is leaving,' he said, picking an apple out of the bowl and taking a big bite.

'He can't be!' I don't know why but Father Tom just felt like a permanent fixture. I hardly dared hope that he might be moving on.

'Honestly,' said Simon, munching hard. 'He told the altar boys this morning.'

I soon discovered he was being sent to a very rough part of London, which I imagine was a bit of a culture shock for him after this leafy suburb, where he had been wined and dined by what my mother, notorious for getting her words confused, would have called 'the many pillocks of the Church'.

Before he left, he came round each class to say his fond farewells. Less fond in my case, but he could hardly miss me out.

I put my hand out to shake his. 'Goodbye, Father,' I said, 'and good luck.' I was sorely tempted to add, 'I think you might need it,' but I somehow bit my tongue.

He shook hands without a word and then turned on his heels and left.

Rarely have I come across anyone who pushed my buttons in quite the way Father Tom had managed to. I'm a calm person by nature, but Father Tom had certainly tested my limits!

I'm pleased to say his successor was a delight: handsome, urbane and a snappy dresser. When Father Rupert came into the staffroom for the first time, he was wearing a lovely white linen jacket. We all introduced ourselves.

'I like your jacket, Father,' Marie said.

'I got it from the local Oxfam for a fiver,' he replied.

'How are you settling in?' I asked.

'Fine,' he said, 'but I'm finding it difficult to keep up the flying hours.'

Flying hours? Well, I thought, there's a breath of fresh air!

It works two ways for teachers and their children when they are at the same school. Your kids might want to pretend they don't know you after you've shared the cornflakes packet over breakfast, but just occasionally you'd prefer to pass them off as passing strangers too. Simon certainly got his revenge for the swimming-gear incident and for being caught up in my contretemps with Father Tom.

We had some very good theatre groups who used to come to the school to perform. Because I taught infants, I used to love taking them to performances, especially in real theatres, where the atmosphere was always electric. Children loved the colour and the spectacle: the real stage and the swishing velvet curtains, the coloured lights and fancy costumes. The pleasure of theatre comes in suspending your disbelief for a couple of hours, and while that can be hard for adults, the magical thing about children is their willingness to believe completely in the fantasy of any story you weave for them. As the lights went down, I loved to look along the row and see them leaning forward eagerly, eyes bright with excitement and anticipation. It was always a really special moment.

Anyway, one day at school a group turned up to perform their version of *Mary Poppins* and all the children got dressed up. The cast were obviously working up to singing 'Supercalifragilisticexpialidocious' and this very tall actor asked the children if they knew any long words. My lot in the infants had a few suggestions.

'Crocodile!' said one.

'Dinosaur!' suggested another.

A flurry of hands went up at the back, where the older children were sitting.

'The lad on the right,' said the actor. 'What long word do you know?'

'Floccinaucinihilipilification,' said the boy, to a rather stunned silence on stage.

The actors looked at one another.

'Well,' said the tall actor, 'and I suppose you know what it means, do you?'

'Yes,' replied the boy. 'It means the habit of estimating as worthless. I also know antidisestablishmentarianism.'

At the interval the cast came into the staffroom for a coffee.

'Who on earth was the smart arse at the back?' said the tall actor.

'Who?' I said vaguely.

'The pain-in-the-neck kid with the big words.'

Should I own up? I thought I'd better, really, because I saw a few grins in my direction and knew someone would give me away.

'Before you go any further,' I said in a rather smaller voice than usual, 'the smart arse is mine.'

Meanwhile, Maureen's reading and writing were coming on in leaps and bounds. She had taken to it with no difficulty at all and could soon write simple sentences. She was a bright-eyed young thing and very little passed her by. She would notice the colour of the head's shirt – 'He wore that shirt last Monday,' she would say – or when you'd had a haircut. When someone in the class was feeling sad, she'd be the first to notice. Her mum was still taking a keen interest in her progress, and although I was always pleased to see parents, I must admit that there were times when I wished Maureen's mum called a little less often.

Later in the year, when the class were able to write a few words, we began to keep 'news' diaries. Every Monday the children would write a sentence or two – or in Maureen's case three or four – about what they had done at the weekend. Then they would draw a picture underneath to illustrate what they had written.

The diaries were, naturally, very simple. The children were writing things down for the first time and sometimes it took a little effort to work out exactly what they were trying to say. Maureen's efforts, though, were always among the best. One Monday she seemed to be particularly intent, her small hand grasping her pencil tightly while she tried hard to form the letters. That night I took the children's news diaries home to mark, and when I opened Maureen's, I burst out laughing.

'On satrday my mumy and daddy had a party and playd pass the parcil. I watchd from stairs and Daddy wun. In the parcil was a bra and pants and daddy took his cloths off and put them on and all thi peeple laffd and mumy saw me and sed got to bed Maureen.'

Underneath was a picture of Maureen's smiling daddy. He was a salesman and I had only ever seen him dressed in a shapeless, well-worn suit. It was a typical childishly drawn stick figure, except it was wearing what was meant to be women's underwear! I know children sometimes make things up. In fact, Reg, our sardonic deputy head, had once written a poster for parents' evening that read, 'We promise not to believe what your children tell us about you if you promise not to believe what they tell you about us.' Nevertheless, while Maureen's mum and dad seemed the unlikeliest people in the world to have a racy party, I must say her story had the unmistakeable whiff of truth about it! I wrote, 'What an interesting weekend!' on her book and gave her a gold star.

The next day Maureen's mum came to pick her up from school and asked me how she was getting on.

'Oh, very well,' I said. 'In fact, she wrote a super little story for her news diary this week. Wait a moment and I'll get it for you.'

Having seen the funny side myself, I thought the story might make her laugh, so I handed her the news diary and Maureen's mum peered delightedly at the page. I went to speak to another parent but caught sight of Maureen's mum out of the corner of my eye. Her eyebrows rose higher and higher up her forehead as she read it and she looked as if she had been shot. Grabbing hold of Maureen's hand, she bolted out of the door. I have to say that I never saw her on the school side of the gate again!

22

Sugar and Spice

It was early 1981, and from the top of the bus in Liverpool's city centre, I could see the landmark Tate & Lyle sugar refinery on Love Lane in the distance. It was a striking building, its marble-faced offices dominating the bleak, redbrick heartland of the city's run-down docklands. Later the docklands would become the centre of the city's regeneration programme, with smart shops and restaurants, but today catching a glimpse of the iconic Tate & Lyle building just made my heart sink. Ninety-day redundancy notices had just been given to its workers and soon another of Liverpool's most important industries would be gone, along with marine engineering and flour-milling.

Liverpool's sugar industry had been founded in 1859 by Henry Tate, who was as important a philanthropist as he was businessman. We had Tate to thank for the Hahnemann Hospital on Hope Street and for the Liverpool University library block. Later he would expand his business to London, and he also donated the Tate Gallery to the capital. It was a golden time, a period of prosperity, and sugar was a major part of Liverpool's affluent past. The industry had also spawned significant spin-off companies, like Hartley's jam, and thriving toffee companies, like Barker & Dobson. Now, though, it seemed the Liverpool sugar industry had no future, and though Tate & Lyle would live on, it would not be in Liverpool.

The woman sitting next to me on the bus shook her head. There were a lot of female workers in the factory and there was little prospect of alternative employment for them in the current climate.

'Sad seeing the news about that refinery,' she said, and I murmured agreement. 'God knows what all those women will do now.'

Things were tough in Liverpool at that time, but the city always had a saving grace: its sense of comedy. Combined with their tenacity, Liverpudlians' gritty black humour makes them very resilient. My new friend on the bus nudged me as we passed a garage.

'Look at that,' she said, and I peered out through the grimy window. There was graffiti spray-painted on a garage wall. 'Free Bobby Sands,' it said. Sands was an IRA prisoner who was in the Maze and had gone on hunger strike. Underneath someone had added, 'With every gallon.' It was so Liverpool: quick, cynical humour.

Liverpool's growth as a city had been largely brought about by its status as a port. In the nineteenth century ships carrying commodities like sugar sailed in and out of the Mersey and an astonishing 40 per cent of the world's trade passed through the city. Liverpool's wealth eclipsed London's at various times in history, but now it was a very different story. Great swathes of land – 15 per cent of the city, in fact – lay derelict and unused, making the place seem like a giant mausoleum of crumbling brick and broken glass. The unemployment rate was among the highest in the UK, with almost one in five people out of work. No wonder Liverpool, which once rivalled London for its number of millionaires, was now being referred to as the 'Bermuda Triangle of British capitalism'.

As the bus trundled through the city, I sighed at the decay I was seeing. Children I had taught all these years ago in my first jobs at Huyton and Woodchurch, kids like Joey and Robbo, would be young men now. What had happened to them? I worried about what kind of future they had in this climate. They were lovely when they were little boys. I hoped they still were.

A few months later, on a hot, sticky evening in July 1981, some friends of mine had been through the Mersey Tunnel, visiting friends in Birkenhead. The husband wanted to get some money from a cash machine on the way home, so they came back through town in the early hours of the morning and drove up to a bank near the university. The route took them up Grove Street, where they stopped at traffic lights. His wife looked up towards Upper Parliament Street as they waited and saw flames licking the sky.

'Oh look,' she said casually, 'there are bonfires over there. There must be a carnival on.'

Her husband looked over to where she was pointing and quickly thrust the car into gear. 'I don't think that's a carnival,' he said, 'and I'm not waiting for the lights,' and with that he sped off.

They learned the full extent of what had gone on in the morning, when news of the Toxteth Riots hit the news-stands and television screens. Over 400 policemen had been injured, and 70 buildings set on fire. A few months earlier major race riots had broken out in Brixton in London, and there were disturbances in English cities over that whole summer in places like Manchester, Leeds, Bradford and Birmingham. Then on 3 July there was more rioting in London, this time in Southall. The next night Toxteth erupted. As government papers later showed, it was Brixton, Southall and Toxteth that saw the most serious and worrying events of that summer of unrest.

Toxteth was the area that my father had worked as a GP, though in those days it was known as Liverpool 8. It was a lively area with an interesting mix of different races. I vividly recall lots of types of black music: calypso and jazz, R&B and wonderful a cappella that you could be lucky enough to hear in playgrounds and on street corners. It had its share of social deprivation back then, but I don't think Dad could have foreseen what would later happen. Liverpool is a city with a distinctive racial and ethnic identity, home to the oldest black African community in Britain, and the oldest Chinese community in Europe, but as immigrant populations all over the world have discovered, at times of economic recession they often suffer discrimination in housing and employment. Toxteth became a ghetto, scarred by poor housing and social problems, and that summer it simply erupted.

The riots were such a terrible thing to happen that they cast a shadow over us all. I think there was a general feeling of shame among Liverpudlians that it had happened in our city, but there was also that immediate backlash of comic defiance that Liverpool excels at. In the playground the next morning, one of the older children came running up to me.

'Have you heard about the policeman who stopped a boy in the riots last night?' he said.

'No, I haven't, Bobby. What happened?'

'The policeman said, "What are you doing with that brick?" and the boy replied, "It's a deposit on a television!"'

I don't think Bobby actually understood the joke, but he was repeating it because he'd heard it. This was a middle-class area and the children here were, unlike the children in the first schools I taught in, protected from the problems that existed in Toxteth and other parts of the city.

The next day I drove down past some of the scenes of rioting. The Rialto, an old dance hall I used to go to, had been burned down, and the Racquet Club, a beautiful grand hotel where I had once been invited to a ball, was also destroyed. I looked around at the smoke-blackened ruins and felt overwhelmed with sadness for my divided city. The lovely Georgian merchants' houses that had once been such a potent symbol of Liverpool's success had been divided into many bedsits and were now a symbol of deprivation. It was hard, that day, to see a way forward.

*   *   *

'Eh, love, look at that lot!'

I had been lost in thought as I walked to school, planning my first lesson, but looked up when I heard the shout. There was a bin man grinning at me. I was walking past the house of the Archbishop of Liverpool, Derek Warlock, which was just down from our school, and the bin man was pointing to a box full of empty wine bottles.

'He lives in there with six nuns, you know! They don't half get through the booze.'

I laughed.

'God knows how many empties there will be when that Pope fella has been,' he continued.

It was not long after the Toxteth Riots and the Pope's visit to Liverpool had just been announced. It was a boost to Liverpool's self-esteem, a sign that despite our troubles we had not been forgotten and were still worth visiting. In all honesty, though, the following months of anticipation got a bit much for some of us. One member of staff, Mrs Kelly, who was a stalwart of the church, became very involved in the preparations. As far as we could make out, most of Mrs Kelly's family were going to meet the Pope, acting either as altar boys or 'acolytes', as she called them, or singing in the specially selected choir. I was very pleased for her, but there was so much talk of the Pope that I almost wished it was all over.

Anna, who was five at the time, obviously thought the wait was going on for ever too. She turned to me at breakfast one morning.

'When *is* that Poke coming?' she demanded.

He was 'the Poke' in our household from that day on.

A date was set for May 1982, but nobody could have foreseen when that visit was planned just how much unrest there would be in Britain at that time. The Falklands War had begun just the month before and for a time it looked as though the Pope's visit would be unable to go ahead lest it be interpreted as political support for Britain's activities in the South Atlantic. It was Archbishop Warlock who worked to ensure that the pastoral visit would go ahead, and as a counterbalance it was arranged that the Pope would visit Argentina soon after his trip to Britain. The Archbishop had invited the Pope, whom he regarded as a personal friend, to stay at his home. It was the only private home the Pope stayed in and the people who lived in the same road started redesigning their front gardens, as if the Pontiff was actually coming to judge Suburban Gardens in Bloom.

On the day of his visit I lined up my class at the door. They were very excited because they knew something different was happening. We herded all the children into the assembly hall, where a large television set that had been specially hired for the day stood at the front. More than a million people had gathered to greet the Pope when his helicopter landed at Speke Airport and we watched the coverage as he was driven the eight miles into the city centre, with the gusty Liverpool wind whipping his zucchetto – or skull cap – from his head. As he stepped down from the Popemobile and went up the steps of the cathedral, known locally as 'Paddy's Wigwam', our deputy head, Reg, called out, 'Who's that guy in white with all the Kellys?'

The head was not amused, but we were!

Such irreverence made me think back a few years, to when I was still occasionally going to church – though not on a regular basis. At one stage a group of us started going to Mass in the city centre, at a church called St Mary's in Highfield Street. There were three priests in the parish who lived in the church house next door, and one of them was Anselm Hurt, the actor John Hurt's brother. He would go on to live at Glenstal Abbey, in County Limerick, where he was responsible for feeding the monks, and he later wrote cookery books. One Sunday we were invited into the church house for coffee after Mass. It was a very old place and apparently overrun with rats, so the priests kept two Jack Russells. We had just sat down when one of the priests stood up, pointed at the dogs and shouted, 'The Pope . . . the Pope . . . Get the Pope!' The two dogs sped off at a rate of knots and a few minutes later each came back with a rat locked between their teeth.

'Good boys!' said the priest. 'You got him.'

Unusually, the real Pope visited two cathedrals on his visit to Liverpool – the Catholic and the Anglican. There had been a lot of negotiations over that, with the Pope's advisers being reluctant to set the precedent of him going into Anglican cathedrals. Liverpool, however, it was argued, was a special case. The city had once been split by Anglo-Irish religious tensions, which had now been greatly eased by the work of Archbishop Warlock and the city's Anglican bishop, David Sheppard. The two were interesting characters and formed a very close bond. Sheppard, who had been a Test cricketer and former England captain, was a great champion of the poor, the unemployed and the marginalised, and he often spoke out against racial and sexual discrimination.

He and Warlock would go on to write a number of social papers together and the unity the two forged, despite their differences on doctrinal matters, surprised many. When Michael Portillo visited Liverpool, he asked the council leader who spoke for the city. Sheppard prompted the council leader to encourage Warlock to speak, much to Portillo's astonishment. He couldn't think of another city in Britain, he said, that would ask a bishop to speak as their representative. Liverpool, however, is not like any other city.

I had been invited to the house of some friends of mine after school on the day of the Pope's visit. The Popemobile was due to pass down their street and there was a bit of a party going on. We all sat on the wide grass verge outside their house and had a picnic with various bottles of liquid refreshment. So many, in fact, that we almost forgot what we were waiting for.

'It's him!' someone shouted.

'Who?'

Then it dawned! We all jumped up, spilling wine in our haste. There was a cheer . . . a brief glimpse of a white figure . . . and it was over. My friend looked at me and I could see she was thinking the same thing. All that preparation!

'More wine?' she said, holding out the bottle.

I gave the answer my mother always gave when offered another glass of wine.

'Well,' I said, 'I might as well be drunk as the way I am.'

*   *   *

I'm not sure who caused the bigger stir in Liverpool that year – the Pope or Yosser Hughes. Every so often a television series comes along that completely captures the zeitgeist of the time, and in 1982 it was Liverpool writer Alan Bleasdale's black comedy *Boys from the Blackstuff*, which was networked on the BBC. It was about a group of tarmac workers, and what the hard-hitting documentary *Cathy Come Home* had done for homelessness in the 1960s, *Boys from the Blackstuff* did for unemployment twenty years later.

'Did you see it last night?' we all asked each other the next day in the staffroom.

'I think Yosser Hughes is based on me next-door neighbour,' laughed one of my colleagues.

The series was set in Liverpool and had many interesting characters, but it was Yosser who stole the show. He was a man driven to the brink of insanity by the emasculating effects of unemployment. His catchphrases 'Gizza job' and 'I can do that' became adopted all over Britain, but despite the laughs, in Liverpool we felt as if at last our plight was getting some sympathetic national recognition. I felt a lump in my throat as I watched the final scenes of the series: three of the main characters witnessing the controlled demolition of Liverpool's Tate & Lyle factory. The familiar building imploded into a cloud of dust, and we all had to hope that another Liverpool would rise victorious from the rubble.

23

Strawberry Fields for Never

'Come in, Lee,' I said, as I unlocked my front door.

Lee stood back hesitantly, his dark eyes swivelling up to my face and back to the ground. When you are a teacher, children find their way into your life in all sorts of ways and Lee was from the local children's home, Strawberry Field. He might as well have had an 'Abandoned' sign round his neck. He was dressed in ill-fitting and faded clothes that were clearly not his own. His khaki shorts hung loosely round his waist, tied with a belt, while his shrunken T-shirt had run in the wash and the colour was mottled and patchy. A sleeveless pull-over that was much too small had been pulled over the top to complete the ragged ensemble. The jumper had a teddy-bear motif on it and I felt so sorry for Lee as I looked at it. He was nine years old and must have hated being dressed in such a babyish garment that was clearly designed for a much younger child.

Lee hung back nervously, reluctant to cross the threshold. I held out my hand encouragingly and spoke softly to him.

'Come on,' I coaxed. 'You'll be OK here.'

Simon and Anna stared curiously at our visitor as he came in. Lee was roughly the same age as Simon, so I asked Simon to take him upstairs and let him choose something to wear. When he came down, he was wearing Levi's and a sweatshirt like any other boy his age. He and Simon seemed to get on well, and Lee already looked more relaxed.

'Why don't the two of you go outside and play?' I said, and when I next looked out, the two of them were happily absorbed with other children in the street.

Strawberry Field Children's Home was closely associated with John Lennon. My childhood home was just round the corner from John's house in Woolton, where he lived with his aunt Mimi. In fact, his mum, Julia, was knocked down and killed outside the park that we used to go to. Opposite that park was the Salvation Army-run children's home and Lennon used to play in the woodland garden behind the house. Later, of course, he would immortalise the place in song and 'Strawberry Fields Forever' was released as a double-A single with McCartney's 'Penny Lane'. Both these songs were seen as the Beatles showing nostalgia for their Liverpool roots, but they were also regarded as the epitome of psychedelic rock. Which I think means everyone suspected they were on LSD when they wrote them!

The original Strawberry Field home that John Lennon wrote about was pulled down and replaced with a modern building. I came across it when good friends of mine, Frank and Jen Moretta, who lived on the Isle of Man, decided to adopt a child. Liverpool had close links to the island and a ferry line ran between the city and Douglas, the Isle of Man's capital. After a period of waiting, Frank and Jen heard that they had been matched with a boy called Lee, who was living in Strawberry Field Children's Home. Frank was delighted as he, too, is from Liverpool and he was glad to have ties with the city again.

For a while, during the adoption process, I was quite involved with Lee. Like most children in care, he had experienced a very troubled start to his life and was in need of a good, secure home. We arranged that at first Frank and Jen would come over to Liverpool every month, for a weekend, to get to know him, and I suggested that on the weekends in between he could come and stay with us.

That first weekend I turned up at Strawberry Field to pick him up, everything seemed quite welcoming. In the hall area, there was a little table with four chairs. There were teddies and dollies on the chair, and the table was set up for a tea party, something that most children find very appealing. So far, so good.

The home itself comprised four units, each with its own dining area. However, for times when there was a big group who wanted to be together, such as Christmas, these four areas could be opened up to form one big room. I had been told which home unit Lee was in and so I went off to try to find what was, laughably, called the family room. There were some children sitting there watching television, even though it wasn't a children's programme. The television was clearly just a babysitter and there wasn't a single toy or book in the room. There was, however, a cage in the corner with a budgie inside.

'Hello,' I called. 'Anyone know where Lee is?'

A little girl looked up at me. 'He'll be 'iding in the bushes,' she said.

I went over and switched off the television.

'What's the budgie's name?' I asked.

''e doesn't have no name,' said the little girl.

Just then the door opened and a woman, maybe in her twenties, lumbered in. She was pasty-faced with small, hard eyes, like shrivelled raisins, and a voice like a foghorn. She was wearing scruffy slippers with slouch socks and had a cigarette dangling inelegantly from her lips.

'Hey, who switched the telly off?' she yelled, shuffling across to switch it back on.

'I did,' I said, and went straight over and switched it back off again. 'Do you know,' I continued, 'that none of these children knows the budgie's name?'

'He hasn't got no name. And who are you? Are you a soshie?'

'What does that mean?' I asked.

The little spokesperson who told me Lee would be ''iding in the bushes' was still standing in front of me, watching with interest.

'She means, are you a social worker?' she explained.

'No, I'm not. I'm here to collect Lee. First, though, I'd like to talk to somebody who is in charge around here.'

I was directed to the captain's office and I knocked on the door.

'Enter!' shouted a very pompous voice.

I walked in and introduced myself to the person behind the desk, a round, pink-cheeked man dressed in Salvation Army uniform, and explained I was here to collect Lee.

'Before I do that, I'd like to talk to you about the woman who seems to be in charge of Lee's home unit. She doesn't appear to have a very caring way about her.'

'Well, my dear,' he replied, 'it's the Army's practice to train our older children to become house parents.'

I couldn't believe my ears! How on earth can you train a child who has had little or no good parenting of their own to be a house parent? Besides, this poor girl had clearly had precious little in the way of training! I was beginning to feel almost sorry for the girl with the 'sliggy' slippers.

'I'm sure there are lots of local mums who would willingly come in to help with the children,' I suggested.

When I left the captain's office, I did indeed find Lee ''iding in the bushes', and that's exactly where he seemed to return to when I dropped him off. Before I took Lee back, I didn't think to ask him to change back into the clothes he'd come in, but the next time I picked him up, he was wearing even worse clothes than before. I managed to corner the house mother and asked her what had happened to the Levi's and sweatshirt.

'Dunno,' she replied. 'The clothes from the four house units all go into the main wash. We never get the same things back.'

In other words, the children never had anything of their own. I knew how that felt. I had never been in Lee's desperate situation, but when I was a child, the only clothes I got were hand-me-downs from my sisters and I longed for something of my very own. On my tenth birthday, I got a new dress and it was such a rare occurrence that I still remember every detail of it. It was pink, with a little black mandarin collar, and I loved it not just because it was pretty, but also because it was mine. If it had gone in the wash and been given to someone else when it came back out, I would have been devastated. I could imagine how Lee felt finally to be given some decent clothes but not get to keep them. It was a terrible system, but there was nothing I could do. Next time Lee was going back to the home from our house, he knew to change back into his motley gear.

In time Lee came to tell me about a Christmas he experienced at Strawberry Field. A group of people – who sounded to me like perhaps they were from the Rotary Club – came to play and sing Christmas carols. When the concert was finished, one of the men dressed up as Father Christmas and came round to give every child in the home a wrapped present.

'Merry Christmas, sonny,' said Father Christmas jovially to Lee, handing him a big parcel. Just as he was about to open it, his house mother intervened.

'You wet the bed last night so you can't have no present,' she said, her thin lips pursed meanly.

He never did find out what was in it.

When Lee was about to leave Strawberry Field, to start his lovely new life with Frank and Jen, a leaving party was held for him. It was to take place on Wednesday 22 July 1981 and I remember it so clearly – for all the wrong reasons. I went along to the party and when I arrived, I was pleased to see the four dining rooms had been opened up to accommodate all the children who lived in the home. Lee also had to say goodbye to his siblings, one of whom had already been adopted and, like Lee, was moving on to be taken care of by a family. It was a poignant day, but I wanted it to be as positive and happy as possible for Lee.

After the usual party food, someone appeared with a big cake iced with the words 'Goodbye and good luck, Lee.'

At least that's a nice gesture, I thought.

'Shall I start cutting the cake for the children?' I asked, trying to be helpful.

'No,' replied the woman carrying it. 'We don't eat it. We just put it back in the freezer, to be iced for the next one leaving.'

I couldn't believe my ears. It really takes a lot for me to lose my temper, but I just saw red.

'Right, children,' I shouted, 'who's for some of Lee's cake?'

I was nearly trampled in the rush.

'Eh, I'll have to tell Captain what you've done with the cake,' said the house mother, who was looking distinctly uneasy by this point.

'You can tell him whatever the hell you like,' I retorted.

Lee changed his name to John when he went to live on the Isle of Man. I'm not surprised he wanted a new identity. He had come from a miserable home life, then a badly run children's home, and I'm sure he wanted to shed his past life like an old skin and allow a new, protective one to grow. Frank and Jen lived in a beautiful lodge on the island and now he had a lovely home, surrounded by cats and dogs to cuddle. Jen used to hear him, sitting on the step talking to the dog, telling it his life story. She would stop and secretly listen to this little vulnerable boy pouring out his heart to the dog, and that's how Jen really got to know all about her new son.

There was, of course, the thorny problem of what he should call them. Frank knew that it might be difficult to use 'Mum' and 'Dad' when John knew he already had a mum and dad, and he didn't want to force him.

'Call us anything you like,' he told John. 'We don't mind as long as it's not rude!'

Then came a very special day that is etched on Jen's memory. John went to the local school and in the evenings kids began to knock at the door and ask him to come out and play. One day they called and he said, 'I'll just ask Jen. Je—' he started, and then stopped. 'Mum, can I go out to play?'

John had got the new start he'd needed, and Frank and Jen had gained a son.

Frank and Jen were both high-school teachers and were registered with social services to help local children, so John wasn't their only success story. One day at school they got a phone call to say that Caroline, a girl in their own school, was experiencing problems. Her mother wasn't coping very well and was neglecting Caroline. Frank and Jen agreed to look after her for a while and Jen went down to her class to speak to her. She wasn't sure how Caroline would respond to being taken from her home. Would it be all right with Caroline if she came to live with her and Frank?

'Yes, miss, great,' she said instantly.

It must have been a relief for Caroline to experience some normality. She and John got on very well and for the next few years the four of them became a new family unit. Once, when they came over to Liverpool, a group of us went out for a meal together for Chinese New Year. One of my friends didn't know Frank and John's situation, but he watched the banter between the two of them across the table and laughed.

'My God, you've got your dad's sense of humour!' my friend told John.

I don't know if my friend caught the look that passed between them at that moment, but Frank look humorously across the table at John, who just grinned back.

John's life was transformed, but he never forgot where he started out. I think there were many traumatic memories from his early life that he found difficult to erase. Many years later, when he was over in Liverpool, he rang me up and asked me to meet him. I assumed he just wanted to catch up, but when I saw him, he told me he wanted me to drive him up to Strawberry Field. I agreed, without asking too many questions. I suppose I thought it was just something he felt he had to do to confront and come to terms with his past.

'I spent every evening in those bushes,' he said, as we drove up.

I stopped the car outside the building and John looked up at it. Then, suddenly, he started yelling.

'Fuck off! Fuck off. Fuck off!' he screamed at the top of his voice.

I sat in stunned silence.

'Right,' he said calmly. 'We can go now.'

In November 1980, the year before John left Strawberry Field, John Lennon had been shot dead outside the Dakota building in New York, where he had a luxury apartment. Central Park is opposite the Dakota, and afterwards a 2.5-acre site in the park was named Strawberry Fields in his honour. Years later I read that his widow, Yoko Ono, was giving around £1 million to the Strawberry Field Children's Home in Liverpool in his name. I suppose the connection was that as well as playing in the grounds of Strawberry Field, John had experienced a very difficult childhood himself. His father was absent from his life for many years and he ended up with his aunt Mimi after Mimi complained to social services about her sister's care of John. He would later say that not being with his parents as he grew up made him realise that parents are not gods.

I appreciated that the donation to Strawberry Field was given with the best of intentions, and was a generous act, but nevertheless I had strong reservations: I doubt Strawberry Field represented anything that John would have wanted for children in care – where I suppose he could so easily have ended up himself had it not been for his aunt Mimi. Somewhat impulsively, I wrote a personal letter to Yoko Ono, telling her of my experiences there. I said if she was going to give money, could it be to demolish it, not keep it open. I never got a reply.

24

Past Times

There used to be so many of my fingerprints to see,
On chairs and doors and window frames, from sticky
little me.
But if you stop and look a while, you'll see I'm
growing fast.
Those little handprints disappear. You can't bring
back what's passed.
So here's a small reminder, to keep not throw away.
Of tiny hands and how they looked, to make you
smile someday.

There are no doubt homes in Liverpool that still have that little poem on their kitchen wall, with a painted handprint of their child below. Every year in my class the children loved choosing a colour and painting the palms of their hands and their fingers, then pressing down on the paper to make a print. And mums loved having the permanent reminder of their sons' and daughters' childhoods. Maybe it wasn't so much at the time that they appreciated it, but in the years to come, when their children had grown, when the exhaustion of parenthood had given way to nostalgia. Isn't that life all over? It's when things have gone that you miss them most and you stop to appreciate what you once had.

Memories are important to all of us. For children, they are the building blocks of their personality. It was one of the reasons that I liked to go on trips out of school: I enjoyed being their tour guide to the world. Reg Mandelson, original as ever, used to write the same thing on his blackboard at the start of every session: 'Knowledge given out daily, from nine to four. Bring your own container.'

Reg was a big man but lean and very athletic. He thought nothing of cycling an hour to school each day. Sometimes I suspected that he bunked down in the school rather than cycling all the way home again if he'd had one too many in the social club next door. Some days his shirts certainly looked like he'd slept in them. The cleaner also mentioned finding two chairs together as if someone had slept there.

At one point I noticed Reg was cycling each morning with a big rucksack on his back.

'What's that for?' I asked him curiously.

He said nothing but tapped the side of his nose as if to say, 'Mind your own business,' so I just shrugged.

'Do you know what's in there?' I asked the others in the staffroom later, but nobody had a clue and Reg was saying nothing. The contents of Reg's backpack became a bit of a standing joke.

It was early summer 1984, and Reg had organised a school trip to Liverpool's International Garden Festival. The weather was warm and sunny, and the children turned up in brightly coloured shorts and T-shirts, swarming excitedly over the school lawns before boarding the fleet of buses. As we drove out of the school grounds and in towards the docklands in town, Georgie, a little boy in my class, jumped up excitedly.

'Miss,' he shouted, pointing out of the window, 'there's our church!' The bus turned the corner past a pub bedecked with hanging baskets. 'And there's my daddy's church!'

I smiled to myself. As children, my dad used to take us to a Polish church in town where we had to sit for hours listening to hell and damnation in a foreign language. Dad would go off to 'park the car' and said he'd see us afterwards if he didn't catch us inside. We all knew he went off to the pub.

'My daddy went to a church like that too,' I told Georgie. I was sitting beside Reg and nudged him. 'You still do, don't you, Reg?'

'Ha!' he snorted.

On the journey, we passed an old school that had recently been closed. There were workmen in the grounds and I noticed Reg craning his neck to look in the skip as we went past and them muttering to himself, 'Very interesting place, that,' he said.

'Why?'

But Reg would say no more. He tapped the side of his nose, as he had done when I had asked about the rucksack, and I rolled my eyes.

'Ooh, man of mystery, Mr Mandelson,' I said.

'That's me!'

It didn't take long to get to the Garden Festival, which was being held on a piece of reclaimed dockland. The festival was a direct result of the Toxteth Riots, three years before. It was also a partial answer to my question about whether a new vibrant Liverpool could grow again out of the rubble of the old city. Of course it could! In the aftermath of Toxteth, it had been recognised that the social problems that were developing in Liverpool could not be ignored and Cabinet Minister Michael Heseltine, who had previously shown an interest in regeneration programmes, had asked to be sent to Liverpool. Later he would be unofficially dubbed 'Minister for Merseyside'.

His mission was viewed cynically by many as a insubstantial plaster stuck over a great gaping wound. Even some within his own government took that view, with Geoffrey Howe, the then chancellor, gripping his wallet tightly and refusing to let the light hit the cash. Spending money on Liverpool regeneration, he had told his colleagues, would be like 'trying to make water flow uphill'. He should have known better than to dismiss a city with so much history, and so much potential, in that way. Liverpool was not a city to be dumped on top of the national scrapheap.

One of Michael Heseltine's proposals for improving Liverpool was to develop some of the wasteground and make the city more appealing to tourists. An extensive site down by the River Mersey was chosen for the Garden Festival, an idea that would later move on to other British cities, including Glasgow and Stoke-on-Trent. The project had a real feel-good factor surrounding it. It attracted three million visitors and was something we could all be proud of, something that showed the city in a good light again.

The children trooped off the buses and ran into what had once been a down-at-heel stretch of wasteground. The regeneration of Liverpool's docklands would see smart offices, shops, restaurants and museums spring up, and the area actually has more Grade-I-listed buildings than any other site in the UK.

'Look, miss!'

'Over here, miss!'

'Look!'

The children chattered constantly as we walked through the festival, voices rising and falling in squeals and exclamations. There were sixty individual gardens, a miniature railway and lots of artwork connected to the city of Liverpool, including a yellow submarine and a statue of John Lennon. The star attraction was the Japanese Garden, a gift from the Japanese government to the people of Liverpool. It was a stunningly atmospheric creation with delicate tinkling fountains, a waterfall, exotic blooms and authentic Japanese lanterns that transported you to the tranquillity of another, gentler culture. Then there was the striking decorative pagoda with its bright red pillars and a roof that was studded with 5,000 patterned tiles. Some of the festival was wasted on the little ones in my class, who gambolled through it like it was next door's back garden, but that's the thing about education: you don't always know which experiences you give children will become precious, delicate glass-bauble memories later in their lives.

A week later we held an International Day at the school to follow up on our visit to the festival. I always felt sorry for parents when we held events like that and blithely sent home letters asking the children to come in fancy dress! Some parents were very skilled at raiding the linen cupboard, or making something quirky and effective out of Granny's old curtains, but not everyone had the time or the imagination. Luckily, I had recently bought Anna a little Dutch girl costume for a fancy-dress parade in Spain, so I didn't have to make too much effort for her, and Simon had by now started secondary school, but there was still my own costume to consider. Having loved the Japanese Garden so much, I wore a kimono . . . of sorts!

'Is that your dressing gown, miss?'

Eh . . . yes!

I took the register in the classroom before we went outside.

'Who's missing?' I asked.

'Hugh-with-the-One-Eye.'

I blinked. Hugh-with-the-One-Eye? Hugh was a little boy who wore an eye patch to correct a lazy eye.

'No, no,' I corrected the class, 'Hugh has two eyes.'

There was a storm of protest.

'No, miss!'

'Honest, miss! He only has one eye!'

Just then the door opened and Hugh and his mum came in. He had been at the eye clinic and I had a quiet word with his mum. Would she mind if I showed the class that Hugh had two eyes?

'Not at all,' she smiled.

She took off Hugh's eye patch and the children gaped. Two eyes! Hugh-with-the-One-Eye had two eyes! It was a miracle.

The party was being held on the school's front lawn and the children looked like colourful flowers in their costumes from every corner of the globe. We played music from all different cultures, including India and China, and banners festooned the school saying, 'Welcome,' in as many varied languages as we could think of. It was an attempt to show the children that Liverpool, which for most of them was their entire world, was only one small part of the universe. There were other places, other lives, other experiences to encounter and embrace. I thought of my brother, Andrew, who was happily settled in Australia, and Helena, who was still living in Canada, and smiled. I loved that about teaching, the way you poured experiences into children as if you were pouring water into an empty glass. Gradually, you filled them up with knowledge and insight and under-standing – and memories.

The Garden Festival was a wonderful success and temporarily restored the city's pride, but sadly, in the years that followed, the Japanese Garden became over-grown and choked with weeds, and the delicate blooms withered and died. Successive years of neglect allowed harsh winters to strip the paintwork from the pagoda, and the tiles became weathered and damaged. It was a sad picture of decay and neglect, a site of vandalism and anti-social behaviour, a symbol of what we could be but had failed to sustain. Regrettably, yesterday's solution had become part of today's problem.

Later I was thrilled when it was announced that the site was to be restored, with some of the area being used to develop new riverside housing. Even the Japanese Garden was to be brought back to life, with experts travelling from Japan to restore it to its former glory. I was glad because that particular garden was a little symbol of Liverpool's continuing relationship with other parts of the world, and because regeneration always brings a surge of optimism and hope. The original Garden Festival had been something positive that had risen from the ashes of Toxteth, and it was nice to see the spirit of that triumph again.

I also couldn't help wondering when I heard the news how many of those children in that old infant class of 1984 would be drawn back as adults in the years to come because of their school experience there. How many would walk nostalgically through and marvel at the restoration, watch the fine, silver firework sprays of water from the fountains again and remember when they ran through this place as carefree five-year-olds. Memories, memories.

My own memories were to be brought back into focus soon afterwards: Jellybean was coming to stay for the weekend. The Four Buddies had all moved to different parts of the country and as sometimes happens in life, by now I had lost touch with Annie as well as Barbara Mc. Although we were down to the Two Buddies, for some reason Jellybean and I never lost touch through the years. Life goes on, the carefree days of college get left behind, and the burdens, joys and responsibilities of jobs and families sometimes take people in different directions, but we had managed to retain a link that survived even though we lived in different parts of the country. I was excited to see her. I had been invited to a neighbour's barbecue that weekend, so I arranged that Jellybean would come too. I also arranged an evening at my home with Maggie Gee and Tweet from our college days and, because I wanted her to meet my new teaching friends, AnnMarie and Bette, also Marie and Reg.

Perhaps it's just as well when we are young that we don't see too far ahead. It would be too overwhelming if we saw the whole picture of our lives. While it's being painted, we can usually cope with each little section of the drawing. Jellybean would go on to marry three times and suffer the death of her much loved husband Julian. She also brought up four beloved children, Roz, Jess, Ursula and Myles, the two youngest having Asperger's Syndrome (or asparagus syndrome as Ursula calls it). All of her children are richly talented, either in music or fine arts.

Music certainly ran in Jellybean's family. Over the years she had built up quite a reputation as a singer, though I had never been able to attend any of her concerts because I lived too far away. Her sister Pat's family, too, were very musical. Pat and John's daughter Anna, grew up to be a very fine pianist and singer.

She went on to study music at Chetham's School of Music and won the BBC Young Musician of the Year in

1982, playing Rachmaninoff. My Simon, a keen pianist himself, thought it was wonderful and took great inspiration from her success. Anna had a number of prizes, including tea with Maggie Thatcher and a cruise, but her most treasured possession was a telegram from Elton John. He had set his video recorder to watch her performance, he said. Elton had gone to the Royal Academy of Music and he told Anna that she had achieved what he had always wanted to.

'Swap places with him,' I said to Anna mischievously. 'Or at least bank balances!'

The barbecue we went to that weekend was a huge affair with several grand marquees. Out in the garden we got talking to a neighbour.

'What do you do?' Jellybean asked him.

'I'm a plastic surgeon,' he replied.

'Ooh, what can you do for us?' joked Jellybean.

'Actually,' he said, 'I only do harelips and cleft palates. What do you do?'

'I'm a singer,' Jellybean said.

'Well, sing something!' he said.

So Jellybean sang 'The Irish Blessing' and we were all stunned. Her voice was simply beautiful.

'I'm going to play Mimi in *La Bohème*,' she told us afterwards, 'but I'll need to lose about five stone,' she added with a grin. 'I'm supposed to be dying in a garret!'

It started to rain then and we all headed to the orangery.

'I believe your friend just sang,' a woman said to me on the way. 'Do you think she would sing again?'

Geraldine said she would sing 'O Mio Babbino Caro', but she didn't want a fuss – no introductions. She didn't need one. This wonderful sound filled the orangery and everyone held their breath. There were at least a hundred people in there, with kids playing snooker and a lot of background noise, but within five notes everything had stilled. It was one of those special moments when everything hangs by a thread in the stillness and you want time to stop. It was enough to send shivers down your spine.

We're fifty years on, I thought. Fifty years on from those daft college girls who played pranks on one another, yet life still took me by surprise, still had things waiting for me to discover. In those years we had lived, loved, lost, and we were still learning.

I arrived at school on Monday morning just as Reg cycled in. He stopped and walked through the gates with me, pushing his bike and puffing a bit, his rucksack still strapped to his back.

'That rucksack looks really heavy,' I said. 'Are you not going to tell me what's in it yet?'

Still Reg just tapped his nose in response.

'Oh, you're so annoying, Reg Mandelson!'

Reg laughed.

'You know the entire staff has a sweepstake on what's in there?'

'I'm inviting everyone round to my house next Saturday night,' he said.

'Seriously?'

'Yep.'

'And all will be revealed?'

'Yep.'

The following Saturday we all arrived at Reg's beautiful Victorian house with bottles of wine, flowers for his wife and sweets for his kids.

'Wow, Reg!' we all exclaimed as we came through the front door, which had vibrant stained-glass panels. The ground floor of the house was covered with beautiful parquet flooring, the kind the Victorians loved but would cost a fortune to install now.

'What a fabulous house!'

Later in the evening the question of the rucksack came up.

'So what was in it?' somebody asked.

Reg just pointed at the floor and we all looked down, puzzled.

It turned out that Reg had been visiting the demolition site of the old girls' school that we had passed on the way to the Garden Festival. Each day he had been climbing in through the window and removing the floor tiles until he had enough for his house.

'That's stealing!' someone gasped.

'No it's not,' retorted Reg. 'It's recycling. They were knocking the place down!' Reg had been outraged at the potential waste. 'After I'd taken it,' he said, 'I went down past the school and do you know what they were doing? Burning the remainder of the flooring in a skip!'

'Good for you, Reg,' I said.

I couldn't help thinking there was a lesson in there somewhere. Something beautiful that had lasted many years had been discarded as worthless and doubtless replaced with something that might last a decade if it was lucky. Sometimes we don't recognise the value of things until it's too late.

Perhaps that was particularly true of politicians when it came to Liverpool. Progress, moving forward, is important – as long as we take the jewels of the past with us.

25

Everyone Out!

Anna and Simon were looking at me with an astonishment that soon turned to sullenness.

'But why?' demanded Anna as we sat round the dining table. 'Why do we have to move? We like it here!'

We weren't rich, but we lived in a comfortable house with a nice garden and they couldn't understand what could possibly have caused this sudden plan to move. Why did life have to change?

I found it hard to understand myself. It was 1985 and a few months before, Jaime had dropped a bombshell. Eventually he confessed he had been hiding something from me: he had taken a voluntary-redundancy package from his job in the offices of Ford Motors.

'Don't worry,' he had said confidently. 'I'll find another job.'

He never did! It was the last day he ever worked, and now we were down to one income, we simply couldn't afford to keep living in our home. We would have to move somewhere smaller.

Unfortunately for us, his redundancy couldn't have come at a worse time. Liverpool's economy was still ailing and there were also frequent industrial disputes. At times, it felt like the whole of Liverpool was on strike:

dockers . . . factory workers . . . car workers . . . and yes, teachers. It was a very turbulent time in education. There had been unrest in schools for a couple of years and things were coming to a head, with a rolling programme of three-day teacher strikes closing schools all over the country.

Teachers, not known as the most radical of workers, were out in force, demonstrating against the education policies of Margaret Thatcher's Conservative government. On the front page of *The Times* that year, there was a picture of Glenys Kinnock, wife of the leader of the opposition, Neil Kinnock, and a teacher herself, joining the strikes.

'Miss, are you going on strike?' asked Katie, a little girl in my class.

'My mum says she's going to lose her pay because she'll need to take a day off,' said Jimmy, not lifting his eyes from a picture he was colouring with big, fat crayons. His hand moved back and forward tirelessly, scribbling ferociously to colour the big space of an elephant's tummy.

'Are you, miss?' said Katie, not to be deflected. 'Are you going on strike?'

I hated the question. It made me uncomfortable because I counted some of the parents among my friends and I didn't want to make life difficult for them. I wasn't very political and I didn't believe in striking, but quite apart from the principle, as the sole breadwinner now, I couldn't afford to strike. Marie and I were in the National Union of Teachers at the time and our fiery union rep said we would have to resign if we didn't join the strikes. We did resign, joining the more moderate NAS/UWT instead.

There is no doubt that teachers' pay at that time had dropped below other comparable groups. There wasn't an independent pay review in operation then and teachers negotiated directly with management through the Burnham Committee, which included the six teachers' unions and local councils. The problem was, central government had introduced controversial rate-capping policies in a bid to keep tighter control over Local Authority spending and there was rebellion in some areas. Liverpool was more affected than most. The council was led by John Hamilton, but the most famous Liverpool face of the period was his deputy, Derek Hatton. Hatton was either an energetic young firebrand or a ranting lunatic, depending on your point of view. With slick suits and an even slicker tongue, he was never short of a few words. He was a Labour councillor but a supporter of the Trotskyist group Militant Tendency, a group later expelled by the Labour leadership.

Under Hamilton and Hatton, the council pledged to spend £30 million that it didn't have, protesting that it was the equivalent of a grant 'stolen' by central government in cuts. Liverpool was on course for collision with London, but inevitably, it would be the council's own paid workers whose blood would be spilled in that particular head-on crash, teachers among them. We were the ones who wouldn't get paid and who would be laid off. In October that year Neil Kinnock gave an impassioned speech slamming the council's policies, which, he said, had ended in the 'grotesque chaos of a Labour council hiring taxis to scuttle round the city handing out redundancy notices to its own workers'.

Our school didn't escape the bloodbath. For us, it was a man on a motorbike who made the redundancy delivery. When he arrived, I was standing in the office having a laugh with Joan, our school secretary. Joan had a tendency to send out letters with typing errors – she once alerted parents to the fact that 'school badgers' would be on sale in her office – and I had just stopped by to tease her about her latest missive. She had given me a fire-drill notice for my room that asked me to 'leave by the back door and assemble on the front lawn where the headmaster will be poisoned under the copper beech'.

Joan's hand flew to her mouth, caught between laughter and horror, when I pointed out the mistake.

'Blimey, Joan,' I said, 'never mind the fire brigade, we're going to need Hercule Poirot out there!'

Just then there was a loud bang as a man in motorcycle gear, wearing a helmet and a tinted visor, barged into the room.

'Bulk mail,' he shouted, throwing a large envelope onto the floor. It wasn't unexpected, but inside were letters addressed to every member of staff, including the secretary, the caretaker, the cleaners and dinner ladies. I opened up my envelope and quickly began to read.

The city council does not have at its disposal the resources which are required to carry out its full range of services or to meet, in full, its obligations to its employees throughout the whole of the remainder of the present financial year. This means that there will be no money very shortly to continue paying and employing you and other council workers. As a result of this situation, the City Council, at its meeting on Monday 16 September 1985, has instructed me to write to you to give notice that your contract of employment will therefore cease to exist with effect from Tuesday 31 December 1985. I have written to all other employees of the council in similar terms. From the beginning of the next financial year, resources will be available to resume the provision of the full range of services and the City Council has decided, therefore, to re-employ you and all the other employees concerned, with effect from 1 April 1986. Employees should report to their normal place of work for duty on that day.

My heart sank. Paid off just in time for the New Year with the prospect of several months without money. With Jaime not working either, how were we going to manage? A second letter was enclosed. This one was from John Hamilton and was full of general ranting about how this was the government's fault and not Liverpool Council's. 'Stay solid,' was the advice. I sighed. I had just become the sole breadwinner of the family and staying solid was not going to pay the mortgage or put food on the table. Our salaries were due in two days later, so it was very worrying, though Reg did manage to give us all a laugh. The day after we received our letters, there was a knock on my classroom door and a boy from Reg's class handed me a large brown envelope.

'What's this?' I enquired.

'I think it's your wages,' he replied with a grin.

When I opened it, I thought the child was right at first because it appeared to be stuffed with fivers. Thank God, I thought. On closer examination, however, I could see my wages weren't going to go far that month. Instead of the Queen's head on the notes, there was Derek Hatton's! The children in Reg's class had spent all lunchtime colouring them in.

Those of us who were worried, spent some time trying to find out if we would be entitled to any benefits but we were told we would have to wait until it happened. Thankfully, it never did. The council balanced its books a couple of months later, in November 1985, with 30 million pounds' worth of loans.

But when I sat down with Simon and Anna, I thought there was really no choice, despite their pleas. In any case, with Jaime not working, things were only going to get worse.

'I am so sorry,' I said, 'but we need to downsize.'

I was struggling on my teacher's salary to pay the mortgage and other bills, as well as put food on the table. It's amazing what you can do with a packet of mince, an onion and a can of tomatoes, but things were still tight. One month I could pay the mortgage and not much else, and the following month I would have to skip the mortgage and catch up with the other bills. The children were shooting up, but I really wished that their feet, in particular, would stop growing! You might get away with a shorter skirt or trousers for a bit, but you can't wear shoes that are too small.

I felt terrible that the kids were losing their much-loved home, but with Jaime out of work, we had no other way of making ends meet. The house was put on the market and sold quickly, and we bought an end-of-terrace with a back yard, just five minutes' walk away. In the weeks that followed we packed our things into boxes. All the detritus of family life was sorted and divided: piles to keep, piles for the charity shops and piles for the dump. Dusty teddies fell from the top shelves of cupboards where they'd been abandoned, long-forgotten treasures were unearthed, and exclamations of 'Wow – remember this?' rang out all over the house.

On moving day we closed the doors sadly behind us, and Anna and Simon both looked at me, their young eyes full of reproach. For some reason, they blamed me for this and not their father. Why?

My mother had a phrase 'when poverty comes in the door, love flies out the window', But love had flown out long time before.

When Simon was a teenager, he had a few money-making schemes of his own. From the age of nine he had been learning to play the piano. His first teacher was a dour Scotsman. He called boys 'laddie' just as my old friend

Father Jock had, but somehow it had a quite different ring to it.

'No, no, no, laddie!' I would hear him say to Simon. It made *me* nervous, never mind poor Simon.

Over the next few months Simon developed a constant tickly cough. I eventually took him to the doctor. He had chest X-rays, but they turned out to be clear. It was all a bit of a mystery.

'I think something is worrying him,' the doctor told me. 'Go through all the things he does and you'll find out.'

That evening I asked him about school and swimming lessons and everything I could possibly think of. No negative reaction. Then I mentioned piano lessons.

'Do you like your piano lessons?' I asked.

'I have to go, don't I?' he replied.

'Of course you don't!'

'But I want to learn the piano.'

'Then I'll find you another teacher,' I said.

I could almost see the relief in his eyes. I knew how important a good teacher was. I loved music as a child, but a piano teacher got angry with me when I made a mistake and slammed the piano lid on my fingers and I remember feeling that everything was spoiled. I found Simon a lovely Dutch music student called Jolande van Bergen and he never looked back. Now he was a teenager and on Grade 6.

'Why don't you start giving lessons yourself to younger children?' Jolande suggested.

Simon didn't need much persuasion once he'd worked out the profit. Jolande charged £6 for half an hour and she suggested Simon should charge half that. It sounded like a great idea, so I went into the first-year junior class at school.

'Who would like to play the piano?' I asked.

Cries of 'Me, me, me!' echoed round the room as hands shot into the air.

'Well, have a chat with your parents and ask them to come and see me,' I said.

By the end of the following week Simon had twenty pupils and was earning £60 a week – enough for lots of basketball boots and trainers! Our school finished at three thirty, and Simon's secondary school at four, so the children who were waiting for their piano lessons would come down to my class for a while. While I tidied up and prepared work for the next day, the children would enjoy being back in the reception class. They would go and play in the Wendy house or the sandpit and it amused me to see them revert so readily to being infants. Then they would walk home with me, have a biscuit and a drink, and do their homework while they waited for Simon.

I stayed with him for the first lesson to help, and it was just as well I did: I ended up having to play the role of interpreter. Simon asked one little girl to close her eyes and listen to some notes.

'Now,' he said, 'are those ascending or descending?'

No reply.

'He means, are they going up or down?' I said, smiling as I recalled all the mistakes I'd made as a young teacher.

In the end, like all teachers, he had to find his own style. His teaching methods were a little unconventional, but that's exactly what children often like.

One little boy, called Paul, loved Simon and used to get really excited about his lesson.

'He can't wait to get here,' his mum told me.

It was some time before I discovered what Paul found such fun – and it wasn't playing the piano. I made a point of watching through the open door for a few weeks when Paul went in.

'Have you got your money?' Simon said, grinning at Paul.

The two of them had obviously built up a little routine.

'No,' Paul would giggle every time.

Simon would then grab him by the ankles, turn him upside down and shake until the money fell out of his pocket!

Paul was very eager to learn and one week his mum said to me, 'I don't know what Simon said to him last week, but he practised every day.'

It turned out that Simon had given Paul two ten-pence coins.

'If you can play that piece next week with a ten-pence piece on the top of each hand,' he told Paul, 'then you can keep the money!'

There were two teachers in the Cubells house now, but I didn't think I'd be adopting the new kid on the block's methods anytime soon!

Andrew was back from Australia for the summer. My hippy brother was now a respectable married man and we all got to meet his wife and their two lovely daughters. All of them had decided they would like to live in the UK and they were back for a test run. Andrew would drive them round Britain and they would take a look at nice houses with lovely English gardens. Unfortunately, it rained. Then it rained some more. Then it bounced off the pavements and battered at the windows. It rained every day for an entire month. The Aussie visitors looked gloomily out at the grey, sodden streets of Old Blighty and wondered if perhaps a lovely English garden came at too high a price. Then they hopped on a plane and headed back to the constant sunshine of Perth, Australia. Can't say I blamed them!

26

Mums United

I had been going to the same hairdressing salon for over twenty years after bumping into an old friend from primary school at a party when I was at college. She and one of her hairdresser friends had opened their own salon and I went along to get my hair cut. Sadly, my friend died very young and it was her business partner, Cheryl, who took over doing my hair. Cheryl and I would become good friends over the years and I soon discovered that she had married Rory Best, one of the sons of Mo Best, who had opened the Casbah. I saw Mo quite regularly after that because she would come into the salon to have her hair done by Cheryl.

Then one day in 1988 Cheryl phoned to tell me Mo had passed away. She had been ill for some time but had died suddenly after suffering a heart attack. It felt like the end of an era. Mo had kept up with young people and new music all her life, and when we turned up at the crematorium for her funeral service, what struck me most was that there were no old people there. The place was packed and the mourners were mostly in dark glasses, an interesting, exotic assortment of hippies and wannabe pop stars who reflected the varied nature of Mo's life.

'I love young people,' she used to say.

She wasn't that old when she died – just sixty-four – but no matter what age she had become, in my eyes she would never have grown old. She was just that kind of woman.

After the funeral we went back to number 8 Hayman's Green, to the original house I had sneaked out to as a teenager. This time I got to see the house as well as the cellar. The rooms were mostly decorated in green or brown, and the sitting-room décor reflected the fact that Mo had been born in India. She was quite an eccentric woman and in the kitchen there was a shelf with about a hundred porcelain pigs on it and another with a similar number of porcelain cows. Sometimes, looking around a home, you become very aware of the owner's personality. Mo kept collections of strange things, like the wire twists used to keep loaves of bread fresh. They were counted into tens, then hundreds, and I looked at the carefully organised piles and couldn't help wondering what quirky use Mo had intended putting them to.

Mo was a legend in Liverpool, but she was also a mum. A group of us, including her three sons, Pete, Rory and Roag – or 'Rogue', as we used to call him – all went down into the cellar that used to be the Casbah. My heart couldn't help quickening a little as we picked our way down the stairs; it felt like entering a time capsule that would make the years spin all the way back to my youth. I looked around and the memories came flooding back. It was all there, just as I remembered it. The tiny cramped cellar. The stars on the ceiling. The Aztec painting by

John. The rainbow painted by Paul. It was the same and yet it wasn't the same. There was no pulsing beat of music, no sensation of being carried by the screaming crowd, no sweat pouring down the walls. It was dark and silent and a little eerie, but there were shared tales and memories and quiet laughs from those who loved its founder. That place carried so many ghosts and so many memories, but that day in particular it carried the spirit of Mo.

It was the Friday afternoon before Mothering Sunday. For Mother's Day, the children at school always made a card and present to take home and I had decided that this year we should make something different: handmade peppermint creams to put in a decorated basket. It seemed like a good idea until the room was filled with a white mushroom cloud of icing-sugar dust as small, excited fingers experimented with how far they could make the powder fly into the air if they slapped their fingers in the bowls.

'Please, miss,' shouted Katie, 'Jimmy's messing up my icing sugar!'

'Jimmy!'

'Sorry, miss!'

I only had to say his name and Jimmy, who was more mischievous than naughty, sloped away sheepishly, covered in sugar. I looked around the room. There were white dots on noses, and white stripes on jumpers, and a thin white film over skirts and trousers. The children looked like a comical posse of miniature OAPs with their white-streaked hair, but we were having fun and a little bit of mess never did anyone any harm.

I clapped my hands. 'Now, everybody stop what you are doing and listen,' I said.

All eyes swivelled towards me.

'This is the green colouring,' I explained, holding up a bottle. 'It's what will make our sweets a nice light-green peppermint colour, but we only need a tiny little drop or it will make the colour too dark. Does everyone understand? A *tiny* little drop. There's a stopper on the bottle to make sure we don't pour too much out.'

'Can I go first, miss?' said Jimmy eagerly. 'Can I?'

I handed him the bottle. 'OK. Now remember, Jimmy, one little drop. So let's see how careful you can be.'

Jimmy nodded. Then he took the bottle, turned it upside down and, before anything could come out, shook it like a salt cellar.

'Jimmy!'

He looked at me indignantly. 'It just came out!'

'Well, it will if you shake it like that!'

'It doesn't come out of the bottle right,' said Jimmy with a frown, fingers fiddling with the stopper. 'See, it—'

The next thing the stopper had fallen into the bowl. There hadn't been much colouring left, but what had been there was now gone.

Jimmy looked up expectantly at me, waiting for the fall-out. 'Doesn't matter, miss,' he said quickly. 'I like green. Me mum likes green too.'

He stirred the colouring in and stained the icing sugar a vicious, dark, horror-film tone.

Jimmy was thrilled. 'Look, miss! Look!' he said, dancing on his toes.

'Never mind,' I said to the others. 'I think the peppermint creams look nice white as well, so let's just decorate the baskets carefully with the paints.'

I laughed quietly to myself, thinking I still had a thing or two to learn, even after twenty years in teaching!

We had an absorbing afternoon, and at home time the children were excited at the prospect of giving their homemade gifts to their mums. There was the usual jumble of jackets to sort, and zips to fasten, but I heard a little voice rise above the mêlée.

'I've got green sweets too, like yours, Jimmy,' said Katie.

What? How did she manage that, then?

'Let me see, Katie,' I said.

Turned out that Katie had gone over to the paint pots when I wasn't looking and painted her sweets green. I had to go out and tell her mum they weren't fit for human consumption. Mind you, the others weren't either!

'Never mind,' said Katie's mum, smiling at her. 'They look beautiful and they'll be a nice decoration on the dinner table.'

It's what mums do, isn't it?

I had cause to think deeply about exactly what mums do soon after. I used to watch a young boy in a wheelchair being wheeled by his mum down to Yates's, a wine bar not far from our house. He always had his Liverpool football scarf and hat on; the family were obviously going to watch the match.

It's common knowledge that Liverpool is a football-mad city. Many years ago Catholics in the city tended to support Everton, and Protestants supported Liverpool. By the 1960s, however, when I first started teaching, much of that had changed and people supported whichever team they preferred. Reg, who coached the school football teams, remarked that it was quite easy to pick out teams at football practice because the boys divided naturally into two. Half were wearing the red of Liverpool, and half were wearing the blue of Everton. What I did used to enjoy seeing on Derby Day, when Everton and Liverpool played, was the number of dads going into the ground with two or three children with an assortment of red and blue scarves on. On the whole, it's a good-humoured occasion. There was, and still is, rarely any trouble at the ground.

Still, my mother remembered the old days and was not pleased when my Simon started supporting Liverpool. Everything Catholic was like an identity badge for her.

Back in the 1960s there was a programme on television about an Irish lady who had a cupboard full of statues. She was referred to as 'the Mammy', and around that time my college friends started calling my mum 'the Mammy'. Somehow it stuck.

Anyway, for some reason – and I am really not sure how this happened – the Mammy had a season ticket for Everton one year. Once a fortnight I would drop her off at Goodison Park and go into town to get my hair done, then go back to pick her up. The season-ticket holder in the next seat to her was a Mrs Jones and over the months my mum got to know all about her, her children and grandchildren, and Mrs Jones got to know about all of us. They brought photographs of their families to the games and had really good chats. One week my mum would take a flask of coffee and Mrs Jones would bring a hip flask of Scotch, and the next time my mum would take the Scotch and Mrs Jones the coffee. A drop of alcohol oiled their chats famously!

They were sitting having a good old gossip during one match when a goal was scored and a big cheer rang out around the ground. My mum and Mrs Jones stopped talking long enough to jump up and cheer. Just then the man in the seat behind poked my mum in the back.

'Hey, love,' he said, 'that goal was for the other side. I don't know why you two come here every match because all you do is chat and look at photos!'

Football was part of Liverpool life and the kids in school were fanatical about their beloved teams. The events of April 1989, therefore, were very difficult for us all to cope with. The Hillsborough disaster was a human crush at the ground of Sheffield Wednesday in which 96 Liverpool fans died and over 700 were injured. It was the worst stadium disaster in British history, and the official inquiry into events concluded that the disaster had been caused by a failure of police control. It was that report which in time would lead to the elimination of all standing football terraces in Britain.

Liverpool people are very united in times of trouble and there was a feeling of solidarity in the city, an awareness that this disaster had affected us all. I have one abiding memory of that time. When the *Sun* started running headlines suggesting Liverpool people had robbed the corpses of the fans killed in the crush, there was absolute fury. The 1980s had been such a difficult decade for Liverpool, but the people are, on the whole, really decent folk and the *Sun*'s suggestions were so deeply insulting that the city closed ranks. Groups of protestors stood outside all the newsagents with placards, urging shoppers not to buy the paper because it had betrayed the city. I certainly wouldn't have liked to have been the person coming out of one of those newsagents with a copy in my hands.

A few days after the tragedy we held a memorial assembly in school with the junior children giving the readings. Some were very poignant and it was obvious that the children had seen it all unfold on television and had been aware that children the same ages as themselves had been crushed up against the barriers. One little girl in the school had a teenage cousin who was crushed. He didn't die, but the poor boy was left paralysed and brain-damaged. It was he who I used to watch being wheeled in his hat and scarf to Yates's. Every time I saw him, I felt so lucky that my own children were safe and well. I always wondered if the cheering and chanting evoked any reaction in him, if it prompted any deep-seated memories inside his brain.

What struck me most, however, was how loving his family were. I always taught children to make the most of their opportunities, but this young boy had had his chances snatched from him in the Hillsborough disaster.

His family had clearly rallied round. They wiped his face so tenderly and looked after him with the utmost care and respect. It was a lesson in life just to watch the way they coped with his disability and it never ceased to touch me. When I saw his mum wheeling him, not long after Mother's Day, I thought sadly of her waving her son off to the match that spring day, little knowing that he would not be returning in quite the same way. Yet when I looked at her interaction with him, I knew that there was one thing that hadn't changed: her love for him. And that was the most powerful, uplifting thing in the world.

27

Good Sports

Hissing Sid's successor, Father Rupert, cut quite a suave figure in the parish for a priest, with his white jacket and pilot's licence.

'So have you managed to do anything about keeping up the flying hours?' I had asked him, a few months after he first started.

'Yes,' he said. 'My brother went to Rome and he let me fly the plane.'

My God, I thought, there must be some money here!

He was also surprisingly down to earth, though. It wasn't his way to lecture the children, or scare them half to death with talk of Hell or the Devil, as Father Tom had done. He was a quieter presence in the room when he came into my classes and preferred to get to know the children – and, just as importantly, allow them to get to know him – by talking to small groups.

He also liked to engage with them in ordinary situations. I think he realised he needed to build a relationship with them before he talked to them about God. I realised how different he was when I saw him crawl into the Wendy house one day.

'What are you doing?' he asked one little girl.

'I'm making the dinner,' she said pertly.

'Well, can I have some, please?'

She had a pot on the cooker – with nothing in it – and pretended to put some food into a bowl. The next thing he knew she had taken a spoon and nearly rammed it down the back of his throat.

'That was lovely,' he choked. 'I'll come again!'

He was just on his way out when he spotted a little group of four children playing happily together.

'What are you doing?' he asked.

'We've been playing a game and I came first!' Darren told him enthusiastically.

'And I came fourth!' said Ben, equally enthusiastically.

Father Rupert looked at me, puzzled. Fourth out of four, I could see him thinking.

'Ehm . . . isn't that L-A-S-T?' he spelled out, looking at me.

'Oh, no,' I said. 'We don't have L-A-S-T in this class!'

Just then there was a short, sharp knock at the door and Reg blew in like a whirlwind. Being a keen cyclist and athlete, he not only took the school football teams but organised sports days.

'Have you seen this?' he fumed, waving a piece of paper. He caught sight of Father Rupert and stopped. 'Oh sorry – morning, Father. Am I interrupting?'

'Not at all,' said Father Rupert. 'Just off.'

'What is it, Reg?' I asked as the door shut behind the priest.

'Another council directive,' said Reg gloomily.

'What have they put their razor-sharp minds to this time?' I asked with a sigh. 'I thought their heads would still be sore from thinking up the blackboard-chalkboard initiative!'

'Have a look,' said Reg, handing me the letter.

My eyes quickly scanned the text. School sports days, the letter said, were to be cancelled. From now on individual sporting achievement was not to be celebrated because it would make non-sporty kids feel inferior. Life, it seemed, was a team game only. Political correctness was well and truly going mad by the late 1980s!

'That's just silly!' I exclaimed, handing the letter back. 'Are the powers-that-be going to cancel all academic tests because it makes non-academic kids feel less good about themselves? I don't think so! Why pick on sport?'

I liked to emphasise children's successes, not their failures. As I had explained to Father Rupert, I didn't like to pit children against one another all the time, but that didn't mean you could remove competition from their lives completely, because life simply isn't like that. My early years at Huyton and Woodchurch had left a deep impression on me. I knew that life wasn't always fair. Some children are born rich, and some are born poor. Some have lots of talents, and some have learning difficulties to overcome. It was important to find whatever a child was good at and praise them for that. It didn't make sense to allow competition in academic exams and not on the sports field. For some children, the sports field was the one place they shone, the one place they succeeded.

'It's mad,' said Reg, shaking his head.

'What are you going to do?' I asked, knowing that he had already spent hours arranging our annual Sports Day.

'Well, I'm not cancelling!' he said vehemently. 'Sports Day is on Friday, so it's too late now. The letters have already gone out to parents.' He screwed the council's directive into a ball. 'I think this will just have to be lost in the post for a bit.'

He threw the paper into the air, caught it with his foot on the way down and in a lucky fluke kicked it across my desk and straight into the bin on the other side.

'Goal!' he shouted triumphantly, raising his arms and running from the room.

The children stared, open-mouthed.

Big kid!

Sports Day started overcast with a few spots of rain at morning break.

'It'll be fine,' declared Reg, despite peering anxiously through the window. 'It'll be blue skies by this afternoon.'

'Did you hear about St Theresa's?' I asked him. St Theresa's was a neighbouring school of roughly the same size as our own.

'No . . . What?'

'They got the directive a bit late too, so they went ahead with their sports day, but when it came to the races, the winners had to stop, wait for the others to catch up and then hold hands to cross the line together.'

'Oh my God,' muttered Reg, rolling his eyes. He was far too robust a character to understand such namby-pamby behaviour.

Something attracted his attention out in the play-ground and he quickly opened the staffroom window. 'Oi! Patterson,' he shouted to one of the senior boys. 'Foul!' He gesticulated wildly with his arm, pointing to an area below the window. 'Over here! Sin bin!'

'I'll go,' I said. 'I don't mind.'

I genuinely liked playground duty. Some teachers removed themselves to sit on the wall with a cup of tea, keeping as far away from the action as possible, but I never minded spending more time among the children. I found the playground fascinating and did a lot of watch-ing. That was their jungle out there. It was where they made friends, and fell out, and sorted out the pecking order. There were coronations and coups and victories and rebellions.

Sometimes you would hear that primitive chanting children do when there's trouble, and cries of 'Fight! Fight! Fight!' would rise like a war cry from the centre of an unruly scrum. If it was a big child and a little one, or it involved someone who couldn't cope, I would always go immediately. If, however, it involved two children who could handle it, I would sometimes take my time and let them get a few thumps in first. That might sound some-what irresponsible, but the playground is a little society, with its own power structure, and children need to work that out for themselves. They can't always be protected, or have their hands held, though I'd be sure to keep a close eye on them. I used to deflate things by saying, 'You sit on that wall and you sit on that one. Sort yourselves out.' They always understood what 'sort yourselves out' meant.

Certain games were banned in the playground because they were too dangerous. One of them was British bulldog. It ends with a long chain of older children sweeping across the playground, knocking the little ones down like skittles. To try and get away with the ban, the children would keep changing the name.

'No, miss, this isn't bulldog! It's called spazio,' they would say, with typical inventiveness.

'I don't care what it's called,' I would retort. 'Stop it!'

Then that familiar cry would go up: 'Aarh ray, miss!'

Today the children were a bit more excitable than usual because they knew it would be an early lunch and then Sports Day. As it turned out, Reg's forecast was right. By the afternoon the morning clouds had been burned away, the sky was blue, and a slow heat was beginning to build. It was enough for Reg to have donned his sunglasses, a pair of mirrored, steel-rimmed glasses that gave him the air of a slightly seedy, ageing pop star.

'Racy, Reg, very racy,' murmured Sindy, a glamorous young thing who was new to the staff.

'You young 'uns know nothing about style,' declared Reg.

The children were spread across the grass, like long-legged young colts in their shorts and T-shirts, running with boundless energy before the events had even begun. Reg went over to the microphone.

'Good afternoon, everyone, and welcome to Sports Day,' he said. 'We're starting with a novelty race, so I would ask all the mums to line up for the mothers' race.'

'Go on, Mum,' I could hear all the kids urge their poor mothers, who groaned loudly, then reluctantly took to the starting line. As the starter's gun sounded, and the mums shot off to a burst of excited screams and cheers, it was impossible not to notice that one rather well-endowed mum was running . . . well, without the usual support, let's say.

Reg looked at me, his eyes inscrutable behind his mirrored glasses. 'I think I'll just go in and have a drink of water to cool down,' he murmured, and I had to laugh.

I walked over to make sure the children were lined up and ready for their races. Adam Speirs, a long-limbed little boy with a very athletic frame, was raring to go and came running up to speak to me. I liked Adam. I had taught him a couple of years before and he was full of mischief and always in trouble – a real boy's boy. He was honest with it, though, and always admitted to wrong-doing. There was never anything sly about him. While other kids would shout, 'I never, Miss, I never!' Adam would shrug like it was a fair cop and say, 'Yes, Miss, it was me.' He was in his element on Sports Day, and today, dressed in his navy shorts and blue striped T-shirt, he was jumping on the spot in anticipation.

'Miss, I can run really fast!'

'I know, Adam,' I smiled. 'You run like the wind – I've seen you.'

Adam was exactly the kind of child who benefited from Sports Day. He had five siblings who were all far more academic than him. Oh, he wasn't stupid and he was a perfectly competent student – he could read and write and count quite adequately – but he wasn't exceptional like his brothers and sisters, and it would have been easy for Adam to end up feeling inferior in their company. Until, that is, he got onto the sports field. There, Adam was supreme. He ran faster than everyone else, jumped higher, threw further and crossed the winning line every time with a glow of pride. It was wonderful to see him find his own special talent and succeed so spectacularly at it.

At prize-giving, Adam would be up on the stage several times with a medal for this sporting achievement and a trophy for that one. I always felt that prize-giving was a very important part of school life. In fact, we used to have special assemblies on Friday afternoons in which we gave out certificates for noteworthy effort. I liked to be able to say to children, 'If you're very good, and try really hard, perhaps you will get a certificate on Friday.' It never seemed very constructive for me to say to a child, 'You'd better behave or else.' Praise and incentives work much better than sticks and threats.

Mr Connolly, the head teacher, used to see me coming with my lists of Friday 'winners' and raise his eyes. 'What is it for this time?'

'Being very helpful,' I would say.

In other words, not thumping anybody.

The drama of Sports Day was not confined to the children. Parents could get very competitive, though it was usually football matches that drew out the worst instincts in the dads. They weren't exactly shouting, 'Cripple him, son,' but they weren't far off. You'd hear roars of 'Bring him down, son' from the sidelines and afterwards Reg would have to go along the line dishing out warnings.

'I'm afraid I'll have to ask you not to come again if you do that,' he'd say.

Though to be honest, I think 'Bring him down, son' wasn't far off Reg's own attitude!

When the starter's gun fired for the next race, I saw Adam's blue striped T-shirt flashing down the field. I smiled as he crossed the finishing line first. Good for him!

I felt a tug at my skirt and looked down to see a woebegone face staring up at me. 'Miss,' sobbed Rosie, one of the little ones from my class, 'Mr Mandelson is giving out the ice cream now and I got one, but it dropped on the grass and he says I'll have to lick it up if I want any ice cream.'

I looked across and shook my head at Reg. That was his idea of a joke. The children often loved his devil-may-care attitude, but many of the little ones didn't understand his dark humour. Reg looked back and raised his hands innocently in a 'what?' gesture.

'Never mind, sweetheart,' I said, taking Rosie by the hand. 'He doesn't really mean it. Come on and we'll get you another.' We walked across to the table where Reg was handing out the ice cream.

'I'll deal with Mr Mandelson!' I said loudly.

Poor Rosie! Like I say, there are always winners and losers in life.

Mr Connolly was giving a little speech before the final race of the day, the teachers' race. It was the usual headmaster stuff: it's not the winning; it's the taking part . . . All that!

Ever competitive, Reg harrumphed quietly beside me. 'Right, Bernadette,' he said, rubbing his hands when the head had finished, 'are you in for the teachers' race? One of us has to beat Connolly!'

'Reg,' I said dryly, 'you're really going to have to work on getting some competitive spirit if you're going to get anywhere in life.'

Reg just laughed.

We had decided that a sprint was a bit too much for the older members of staff.

'That means you, Reg,' teased Sindy.

'I think you'll find I am in perfect physical shape, Sindy.'

Instead of a sprint, we all lined up for the egg and spoon race. On the starting line, I became aware of a striped blue T-shirt down at the finish. Young Adam was clearly taking a close interest in the race.

'Come on, Mrs Cubells!' he shouted.

'Ready, George?' said Reg to Mr Connolly, with some relish.

The two men lined up at opposite sides and we were off, careering down the field with our eggs tumbling from the spoons every few seconds. Most of us were helpless with laughter, apart from Reg and Mr Connolly, who were concentrating on the task with grim determination. A few yards from the end, Reg, who was in the lead, dropped his egg and a loud wail filled the air.

'Nooooooo!' shouted Reg.

That was enough for the rest of us. Reg's reaction was so ridiculous that we all failed to finish we were laughing so hard. Sindy ended up rolling on the ground, her lovely blonde hair covered in blades of grass. I felt like telling Mr Connolly to wait and hold hands with Reg before crossing the line, but our head, who only minutes earlier had lectured on good sportsmanship, was waiting for nobody. He crossed first and looked round triumphantly at the dejected Reg.

'Never mind, Reg,' I said, patting him on the shoulder. 'It's not the winning but the taking part . . .'

We were just congratulating the head when a little voice could be heard protesting, 'Aarh ray, miss! He cheated!'

It was Adam, pointing accusingly at Mr Connolly.

'He had his thumb on the egg!' he said indignantly.

The rest of us turned to the head. Reg raised his eyebrows, placed his hands on his hips and looked accusingly at him.

'No I didn't!' Mr Connolly spluttered, sounding more like one of his pupils than the headmaster.

'Yes you did,' retorted Adam. 'I saw you!'

Sadly, despite all the laughs, it was our last proper Sports Day for a good few years. At prize-giving, Adam's brothers and sisters continued to walk across the stage, but Adam did not. He had lost his time to shine.

'It's as if his light has gone out,' his mum told me, and I thought that was very sad. Education should be about switching lights on, not flicking them off.

28

Fond Farewells

'Anna, what are you doing!' said my mother sharply.

It was 1 June 1990 and we were all standing at my father's grave, as we did every year on the anniversary of his death. My mother was upset, so when Anna had started digging with a spoon at the corner of the grave, I had tried to ignore her and not attract Mum's attention.

'I'm just burying Popov,' said Anna.

Popov was a goldfish she had won just two days before at a fair. We had gone and bought all this stuff to house and feed him, but the poor thing hadn't survived long. Anna had placed him in a matchbox and brought him along to bury beside my father. I'm not sure which one she thought needed the company more – Popov or her granddad.

'You must have known he was going to die if you called him Pop-Off,' muttered Simon unhelpfully.

My mother was distinctly unimpressed by Anna's plans and refused to let her bury the fish.

'Don't worry,' I whispered to Anna. 'We'll come back by ourselves and you can bury Popov.'

Children have their own way of dealing with death. Your instinct as an adult is to protect children, to spare them pain, but you can't always. It's very poignant when you see them struggling to come to terms with the big issues of life that there are simply no answers to, but it's all part of their development. Although I was no big fan of some aspects of the Church, I did recognise that religious terminology could be very helpful for children. It gave them a sense of meaning in an otherwise chaotic universe.

There was a little Irish boy called Conor in my class that year and he had such a lovely turn of phrase that I often wonder if he became a writer. He arrived in school one day looking quite sad, so I waited until he was settled, then sat down beside him.

'What's the matter, Conor?' I asked gently.

'Coming to school,' he said, 'I saw a hedgehog lying on the grass. His eyes were open and he wasn't looking. There were things crawling on him, but he couldn't feel them. I think it's time he went to Heaven, don't you?'

What was much more difficult was dealing with children who had to cope with family bereavements. That year I also had a little boy called Paul in my class and one day his dad came up to talk to me at playtime.

'Steve Smith,' he said, holding out his hand. 'I'm Paul's dad.' He seemed pale and on edge and I could tell from his expression that he had something difficult to talk about. 'I'm sorry,' he added. 'Am I keeping you from your cup of tea in the staffroom?'

'Not at all,' I said, sensing he was upset. 'I'll make us both one and we can have it in my room.'

A few minutes later I noticed his hand was shaking slightly as he picked up the mug of tea I brought him.

'I need to talk to you about Paul,' he said. 'About what's happening at home. He might not be quite himself . . .' He paused and took a sip of tea to steady himself. 'My wife is dying of cancer.'

'I am so sorry,' I said quietly, and my hand instinctively reached out to touch his arm. It was just a momentary gesture, yet I could feel his rock-like tension, the supreme effort he was making to remain calm.

'I don't think it's going to be long now,' he continued, 'but I don't know how to tell Paul.' He had avoided my eyes, but he looked up at me helplessly now. I felt desperately sorry for him and didn't envy him his task. How do you tell a child that their mum won't be with them for much longer?

'I don't know how much good it will do,' I said slowly, 'but I could try talking to the class about people dying.'

'Anything you can do to help him,' he said, 'I'll be grateful for.'

The next day I sat the children down for storytime, which was always a good opportunity for a little chat. They all gathered round me; the physical proximity allows you to talk a bit more intimately. I confess I told them a lie that day, but it was for the very best of reasons.

'You know,' I said, 'when I was a little girl, my mummy was very ill. The doctors couldn't make her any better. In the end, God said, "Well, I know she's in a lot of pain, so maybe she should come up to Heaven with me. I'll look after her." '

The children were all listening intently. They always liked it when you talked about your own life and told them stories of when you were a child.

'I knew she was up in Heaven watching me when I was growing up, and I know she's still up there now,' I continued.

I'm not sure I believe in Heaven, but it's a very useful concept for young children. They find it incredibly difficult to understand that someone who has died isn't *ever* coming back. They can't really get their heads round 'for ever', but they find it relatively easier to imagine a concrete place where their loved ones have actually gone to.

The next day Paul came running in, desperate to tell me something.

'You know how you told us about your mummy?' he said breathlessly. 'Well, when I went home, my mummy was dead!'

Children are very resilient, young ones in particular, but of course it hadn't all sunk in yet for Paul. There would be difficult days ahead. I sat him on my knee.

'Your mummy is watching you from Heaven now, Paul,' I said to him, 'and she wants to see all the things you are going to do, because you are very clever. All those good things, your mummy will see and know about.'

I don't know if he was comforted or not, but he seemed to be, and for a moment his head dropped against my shoulder and I held him tight.

Strangely, it was just the following year that my own mum suffered a very serious stroke and became gravely ill. I thought a lot about Paul during that time. I was an adult and had been lucky enough to have my mum around all my life, yet I still struggled. Paul was just a little boy and had been given a mum for only a few years. It was yet another of life's injustices.

Simon had left school now and was reading maths at Oxford University, later switching to modern languages and linguistics at Cambridge. He had always been close to Mum and came home to see his grandma. I was so glad to see him. It had been hard to wave my eldest off to university. I had tried to be very practical, so that it was easier for all of us, but I missed Simon, and I knew Jaime and Anna did too. Nothing quite prepares you for your children flying the nest.

Nothing quite prepares you for watching your parents grow old, either. Mum was in Walton Hospital, the area's centre of excellence for neurological conditions, but the first Gulf War was by now in full swing and was complicating things.

'I'm very sorry,' a nursing sister said to me. 'Normally we would keep your mum here, but we have to clear two floors in case of war casualties.'

As I was working, caring for Mum at home wasn't an option, and she needed round-the-clock help anyway. The sister handed me a list of nursing homes that had supposedly been rubber-stamped by the health authorities. The hospital would look after Mum in the meantime. I looked at the list and felt overwhelmed, uncertain where to begin or how to deal with this new turn of events. If I was perfectly honest, my relationship with my mum had never been quite as close as I would have liked it to be, but of course I loved her. She once confessed to

Aideen that she had never really been very maternal and didn't want all these children who kept coming along. I think subconsciously I had always known that, and the little girl who longed for her love and approval was still trapped inside me.

I felt the need to do everything I could for her, to be as loving as I could possibly be. I wanted the end of our relationship to be right even if the start hadn't always been. If I wasn't on dinner duty at school, I would rush to the hospital at lunchtime. It took me twenty minutes just to get there, so I was only able to spend a very short time with her before rushing back. Then I'd return in the evening. I became very stressed and eventually it just got too much. En route to the hospital one day, I stopped the car. Despite travelling this route twice a day for three weeks, I had no idea where I was. It wasn't simply a question of which road I was on; I felt lost in every way. This was back in the days before everyone had mobile phones, so, feeling completely at sea, I went up to a door and asked if I could call a friend.

'Don't worry, queen,' said the woman kindly, 'I'll tell you where you are.'

But I needed a familiar face and phoned my friend AnnMarie. By the time she got there, I was in bits and it was AnnMarie who had to take me home and put me back together.

I started looking at homes for Mum and some were truly awful. I went into one where the matron showed me round and all she could say was things like 'This used to be the Lord Lieutenant of Liverpool's house.' Or 'This painting is of so-and-so.' Like I cared. I was much more concerned about the old man in a wheelchair who was sitting with his pyjamas open for the entire time she showed me round. By the time we got back from the lovely gardens half an hour later, he hadn't moved. I went over, pulled his pyjamas together and turned to the matron.

'My mother won't be coming here, thank you,' I said.

I found a wonderful place run by three Irish sisters, all nurses. When I asked what time I could come to see round the home, the reply was, 'The door is always open.' It was so different from everywhere else I had approached and I liked them before I even got there. The staff were kind, patient and caring, and some of the young girls who helped out were nieces of the three sisters who ran the place, so it was a real family affair. Sadly, my mum only lived for another four weeks. She contracted pneumonia and my lovely GP, Sean, was called out to her. I met him outside the school one day.

'You know pneumonia is a friend to elderly people?' he said.

I knew he was telling me that it was better if my mother slipped away.

One morning shortly after, I had just come out of the shower when the phone rang. It was the nursing home saying my mum's condition had deteriorated and I should come down immediately. My hair was dripping wet, so I wrapped a towel round my head and sped off. I had only been there with her about ten minutes when the sister came in and looked at her.

'I think she's gone,' she said quietly.

I stood up and kissed my mother.

'Goodnight, God bless, Mammy,' I said, just like I had as a child.

Sean came in. 'Do you want me to give you something to make it easier?' he asked kindly.

'No, I'm all right,' I said. 'I just need to sit for a bit.'

I needed some quiet time on my own before I would have to start ringing my family and sharing the sad news with them. There were so many memories and emotions to process.

You might think that it would be difficult to teach a class of kids when bad things are happening in your own life. After all, it's not as if you just sit at a desk and get on with things quietly on your own. You have to interact with all these children, give them time and energy and patience, keep order. Somehow, though, I always kept going and found that when I walked through the school gates, everything else got mentally switched off. I was there to be with the children and that was that. Perhaps that protected me emotionally in a way.

There was a lovely teacher who taught in the room next to me. One day we were talking about one of our colleagues who had difficulties at home but who took it out on the children. She was always angry and impatient with them.

'I couldn't do that,' my friend next door said. 'I have an awful home life but I shut that door and leave it behind when I come here.'

That was my way too. You can't take your own problems and difficulties into school, though I never shied away from letting them see I had an existence outside school. Children sometimes found that hard to grasp. When they first came into the school, I used to make a point of taking my class round all the different classrooms and showing them the secretary's office and head teacher's room. I even showed them the teachers' toilets – yes, teachers wee too! – and the staffroom. 'This,' I would tell them, 'is where the teachers have their cup of tea.'

I remember taking one little girl into the staffroom with me for something one day.

'Where do you sleep?' she asked, looking around curiously for any sign of beds!

So many memories passed through my head after Mum died, some of them sad and some of them comical. You know what they say: 'The world doesn't stop being funny when people die, nor does it cease being serious when people laugh.' The Mammy had some very strange sayings indeed. 'The curse of the seven snotty orphans on you,' she would say. Or, 'The sights you see when you haven't got a gun.' Or, 'We're all together like Brown's cows.' We didn't have a clue what she was talking about half the time.

Aideen came over from Dublin to help me with the funeral arrangements and with her being 'in the business', so to speak, I left all the holy stuff to her – hymns and readings and so on – but my colleague Frances, who was head of music, asked if I would like the school choir to sing at the funeral. It was a lovely thought, one that would have delighted my mother, and they sang really beautifully. Children's voices are so poignant on occasions like that, their innocence piercing through the sadness in such a bittersweet way. I rewarded them all with a big bag of sweets to share the next day.

My hairdressing friend Cheryl and her husband, Rory Best, were there too, and after the service the house was busy. That morning three nuns from Aideen's order had flown in to be with her, and when we got back from the cemetery, they took up residence on the sofa. Rory sat at their feet.

'Would you like a drink?' I asked one of the nuns. 'Tea . . . coffee . . . a soft drink . . .?'

'Sure, I'll have a vodka and white, with a twist over ice,' she replied.

I went to the kitchen and found Aideen. 'What's a vodka and white with a twist over ice?'

'Vodka with white lemonade and ice and lemon,' she said, looking at me incredulously, as if my education had been sorely lacking. I didn't go to a finishing school, but perhaps I should have gone to a convent.

I took the drink back to the nun and found Rory gazing up at her. Rory had a smooth way with the ladies – or so he liked to think – but his flirting was harmless, so Cheryl ignored his playful ways most of the time.

'Has anyone ever told you that you have beautiful eyes?' he said.

Aideen got hold of me. 'Could you get Rory out of there?' she whispered. 'I think he's embarrassing Sister Veronica.'

I went in as discreetly as I could and crouched down beside Rory.

'She's a nun!' I hissed. 'Do you want to come into the kitchen now?'

Instead of being embarrassed and beating a hasty retreat, Rory just looked curious. 'How was I supposed to know you were a nun?' he asked her.

'Well, we don't wear a habit any more,' conceded Sister Veronica, 'but we have a wee badge so people will know.'

'Can I see it?' asked Rory.

She pointed to a small silver cross on the lapel of her jacket.

'Well,' he said, unimpressed, 'I thought it would be a badge saying, "I am a nun." '

Oh, Rory, I thought. Get out of here!

But Sister V obviously had a soft spot for him. The next time Aideen saw her, she said that if Rory was ever in Dublin, it would be nice to talk to him.

'Sure, he misses his mammy,' she said.

It was a simple truth for all of us: for Peter, for Rory, for me – we missed our mammies when they were gone.

The cemetery is always a bleak farewell to someone you love and yet there was a moment when I couldn't help smiling through the tears as we stood at Mum's grave and a memory suddenly took hold of me. You see, Anna and I *had* gone back alone to my father's grave to bury Popov. We had dug a small hole at the corner and buried him in his matchbox because I thought it would help Anna to do so. Sometimes ritual is important, though in the years to come I realised that the fact that Anna and I had been close enough to deal with it together was the most important thing of all. I loved being close to my daughter in a way that I hadn't really managed to be with my own mum.

The next visit we'd had with Mum after Anna and I buried Popov had been just before Christmas, on my father's birthday. Mum had washed the gravestone and put fresh flowers down. Then she'd clasped her hands together.

'Now let's say a quiet prayer for Granddad,' she said to Simon and Anna.

'And Popov,' said Anna.

Thankfully, my mother didn't seem to hear.

Mum had always wanted to be reunited with my dad and I was glad they were buried together. Whether she was quite so pleased to discover she was sharing the space with Popov was another matter.

29

Family Additions

I was walking through town one day when I heard a voice that I hadn't heard for many years.

'Mrs Cubells!'

I turned to see Veronica, who was the mum of Robert, the little climber from Woodchurch.

'How lovely to see you, Veronica! How's Robert doing these days?'

Veronica smiled. 'I don't think it will surprise you very much to know that he's become a climber and paragliding instructor. He lives in the South of France.'

'How wonderful!'

Robert had certainly used his natural talents and that gave me as much satisfaction as if Veronica had told me that he was a professor at Oxford.

'You must miss having him at home.'

'Yes,' she said, 'but the house is still full.'

I looked at her in surprise. Veronica and her husband had actually adopted Robert. They'd had one child of their own in the early years of their marriage but had been told they couldn't have any more. To expand their family, they had adopted Robert and a little girl they called Felicity. Life has a way of surprising you, however, and it seemed that in the years since I had seen her, things had taken an unexpected turn for Veronica. The doctors who had told her that it was impossible to conceive had got it wrong and she had become pregnant naturally. From a prediction of just one child all those years ago, Veronica and her husband had actually gone on to have four. They were a lovely family and they had clearly coped very well with their surprise late addition. After the initial shock, their new little girl had brought them a lot of joy.

It's funny how life works out. Not long after this conversation, my own family gained a surprise addition: a fully formed teenager to add to the two I already had. Alexis had been Anna's best friend for many years. They had first met, aged three, at nursery school.

'I have a friend,' Anna announced one evening, 'and her name is Electric.'

Unlike Anna, Alexis didn't go to the primary school where I taught, so the friends lost touch for a while. They were to meet up again at senior school, however, and quickly became close once more. They gravitated towards the same type of music (awful, if you ask me, which they usually didn't), and eventually they started hitting the clubs in town together.

It was the summer holidays, a scorching day in July, when Anna came to find me in the back yard where I was watering some pots. I was pulling the flowers over into the shade against the wall when I heard the click of the back door. Anna was dressed in shorts and a vest top and I had launched into a warning about putting some sunscreen on when I suddenly realised something wasn't right.

'What's the matter, love?' I asked, seeing her tear-stained face. I left the pots and hurried towards her on the back step. 'What's happened?'

'It's Alexis,' she said. 'Her mum has died.'

I was too stunned to speak and just put my arms round Anna. Alexis was one of six children. Her father had a good job and the whole family spent a month in the summer each year in their villa in Menorca. They had only left the week before, but Alexis's mum had suffered a bad asthma attack in the shower and died before an ambulance could reach her. She was buried in Menorca and her children, one of whom was only five years old, had had to endure the heart-breaking journey home without her.

From then on Alexis began to spend every weekend at our house, staying at least one night and sometimes two, though if she stayed on a Sunday night, she would always get up early to go back home and check up on the younger children. She wanted to make sure they got out in time for school and that they had money for their lunch. Alexis enjoyed being with us and fitted in very well, so sometime after her sixteenth birthday I had a quiet chat with her.

'I've been thinking,' I said tentatively. 'Would you like to come and stay here all the time?'

'Yes, please!' she said instantly.

It never even occurred to me that it wouldn't work out. Families expand and contract, change shape and adapt all the time, and Alexis seemed like a natural addition to ours. She and Anna were the best of friends and that didn't change when Alexis moved in. Simon was at

Cambridge University by now, so he was already out of the house. Jaime has a soft heart too, so he didn't mind, and I was more than happy to have Alexis stay with us. She came one weekend as usual, then simply stayed on afterwards.

The very first night she walked in from school, she reached for the cereal packet, as she normally would have done at home.

'No, don't fill up on that,' I told her. 'Have an apple or a banana because we are going to have dinner soon.'

Shortly after, I called her and Alexis downstairs and they came into the kitchen to eat.

'Do you do this every day?' Alexis asked.

'What, eat?' said Anna.

'No, sit down to eat together.'

'Yes,' I said, 'and we don't have the telly on either, because eating is a social occasion.'

I knew I couldn't replace Alexis's mum, but I could teach her things and be there for the girly chats that she so missed. When she was going out, Alexis would come downstairs to check her outfit with me. A few weeks after she came to stay permanently, she was going out to a party and clip-clopped downstairs in her high heels to show me a fitted emerald-green dress.

'What do you think?' she asked uncertainly.

'Oh, that's beautiful,' I said. Alexis is a gorgeous-looking girl, with olive colouring and lovely naturally curly hair, though to look at it, you would swear it had been permed. The vibrant colour of the dress suited her perfectly.

She seemed satisfied, but a few minutes later she came down in a little black number with a lace top and full skirt.

'Oh, that's beautiful too,' I said.

'Which do you prefer?'

'I like them both . . . You won't go wrong in either.'

'I think I'll wear this one,' she said.

'It's lovely,' I agreed.

I thought she was finished, but a moment later she came down again with different shoes.

'These or the other ones?' she said with a frown.

'Those,' I said.

'Good. I thought these too.'

She went to collect her bag and then looked at it before turning to me. 'Do you think—' she began.

'Do you know what I think, Alexis?'

'What?'

'I think you would look stunning in a black plastic bin bag.'

A few weeks later she went to the boat show at the NEC and came rushing home full of excitement, waving a card.

'Look,' she said, handing it to me, eyes shining.

It was a card from a modelling agency. Apparently somebody had approached her, wanting her to come to London.

'Well,' I said, 'that's very flattering.'

I couldn't hide the unease in my voice. I'm a teacher. My heart just sank at the prospect of her throwing all her potential away on something as transient as modelling.

'But . . .?' said Alexis, sensing my hesitation.

'You're a very bright girl, Alexis, and you can go to university. You can always do modelling afterwards if you want.'

She took the advice without a quibble. It may have been that she saw the sense in the argument about education, but I think it was also that London didn't really appeal. After all the upheaval in her young life, she had found herself a home and she didn't want to leave it.

I had looked after young children all my life, but teenagers are a different matter. With little ones, there's not that much to seriously challenge you, though there are times that are more difficult than others.

'Miss,' said little Pamela in my class plaintively, 'I don't feel well.'

She was standing in the cloakroom like a tiny ghost, her face drained of colour and her dark eyes standing out like big black ovals.

'Oh dear,' I said, taking her in my arms. 'What's wrong, Pamela? Is it your tummy?'

Before she could even answer, she had vomited all over my front and down my cleavage! Strangely, when it is a little child, things like that never bother me. I certainly forgave Pamela before I forgave Mr Connolly: I went along to his office after dealing with Pamela.

'I need to go home to get changed,' I said.

He looked at my sick-spattered attire and apparently didn't notice any difference from normal.

'Why?' he said, frowning.

At home, teenagers were proving far more challenging than infants. One night I sat Anna and Alexis down. The two of them were sitting A levels and should have been studying hard, but they were a very glamorous pair and were forever getting themselves dolled up and heading out to the clubs during the week.

'There are going to be new house rules,' I warned them. 'You can go out on Friday and Saturday nights only. The rest of the week is for homework and early nights.'

The two of them exchanged horrified glances.

'Oh, come on, Mum,' said Anna, 'be reasonable!'

'Friday and Saturday only!'

'It's like living with the Gestapo,' muttered Anna crossly.

For the first two weeks they didn't resist, but by the third week they were beginning to get desperate. They knew that arguing with me, or making a fuss, would be a waste of time. They had to be cleverer than that. Unfortunately, they weren't clever enough!

I was lying on the bed one evening, doing my cross-word puzzle, when there was a knock at the door. To my surprise in came Alexis with a cup of tea.

'Are you OK?' she enquired solicitously. 'Do you want anything?'

'No, I'm fine, thanks.'

Hmm. Very thoughtful.

A few minutes later there was another knock at the door. This time it was Anna who popped her head round.

'Are you OK, Mum?' she asked.

I didn't even look up from my puzzle.

'Whatever the question is, the answer is no,' I said, filling in an answer.

Nice try, girls!

That weekend Alexis's sister, Melissa, who lived with her uncle, came to visit us for a few days. On the Monday morning she came down dressed for school but complaining about the fact that she was very hot.

'Why is that?' I asked.

'Because I have two pairs of tights on,' she said. She explained that she had cut the leg off one pair because it had ladders in it, then cut the leg off another pair that a hole in it and was now wearing two separate legs with the tops of two different pairs. No wonder she was hot!

'I'll get you some new tights,' I said.

'It's OK,' Melissa replied quickly. 'I don't want to put you out. If you give me the money, I'll just nip into Ethel Austin on my way to school.'

'Melissa,' I said, 'school starts at nine o'clock. Ethel Austin doesn't open until nine o'clock. I will get you the tights.'

'You had me sussed,' Melissa laughed when I saw her again, years later. 'You knew I wanted the money for ciggies, didn't you?'

Well, I wasn't born yesterday! And I had been teaching long enough to develop a sixth sense.

I made the mistake of thinking I could use my well-honed teaching skills to teach Anna and Alexis to drive.

I should have stuck to infants. I used to meet Alexis in town and let her drive home. Once, a taxi beeped at her for some reason or other and she slammed on the brakes.

'Right!' she shouted, beside herself with road rage. 'I'm going to give him a piece of my mind!'

'If you do, then this is your last lesson,' I replied.

I always dreaded seeing cyclists, which were her pet hate.

'Get out of the bloody way!' she would yell out of the window.

I would close my eyes and slink down the seat.

Anna was no better. It was so nerve-wracking having them out on the road that I decided to go to the Ford factory for a quiet lesson. I knew they had big car parks and also traffic lights and zebra crossings, but it was safely away from the main road. The more I can keep them away from other road users at this stage, the better, I thought. I was just getting Anna to reverse into a parking space when there was a knock on the passenger window. I wound down the window and there stood a security guard.

'Eh, love, are you giving driving lessons here?'

'Sort of,' I replied.

'Well, this is private land, so you can't. Clear off!'

They did both pass, but I was a wreck by the end of it. Whatever I saved in money I certainly paid for in frayed nerves.

One by one my chicks were fleeing the nest. Simon had gone, of course, but now Anna was applying to university. At first, she said she wanted to study modern languages. Strange, I thought, how both my children are gravitating towards what my father had always secretly wanted to study. Just before sitting her A levels, however, Anna had a change of heart.

'I want to do something different,' she declared. 'Like Japanese.'

Typical Anna!

Alexis was keeping rather quiet.

'Where do you want to go, Alexis?' I asked.

'I'd rather stay in Liverpool,' she said, looking anxiously at me. 'Do you think that . . . well . . . I could maybe stay here?'

'Of course you can!'

One chick left at home.

The best university for Japanese is Durham because it's twinned with Tokyo University. We drove up there, but when we arrived, Anna looked out of the window in horror.

'Oh my God,' she said, 'sheep!'

On the main noticeboard it said that if you liked night life, Newcastle was only forty minutes away. Anna liked night life, but she liked it close by. So instead, she headed to Sheffield University, which she loved. I consoled myself that it wasn't too far to go to see her.

Alexis didn't regret staying at home and her next birthday was very special. She had opened her presents, but I told her I had one special one that I had kept for last.

'If you don't like it, I'll keep it,' I told her, 'because I can't take it back.'

Alexis tried not to look horrified as I spoke. Oh God, I could see her thinking, it's something to wear! And if she says she'll keep it, then . . .

She tried to keep a smile plastered to her face as she waited for me to present her with some ghastly garment that she would need to pretend to love, but it wasn't something to wear. It was something that I knew would make her know that this was her home now, that she really was part of the family.

It was the cutest little black-and-white kitten you've ever seen. I'd tried to put it in a gift bag, but it wasn't cooperating, so I decided just to hold it in the palm of my hand behind my back. When I brought my arm round and Alexis saw this little ball of fluff and fur perched on my hand, she burst into tears. She called him Charlie and she adored him. So when I say my family expanded by one that year, it's not entirely true. It expanded by two: the lovely Alexis and the almost-as-lovely Charlie.

30

Sudden Slips

The mood in the staffroom in February 1993 was sombre. Grainy CCTV images of a toddler being taken by the hand and led out of a shopping centre in Bootle, near Liverpool, by two ten-year-olds were etched on all our hearts and sparked intense discussion. Two-year-old Jamie Bulger had been shopping with his mum when he got separated, and despite taking his hand as if they were protecting him, the two boys, Robert Thompson and Jon Venables, had led him to his death. Again and again the footage was played on news programmes and yet you could never become inured to the horror of it. Each time was like the first. The knowledge that Jaime had been murdered by two such young boys horrified the entire nation.

Perhaps it's understandable that people's fear and revulsion made them turn on the two ten-year-olds, but I felt uneasy because I knew that the murderers were little more than children themselves. They were still at primary school. They were only four or five years older than the children I taught. If they had gone wrong, who was to blame? Wasn't it the adults around them? To an extent, children are a mirror of the society they come from, and those two ten-year-olds were clearly damaged boys. For those of us who worked with children, it sparked all kinds of discussions. In the staffroom we debated whether children could be born evil. The general consensus among those of us who spent our entire working lives with children was that they couldn't. They were made evil by circumstance.

It was a difficult tightrope to walk because obviously our sorrow for Jamie and his family was paramount. A two-year-old boy would now never grow up. His life had been stolen and that was a justifiable reason for anger. Nevertheless, simply focusing on the two boys as 'evil' let us adults off the hook. When an online petition demanding the two boys be kept in permanent custody and never be released was forwarded to me, I agonised but didn't add my name. Nothing could bring Jamie back from the dead now. Lessons had to be learned; I just hoped they were the right ones.

'Happy birthday to you. Happy birthday to you. Happy birthday, Mrs Cuu ... be ... ells. Happy birthday to you!'

Reg and another colleague had come into my room and were leading my reception class in song.

'Well, thank you,' I smiled. 'How beautifully you sang that!'

Glowing faces beamed up at me.

'Will you have a birthday cake, miss?'

'Ooh, I hope so, Darren. I love cake, don't you?'

'What age are you, miss?' asked Sally, a little round-cheeked girl who had an almost permanent frown of concentration on her forehead.

'I'm fifty, Sally,' I replied.

Sally's eyes opened wide.

'Is that almost the last number, miss?' she asked.

Reg guffawed.

'I hope not, sweetheart!' I said. 'I really hope not!'

Life was rolling along, but sometimes things happen so suddenly that it feels like there's only a heartbeat separating your old life from a new one. A twist, a turn – or, in my case, a slip – and all of a sudden everything changes. One minute things are set out in a particular way, the next everything has gone up in the air. When it falls and settles again, the pattern is quite different. Life is like a constantly twisting, colourful kaleidoscope.

I expected to teach until retirement in the usual way, but it was not to be. I had a student in my classroom and had left her to take the class on her own while I carried some marking to the staffroom before helping her clear up at the end of the day. It was summer and the children had a really bad habit of putting paper towels under the tap and using them to wipe themselves down when it was hot.

'In the bin . . . now!' we always said, because the towels got discarded everywhere and made a real mess.

But now, hurrying back to help my student, and with my arms full of marking, I didn't spot a paper towel that was lying in a soggy heap in the corridor. My heel caught it awkwardly, my books flew up into the air above me, and when they – and I – hit the ground, nothing was the same again. There was a bookcase to my left that might have broken my fall if I could only have grabbed hold of it, but it was all so sudden. I knew immediately the damage was severe and I lay there unable to move. Little Sally came along then, peering down at me with her characteristic frown as I lay flat out on my back.

'Hello, miss,' she said. 'Are you having a lie down?'

'No, darling. Could you get me some help?'

In actual fact, though, I managed to crawl – literally – to the nearest classroom before Sally came back. My colleague, Rosemary, helped me into a chair, then went off to tell the student what had happened and check with the head that she could leave a little early to take me home in her car. I usually walked, but I wasn't going to be walking anywhere for quite some time.

She called for the doctor and he came to the house quite quickly and gave me strong painkillers. That night, I had a very disturbed sleep, punctuated with terrible nightmares full of writhing snakes. When the doctor returned in a couple of days, I still had unbearable pain in my left leg and couldn't feel my toes. It was clear that whatever had happened in the fall was not going to right itself with some rest. An ambulance was called and I was taken to hospital, little realising that I would be stuck there for the next four weeks.

A lumbar puncture, which involves withdrawing fluid from the spine to test it, was done and the specialist came to talk to me about the result.

'You have a prolapsed disc and I'm going to do a procedure called chemonucleolysis,' he explained. 'First, though, I have to ask you if you have been in America recently and eaten American beef.'

I was puzzled. 'No, I haven't – but why?'

'Well, chemonucleolysis involves injecting enzymes into the disc in the hope of shrinking it. The Americans use these enzymes to tenderise their steaks and we couldn't have gone ahead if you'd already had exposure to the enzymes.'

After the injection, the centre of the disc would go fluid and that fluid would be drawn off. In the weeks and months after, it was hoped that removing the fluid would make the disc shrink.

Unfortunately, it didn't work.

'The only answer,' the specialist told me, 'is an operation. Unless you have a spinal fusion, the pain is going to be there for ever.'

My heart sank and after he'd gone I turned my face into the pillow in despair. Spinal fusion is a technique that basically welds faulty vertebrae together to make a solid bone, but it does carry a risk and I was too frightened to go ahead. I'd heard about someone who had ended up using a wheelchair after a spinal-fusion operation. I couldn't bear it if that happened to me. Surely there was an alternative we could try first?

I couldn't sleep, the combination of pain and worry making me both alert and miserable. I knew I just didn't have the courage to say yes to the operation. I talked it over with Jaime, but my mind was made up.

'I can't do it,' I told the specialist when he came back to see me. 'I'll do any amount of physiotherapy,' I pleaded. 'I'll work really hard if it means I don't have to have surgery.'

I could tell from the specialist's reaction that although he understood my fears and misgivings, he didn't think there was much chance of my problems being solved without surgical intervention.

'We can try, Bernadette,' he said, 'but you have a battle on your hands.' He looked at me with compassion and shook his head. 'You will change your mind,' he warned as gently as he could. 'You will ring me when you are on all fours.'

I was so relieved that he was agreeing to try physio that I didn't pay as much attention to those words 'on all fours' as I should have. I would be the exception to the rule, I told myself. I would make myself walk again through sheer effort.

The period after I came out of hospital was a difficult one. I am a positive person and attacked physio with energy and determination, but the results were slow, the improvement negligible, and gradually I felt the energy sapping out of me like a punctured tyre. I wondered where my life was going. What did the future hold for someone like me? I was beginning to feel useless, as if everything was over, but I was only fifty and it felt too young to be on the scrapheap. To make matters worse, my relationship with Jaime was becoming strained. I felt like everything I had known hung in the balance as I tried to weather the storm.

My friend Carole, who ran a nursery, came to my aid, offering me a lifeline just as I was spiralling downwards. Her nursery was called Bluebell and was situated in an old chapel near Penny Lane. She asked if I'd like to come down, even just for an hour once in a while, to read a story. I think Carole knew the therapeutic value of children. The walk to the nursery would normally take twenty minutes, but I was still using a walking stick and had to take longer, stopping frequently to look in shop windows for a breather.

The whole experience worked wonders for me. I had a new persona in the nursery. Carole introduced me as Miss Bernadette, though one little boy translated that into the much more exotic Miss Benadotti. Carole showed me a small empty room that I could use if I wanted to work with a group and I immediately thought of the bright posters I still had at home, colourful alphabet and number friezes. All my teacher's instincts kicked in; that's something that doesn't go away. The young girls who worked in the nursery were doing NVQs and they sometimes asked my advice about coursework and I enjoyed the feeling of being consulted. I chatted with them about targets and outcomes, and got them to write down their experiences with the children. Helping them made me feel useful again.

The biggest boost I got, however, was being back among children again, even for a short time. The comfort of the familiar washed over me and it lifted my spirits. There was one little boy who had not settled in well to nursery life. He got upset easily and was clearly not comfortable in this new environment. After a while, though, when I walked in the door, he would light up and runs towards me.

'It's me mate!' he cried. 'It's me mate!'

His words were the best painkiller ever.

As soon as I was able to do a full day, I went back into school, hobbling around with my stick as best I could. Somewhere inside myself, I knew it wasn't going to work, but I refused to admit it. I wasn't ready to admit defeat. The reality was, though, that I couldn't even walk upstairs for a cup of coffee with the rest of my colleagues and it felt isolating to be cut off from the staffroom and all the normal banter. Even in the classroom, it was hard. I couldn't sit on the small chairs with the children any more because I would never be able to get up out of them again. They had to come to me when I wanted to teach a group and it made me feel limited and immobile.

After a few weeks I received a letter asking me to go and see one of the council's medical officers. I felt nervous and anxious walking into his room, as if I knew what was coming. He was a middle-aged man with a compassionate manner and I wilted under his scrutiny.

'You can't go on like this,' he said seriously. 'I am amazed you are actually getting to school each day.'

'I manage,' I said, refusing to look him in the eye.

'Bernadette, you are not fit to be working in a school.' He hesitated, choosing his words carefully. 'The thing is, we don't have insurance for you to work in a state like this.'

'What do you mean?'

'I mean that I want you to consider retirement on the grounds of ill health.'

I felt as if my world had shuddered to a complete stop.

31

Happy Endings and New Beginnings

Retirement day. All packed up and ready to go, I took a last walk around the school, past the gym, through the assembly hall and down into the infant department, hearing the ghostly voices of all the children I've taught ringing in my ears.

'Miss! He's hitting me!'

'Miss! I feel sick!'

'Please, miss!'

The infant corridor was hardest to leave because this was the place I loved most, but I am a positive person and you can't live in the past. Besides, there is no point in fighting something over which you have no choice. Today had been tinged with sadness, but I looked forward to a whole new future opening up. Isn't that what I had taught children all my career? There are always new possibilities if you look for them.

It had been a day of mixed emotions, but like every other day of my career, it had its funny moments and it was the comedy of young children that I knew I would miss the most. That afternoon I had been given a presentation by the children and staff. I stood in the hall and looked out at the sea of young faces, with my lot at the front.

'I first came to this school in 1948,' I told the children. 'Do you think I came here as a teacher or as a little girl?'

'A teacher! A teacher!' shouted all the little ones.

I could see the juniors at the back working it all out, thinking, My God, how old *is* she? A hand at the back went up.

'I think you came as a little girl.'

Well, thank goodness for that!

'I did. I came here as a little girl first and then I became a teacher, but I am leaving today and I know you have all been very kind and bought me a present because I can see it sitting on the stage. It's beautifully wrapped, isn't it? I keep wondering what it is.'

'It's a cassette player!' shouted David, one of the infants at the front, who was unable to contain himself.

'Shhhhh!' shouted the others, outraged at his indiscretion.

I pretended I hadn't heard.

'It looks a bit like a microwave,' I mused.

'It's a cassette player!' shouted David, more urgently.

'Shhhhh!'

'But then again . . . it could be a television.'

'IT'S A CASSETTE PLAYER!'

'Maybe I should just open it and see.'

I ripped the paper from the box as the children watched.

'Oh, wonderful! It's a cassette player, which is just what I need.'

'I *told* you it was a cassette player,' muttered David, with the slightly aggrieved tone of a man who should have been listened to in the first place.

After the presentation, once all the children had left for the day and I'd said my farewells, I couldn't resist going back to my classroom for a final goodbye. I could hear the cleaners out in the corridors, buckets and mops clanking. It was time to go. A last look at the walls, a smile at some of the children's drawings that were still pinned there. We were taught at college never to ask a child what their painting was of. It should be obvious to all! I used to get round it by saying, 'Tell me about this lovely painting you've done.' I remember asking that question and the young artist replying, 'It's Leonardo.' I couldn't believe my ears. A genius at last! 'You know,' she continued, 'Leonardo the Ninja Turtle.'

But I was never really looking for geniuses. I was just looking to help ordinary children be all that they could be. I wanted them to seize their opportunity to make something of themselves, to find happiness in whatever way they could. The only problem was, how was I going to do the same?

Almost everything in my life was changing but one thing remained the same. From the earliest days of our relationship, Jaime had been very suspicious of even the most innocent things that I did. One morning, when I walked down to the butchers, I bumped into the father of a boy I had taught many years before. I always loved to catch up on news about former pupils and spent five minutes talking to him about his son. When I got home, I was stunned when Jaime started interrogating me. Who was that dark haired man with glasses that I had been talking to? How did I know him? I was used to this behaviour but for some reason, I think that day I just snapped inside.

It kept going round and round my head and that evening, as I prepared dinner and waited for Alexis to arrive home from university, I asked Jaime a question.

'In an ideal world, what would you have wanted for you and me?'

His answer sent a shiver down my spine. 'You and me in this house. Nobody going out and nobody coming in'.

And that was what finally made up my mind. I knew I had to leave him.

I didn't discuss things any further with Jaime because I knew how he would react, but I started looking at flats. I soon found a really nice little place to rent and chatted to Alexis about my plans. By now she had a lovely boyfriend called Shaffi and in a way, it was time for us all to move on. Alexis and Shaffi soon found a house to rent and were as happy as sandboys! I started packing, just a few things, in a suitcase which I hid in a wardrobe in the spare bedroom. Besides clothes I took very little . . . just my photo albums, which I'd built up over the years. They had sustained me through the bad times and now they moved on with me, to hopefully a much happier life.

That Friday, when Jaime went out to buy cigarettes, I took the case out of the wardrobe. I walked slowly down the stairs and opened the front door. I stepped out, slammed the door, locked it and then posted the keys through the letter box. I didn't leave a note. There was nothing left to say!

*   *   *

Even when things are at their toughest, there are still those moments in life when you just can't help laughing, despite the pain. Following my accident, I had a plaster cast on my back for a while, but one day my leg swelled up uncomfortably. Eventually, I rang my doctor and made an appointment.

When I walked into the surgery, I felt like a turtle.

'Let's have a look,' said the doc.

He was only a young chap, but he had to help me in and out of my trousers because I was encased in a shell and couldn't bend properly. After examining the leg, he held the trouser leg open for me. I was stepping gingerly in when I felt myself lose balance.

'Oh, no!' I shouted, wavering desperately, and the next minute I had toppled to the floor.

The doctor had broken my fall a bit, but as I rolled around on the ground, like a beetle on its back trying to right itself, all the fruitless rocking from side to side destabilised him and he ended up on top of me. I felt so embarrassed as we tried to disentangle ourselves from this sprawl of limbs, but as our eyes met, I noticed a glint of humour in the young doctor's eyes.

'Please God,' he said fervently, 'don't let that door open . . .'

It lightened the moment and we both giggled.

I wasn't laughing a short while later, though. That hospital specialist had known what he was talking about: a morning came when I simply could not get out of bed. I rolled onto the floor and literally crawled my way pain-fully to the toilet. His words came back to me then. 'You will ring me when you are on all fours.' I picked up the phone and dialled his number.

I gasped when I looked out of the window. It was the most beautiful machine I had ever seen: low, sleek, gleaming red, the curved contours of the body creating lines of perfection. Outside, Simon grinned and waved at me as he showed off new toy. It was his twenty-fifth birthday and I had got out of hospital the day before, after back surgery.

I picked up the phone and dialled.

'Hello?'

'Hi, Marie,' I said. 'It's Bernadette.'

'You're out! How are you?'

'Fine but taking things slowly. Are you doing anything this morning?'

'Just enjoying the fact that it's Saturday. Why?'

'Do you fancy coming round for a coffee?'

'Lovely!'

'It's Simon's birthday and there's something I want you to see. Cast your mind back. Do you remember that essay he wrote at school? The one that said what he wanted for his twenty-fifth birthday?'

Marie laughed. 'Oh, yes! The red Ferrari!'

'Well, come and see what's parked outside.'

'You don't mean he . . . You're joking!'

'Just come!'

When Marie arrived, I managed to hobble out onto the pavement and the two us stood side by side, gawping. We walked round it reverently, looking at the iconic rearing-horse logo on the bonnet. Anna was still at university, but Simon now worked in the City as a trader and the fruits of his labours were plentiful. Still, a Ferrari . . . already . . .

Marie looked thoughtful. 'Do you think we've wasted our lives stuck in dusty old schools with kids?'

We looked at one another seriously, then burst out laughing at the same time.

'Nah!' we both said, and shook our heads.

It was not long after that Simon got another high-powered job in banking in Hong Kong and Anna graduated with a good degree that would see her move to Japan to live. It was then, after a long, difficult time, that my marriage to Jaime finally limped to a close. Sadly, like many couples whose children have fled the nest and settled elsewhere, we found that we had little in common. I felt that we were very different people and wanted different things and would therefore be happier apart. But we did come together for Simon and Tamzin's wedding, and despite everything that had happened, we tried to be united on the day for our son. The wedding also provided a long-overdue opportunity for a family reunion. Andrew came all the way from Perth, Aideen came from Dublin, Helena from Canada, and Kathleen from down south, so it was also a rare opportunity for all four Tierney girls to get together for the day.

It was interesting the way friends reacted to the separation. Some felt they had to take sides and choose only one of us to remain friends with, but my friend AnnMarie and her husband, Hedley, were there for both of us and I really appreciated that. On the day of the wedding, Hedley put his arm round Simon. 'I'll look after your old man for you,' he said. Inside, I felt glad that someone would look out for Jaime in a way that I no longer could. I'm sure it was a comfort to Simon too. He and Anna loved their dad. They were very close to him and I knew how concerned they were about him.

It would be years before Jaime and I sat down together in the same room again. We had been apart for five years when I finally told him I needed to speak to him about a divorce. We met in a café, neutral territory, and I explained over a coffee that it was best for both of us if we formalised everything. Reluctantly, Jaime agreed and signed the papers I had brought.

It was a nice café, with little miniature pots of jam for scones on the table, and as I looked at them, a sudden memory made me smile. I picked up the jar.

'Remember the first time I came to your house?'

We both smiled.

'It wasn't all bad, Bernadette,' he said.

'No, it wasn't all bad.'

'Two lovely children to show for it.'

He nodded.

'Do you know what the kids used to call us?' I asked.

'What?'

'Florence and Sherlock. Florence because I was always concerned about what they were up to and Sherlock because you were always searching for clues, trying to find out everything!'

He laughed.

We both loved Simon and Anna so much, and were so proud of them, and that would always be a unifying bond between us. I stood up, anxious not to make the moment longer or more difficult than it needed to be.

'Good luck, Jaime,' I said and walked swiftly from the café.

I knew it was the right thing for both of us, but sometimes doing the right thing can be painful. You don't walk away from thirty years with a person without immense sadness and regret. But, just as constant dripping wears away a stone, constant jealousy wears away love.

To cheer me up, my friend Bette and her husband, John, took me out to a club to see the Merseysippi Jazz Band. It became a regular thing on a Monday night with a group of us, and one night, quite some time later, John said he was going to call his friend Robby and invite him along.

'It's a year since Robby's wife died and he always loved jazz,' he said. 'Maybe he'd like to join us.'

I thought no more about it. John and Robby had met when they were eighteen and were trainee pilots at Cranwell. They had gone their separate ways and hadn't seen each other for forty years. When Robby had retired from his job as chief test pilot for British Aerospace, however, he had got a job teaching pilots in a simulator. One day he heard another tutor's voice down the corridor and recognised it instantly.

'John?' he shouted.

'Robby Robinson!' exclaimed John.

They had both changed beyond recognition, but they recognised each other's voices immediately. Having been lucky enough to re-establish contact, they resolved not to lose touch again.

Over the years that I'd been apart from Jaime, there were embarrassing times when I had to politely grin and bear it when I turned up to dinner with friends and found they had 'matched' me with some poor guy who was no doubt suffering similar embarrassment to my own. The night at the jazz club was different, however. We were in a group, of course, but what's more, within half an hour I felt as if I'd known Robby all my life.

He'd been through difficult times, as I had, because he had lost his wife to cancer, but like me, he knew how to laugh – even in the face of adversity – and he won me over with his funny stories.

Because he's a retired test pilot – or 'pest toilet', as he calls himself – he has endless interesting tales about flying. He's a mixture of a complete gentleman and a mischievous boy, a combination I love. The night we met, he told me a story about Farnborough Air Show over a gin and tonic.

'After my display my secretary came up to me,' he said. 'She was raving about the Red Arrows and said she wished she could meet them, so I said I knew them and could perhaps introduce her.'

'And did you?' I asked.

He grinned. 'Oh, yes. There was a reception at the president's marquee that evening, so I took her along. I knew the Red Arrows were bound to be there and they were. I knew one of the ones who had turned up and I told my secretary all about him. "This guy is really interesting," I said. "He had to eject from his aircraft at high speed last week." '

'Wow!' I said, taking a sip of gin.

'Yes, that's what she thought. She looked up at him in absolute awe and said, "I believe you ejaculated last week." '

I spluttered, the gin catching in my throat and going up my nose.

'And he said, "Yes, my dear – and I hope to again soon," ' laughed Robby, delighted by my response.

I really didn't expect this second chance at love in my life, but a whole new world opened up to me with Robby and we began to see each other regularly. I knew it would be hard for Simon and Anna to accept a new man in my life – and they are, quite rightly, very protective of Jaime – but luckily, they both get on very well with Robby. When Simon came to meet him for the first time, he and Robby ended up going to the pub for a drink. They disposed of any awkwardness in a typically male way. It was just after the 2003 Rugby World Cup and Simon had actually been in the stadium for the final to see Jonny Wilkinson's winning drop goal in extra time against Australia, so they had plenty to talk about.

'I just want to say one thing, Simon,' Robby said as they stood at the bar. 'Meeting your mother has made a great difference to my life.'

'Yes,' said Simon, 'and I think it has to Mum's too. Now, about the rugby . . .'

Epilogue

When I was a little girl, I spent many hours listening to old 78 records. I had some with musical versions of fairy tales, like 'Snow White' and 'Sleeping Beauty', and my favourite song was 'Someday My Prince Will Come'. After my divorce, I didn't really believe in princes, but at the age of fifty-nine, I felt as if one had finally walked into my life and it was worth the wait.

A year after we met, Robby proposed and everything that had not been quite right about my life slotted into place. It was as if all the little pebbles in my shoes that I'd been walking around with for years were emptied out and I felt comfortable and at peace. Our wedding was one of the happiest days of my life, surrounded by so many of the people who were special to me. Simon, Anna and Alexis were there, of course, but Aideen also made it over from Dublin, which was lovely. It made me reflect on all those years we were out of touch because she was locked away in the convent. These days she lives in a flat owned by the order, has her own front door and can come and go as she pleases. All my friends from over the years were there too: Jellybean, Tweet and Maggie Gee, AnnMarie and Marie, and, of course, Bette and John, who introduced us.

We got married in a place called Sutton Hall, a nice old building that was the former home of the earls of Lucan and was also once a convent. On the big day it was inevitable that my mind would briefly flit back to the past and to those we had loved who couldn't be with us. I turned to Aideen as we left the house.

'What do you think Mum would say about me getting married in a civil ceremony in a former convent?'

'Oh, the Mammy would be fine with it!' said Aideen soothingly.

We may have been a more mature bride and groom, but it was still a romantic day, with Robby singing a love song to me at the reception. At least, it was romantic until poor Tweet collapsed during the chorus, but thankfully, it was just a sudden and temporary drop in blood pressure due to some medication she was taking.

'I don't usually have women falling at my feet,' said Robby, who is rarely serious for long.

'Well, I thought it was lovely when you sang, Robby,' Aideen said approvingly.

'Yes, there wasn't a dry seat in the house!' he declared.

I may have stopped teaching, but I meet up with teacher friends every month and children remain a big part of my life. I do a school run and I also still go in occasionally to help in schools. Most exciting of all, I have several grandchildren now. Simon and Tamzin have two adorable little boys – three-year-old Oscar and baby Hugo, who is one – and Alexis has also had her first child, a beautiful dark-haired little girl called Sofia.

Simon went from Hong Kong to Tokyo but is now back in Hong Kong, where he works as a trader for a bank. I would love to see more of the children growing up, but I see them each year in the summer for a few weeks and we Skype regularly. Oscar always puts his foot up to the screen for me because he remembers that the last time I saw him, I played 'Tick Tack Toe' with him.

'Kiss Grandma goodbye,' Simon says, and Oscar runs to the computer, putting his little pursed lips to the screen.

Anna works in banking too these days, also in the Far East. She is in Tokyo and is unmarried – 'Take your time!' I tell her – but she is loving life in the Japanese city, which she says is one of the safest in the world. I love it when she comes home, but as long as she's happy out there, then so am I. At least Alexis is still here in Liverpool.

'What do you want the baby to call you?' Alexis asked me when she was pregnant.

'Why, "Grandma", of course!'

'I was hoping you would say that,' she said.

I have been so lucky. I have been 'Miss' to hundreds of children in my life and am now 'Grandma' to three very special ones. Actually, though, I believe all children are special. As one of literature's most famous teachers, Muriel Spark's Miss Brodie, said, 'Deep in most of us is the potential for greatness, or the potential to inspire greatness.' I think that's true. I often wonder where all 'my' children are now and how many of them have gone on to truly fulfil the potential they have inside.

'What do you do?' new people often ask when we first meet. My reply is always the same.

'Well, I used to be a teacher, but I'm all right now!' I joke.

The truth is that I wouldn't have swapped a moment of it, and I can't imagine a time when my life won't be full of children and stories. I loved those fairy-tale records when I was small. No matter how difficult or dark the story got, I waited optimistically for the happy ending to arrive. I think it finally has.

Acknowledgements

I would like to give my heartfelt thanks to Catherine Deveney for all her hard work and perseverance, in bringing structure to my book.

Also a big thank you to Ajda Vucicevic at Luigi Bonomi Associates, who was the first person to read my book and somehow saw potential in it!

Last but certainly not least, I owe a special thanks to Fenella Bates, from Hodder and Stoughton, for going out on a limb and agreeing to publish my book.